WITCHCRAFT CONTINUED

Published in our
centenary year
∾ **2004** ∾
MANCHESTER
UNIVERSITY
PRESS

WITCHCRAFT CONTINUED

Popular magic in modern Europe

edited by
Willem de Blécourt and Owen Davies

Manchester University Press
Manchester and New York

distributed exclusively in the USA by Palgrave

Copyright © Manchester University Press 2004

While copyright in the volume as a whole is vested in Manchester University Press, copyright in individual chapters belongs to their respective authors, and no chapter may be reproduced wholly or in part without the express permission in writing of both author and publisher.

Published by Manchester University Press
Oxford Road, Manchester M13 9NR, UK
and Room 400, 175 Fifth Avenue, New York, NY 10010, USA
www.manchesteruniversitypress.co.uk

Distributed exclusively in the USA by
Palgrave, 175 Fifth Avenue, New York, NY 10010, USA

Distributed exclusively in Canada by
UBC Press, University of British Columbia, 2029 West Mall,
Vancouver, BC, Canada V6T 1Z2

British Library Cataloguing-in-Publication Data
A catalogue record for this book is available from the British Library

Library of Congress Cataloging-in-Publication Data applied for

ISBN 0 7190 6658 1 *hardback*
EAN 978 0 7190 6658 0
ISBN 0 7190 6659 x *paperback*
EAN 978 0 7190 6659 7

First published 2004

13 12 11 10 09 08 07 06 05 04   10 9 8 7 6 5 4 3 2 1

Typeset in Monotype Bell by
Carnegie Publishing Ltd, Lancaster
Printed in Great Britain
by Biddles Ltd, King's Lynn

CONTENTS

CONTRIBUTORS

Willem de Blécourt is Honorary Research Fellow at the Huizinga Institute of Cultural History, Amsterdam. He has written numerous articles on witchcraft, popular culture and irregular medicine, published in Dutch, German and English journals such as *Social History*, *Medical History* and *Gender & History*. His most recent book is *Het Amazonenleger* [*The Army of Amazons*] (1999) which deals with irregular female healers in the Netherlands, 1850–1930. He is currently writing a book on werewolves to be published by London and Hambledon Press. He is also working on a history of witchcraft in the Netherlands.

Owen Davies is a Lecturer in History at the University of Hertfordshire. He has published numerous articles on the history of witchcraft and magic in eighteenth- and nineteenth-century England and Wales. He is also the author of *Witchcraft, magic and culture 1736–1951* (Manchester University Press, 1999) and *A People Bewitched* (1999). His most recent book is *Cunning-Folk: Popular Magic in English History* (2003).

Nils Freytag is an assistant professor at the University of Munich. He is the author of *Aberglauben im 19. Jahrhundert. Preußen und seine Rheinprovinz zwischen Tradition und Moderne 1815–1918* (2003), and along with Diethard Sawicki is currently editing *Entzauberte Moderne?*, a collection of essays on the occult in nineteenth- and twentieth-century Europe. His research interests include the social, cultural and environmental history of Germany in the eighteenth and nineteenth centuries.

Susan Hoyle took early retirement from British Rail in 1996 after a varied career, mainly concerned with public transport. She is now an independent scholar and writer, and amongst other projects is working on narratives about the battle of Trafalgar, as well as Victorian witches and detectives. She lives near Land's End.

Richard Jenkins is Professor of Sociology at the University of Sheffield. He has carried out ethnographic field research in Northern Ireland, England, Wales and Denmark. Among his recent publications are *Pierre Bourdieu* (2nd edn, 2002), *Social Identity* (1996), *Rethinking Ethnicity* (1997), *Questions of Competence* (1998) and *Foundations of Sociology* (2002).

Sabina Magliocco is Associate Professor of Anthropology at California State University, Northridge. She is the author of *The Two Madonnas: The Politics of Festival in a Sardinian Community* (1993), *Neo-Pagan Sacred Art and Altars: Making Things Whole* (2001), and numerous articles. A recipient of Guggenheim and National Endowment for the Humanities fellowships, she has done fieldwork in Italy and the United States on ritual, festival, folk narrative and material culture.

Stephen Mitchell is Professor of Scandinavian and Folklore at Harvard University. His research in recent years has focused on witchcraft and performance in medieval Scandinavia and includes 'Nordic Witchcraft in Transition: Impotence, Heresy, and Diabolism in 14th-century Bergen' (*Scandia*), 'Blåkulla and its Antecedents: Transvection and Conventicles in Nordic Witchcraft' (*Alvíssmál*), 'Anaphrodisiac Charms in the Nordic Middle Ages: Impotence, Infertility, and Magic' (*Norveg*), 'Folklore and Philology

Revisited: Medieval Scandinavian Folklore?' (*Norden og Europa*), and 'Gender and Nordic Witchcraft in the Later Middle Ages' (*Arv*).

Enrique Perdiguero is Senior Lecturer of History of Science at Miguel Hernández University, Alicante, Spain. His main research interests are the interplay between popular and academic medicine and the development of public health services. Recent publications in English include: J. Bernabeu, R. Huertas, E. Rodríguez and E. Perdiguero, 'History of health, a valuable tool in public health', *Journal of Epidemiology and Community Health* (2001); J. Bernabeu and E. Perdiguero, 'At the Service of Spain and Spanish Children: Mother and Child Healthcare in Spain During the First Two Decades of Franco's Regime (1939–1963)', in I. Löwy and J. Krige (eds), *Images of Disease: Science, Public Policy and Health in Post-war Europe* (2001).

Éva Pócs has published widely on South-Eastern and Central European beliefs concerning fairies, magic and witchcraft from the medieval to the modern period. Her most recent major English-language publication is *Between the Living and the Dead: A Perspective on Witches and Seers in the Early Modern Age* (1999). She is also the editor of *Demons, Spirits, Witches: Church Demonology and Popular Mythology* (Budapest, forthcoming).

Laura Stark is a researcher at the Academy of Finland and a docent in the Department of Folklore Studies at the University of Helsinki. Her recent publications include *Magic, Body and Social Order: The Construction of Gender Through Women's Private Rituals in Traditional Finland* (1998), and *Peasants, Pilgrims and Sacred Promises: Ritual and the Supernatural in Orthodox Karelian Folk Religion* (2002). Two current research topics include concepts of body as self represented in the magic beliefs and practices of nineteenth-century agrarian Finland, and how modernization was experienced by the Finnish rural populace between 1860 and 1960.

Introduction: witchcraft continued

Willem de Blécourt and Owen Davies

The study of witchcraft accusations in Europe during the period after the end of the witch trials is still in its infancy. The present volume, together with its companion *Beyond the witch trials*, intends to develop the field further by presenting a plethora of studies from across Europe and, most importantly, to inspire new research. Whereas *Beyond the witch trials* focused on the period of the Enlightenment, from the late seventeenth through to the end of the eighteenth century, here we pay attention to the nineteenth and twentieth centuries. Once again we have sought to bring together an interdisciplinary group of scholars, whose contributions demonstrate the value of applying the analytical tools of sociology, anthropology, folkloristics and literary studies to historical sources. Above all they show that the history of witchcraft in the modern era is as much a story of continuation as of decline.

The nineteenth century stands out as the great unknown in witchcraft studies, although this differs from country to country. Flanked on one side by the eighteenth century, during which the pyres still flared occasionally in countries such as Germany, Switzerland and Hungary, and the Mediterranean Inquisitions were still active, and on the other by the twentieth century, during which anthropologists, folklorists and legal researchers generated volumes of new witchcraft material, the 1800s have often escaped extensive scrutiny.[1] This is at least the case when we look at witchcraft studies on a European scale. England is a notable exception, but compared with much of the continent it received little attention from twentieth-century fieldworkers.[2] The question is whether this primarily reflects the state of research or the actual historical situation. The English case is complicated, moreover, by the invention of witchcraft as a pagan religion during the 1950s, which, as Gustav Henningsen wrote, had 'nothing to do with witchcraft in the traditional sense'.[3]

It is very plausible to argue that witchcraft as a modern DIY religion could only emerge when its namesake had become largely irrelevant. But then we have to bear in mind that most of the people who were and are drawn to the religion came from social classes whose members had already largely abandoned witchcraft as a mechanism of accusation by the eighteenth century. A comparative approach may shed some more light on this, because at present the religion is hardly studied outside England. Continental instances nevertheless appear to be strongly influenced by the English paradigm, contradicting continuity with local traditions more clearly. The English example also indicates the possibility of several mutually exclusive meanings of the term 'witchcraft'. For instance, there were, and still are, thousands of magical practitioners of a great variety spread all over Europe, Britain included. They are sometimes addressed with terms that translate as 'witch', but it would be highly confusing to equate them with the women, and to a lesser extent men, who were accused of causing harm to their neighbours by spells or mere body language. We can also consider another contemporary usage of the term 'witchcraft' signifying ritual black magic, as in the newspaper reports that form the basis of Richard Jenkins's contribution to this volume. This takes the harmful aspect of traditional accusatory witchcraft and contaminates it with ideas about paganism. All three recent connotations of witchcraft have the 'craft' element in common, the peculiar notion in the English language that witchcraft should somehow be 'doable'. Again, this is a far cry from witchcraft as a device of ascribing misfortune to others, which is not to say that black magic cannot be ascribed or even practised. As it is, most of the contributions to this volume can be situated in the field of tension between story and action in which either the witch or the people bewitched play the main role.

The potential of future witchcraft research can be outlined by discussing the various aspects of the most prominent problem pervading witchcraft studies after the end of the witch trials: did witchcraft decline, and if so, how and why? In order to recognize a possible decline, it is necessary to establish how nineteenth- and twentieth-century witchcraft is best characterized. Physical violence against suspected witches stands out as one of the most prominent traits of witchcraft in the period. Taking it as defining, however, would give an overall picture that would be both distorted and exceptional. Only in particular circumstances does violence reveal an essential reaction to bewitchments and an important indicator of historical change. Indeed, asking whether witchcraft is slowly but inevitably disappearing in Europe implies focusing on possible changes. So far these have been found in the content of the accusations, the kind of people accused, those who acted as accusers, as well as in the contexts in which the accusations occurred. Far from constituting a monolithic, stable entity, witchcraft was subject to adaptation and alteration. But as our view is partly clouded by the nature of the sources documenting witchcraft, explanations have to remain tentative. Moreover, much depends on the specific angle from which witchcraft is approached and from the overall category it is placed in.

Nevertheless, reading nineteenth- and twentieth-century witchcraft reports can easily convey the impression of extreme, sometimes even deadly, violence. As the essays in this volume show, witches were scratched in England, swum in Germany, beaten in the Netherlands and shot in France. In her seminal review of witchcraft studies concerning the continuation of witchcraft after the end of the witch trials, Marijke Gijswijt-Hofstra made a similar observation. She introduces her itinerary through European witchcraft research with a number of cases 'from Ireland to Russia' in which witches were burned as a result of lynching, and she cites numerous other violent incidents. It has become abundantly clear that, more often than not, the witch trials were instigated 'from below', though allowed and sometimes even stimulated by the secular authorities. Is it possible, then, to interpret the later manifestations of communal violence as a mere continuation of the early modern persecution? Continuing the same line of thought, should we interpret more individualistic acts of violence against witches as yet another step in the declining support for physically exterminating them? There are several caveats to this line of reasoning, such as the problem of representativity and the relation between magical and physical solutions to a bewitchment. Both points of caution are raised by Gijswijt-Hofstra, but a little more can be said about them.

We can safely assume that instances of violence against witches were 'tips of the iceberg', and they are thus only the extreme expressions of a much wider dispersed witchcraft discourse – a shorthand note denoting the whole complex of 'thinking and acting in terms of witchcraft'. Violent incidents come to the fore because they were, by their very nature, more prone to publicity than cases that ended more peacefully. Sensationalist press reporting of such cases is already identifiable in the early modern period, if sensationalism was not already part and parcel of the very development of the press itself. The ingredients of witchcraft and popular justice, which were condemned by journalists and deemed offensive to middle- and upper-class norms, curiously mixed with a certain condoning through the provision of detailed descriptions, provided a cultural weight that exceeded mere numbers of incidents. Cases of violence, we argue here, thus had a greater impact on the sense of witchcraft's place in history, be it contemporaries' or later historians', than all those instances that have remained largely hidden from the public gaze. Whether that place is justified, remains to be seen.

The other point concerns the relation between violence and unwitchment. As Gijswijt-Hofstra put it: 'Whether taking the law violently in one's own hands represented a last resort, after self-medication, counter-magic and/or consulting healers or unwitching specialists – in so far as they were available – had all come to nothing, cannot always be discovered, although this seems likely'.[4] This statement, however, presumes violence to be outside the witchcraft discourse, as something 'non-magical'. This is debatable when it concerned the witch trials, which certainly had their numinous dimensions. It is also debatable in the case of the water test, which grew out of a divine ordeal without becoming more material in the process. There is also an additional complication with swimming, as in many cases it was performed at the behest of those suspected of bewitchment in order to clear their names. We can also question the statement with regard to those unwitchment rituals in which both the luring of the witch and having her bless the victim pervaded the physical aspect to such an extent that it is hard to point out any clear boundary. Blood too may have been extracted by force, but its healing qualities put it squarely in the magical domain. This all makes it difficult to classify violent reactions as mere violence or as a 'last resort'. Furthermore, violence was used all the time after the witch trials, and considering these had already largely ended in some regions like the Dutch Republic by the early seventeenth century, it surely cannot be seen as a sign of witchcraft's continuous decline. Moreover, as de Blécourt discusses, it seems that in the Netherlands orthodox Protestants reacted more violently to bewitchments than orthodox Catholics. This probably indicates a much more profound European difference between the two Christian denominations where witch-craft is concerned. And while it certainly shows that the range of counter-measures was much wider for Catholics, it does not follow that Protestants had depleted the available options; they simply did not have any other. Violence thus emerges as a course of action embedded in a religious repertoire – the distinction between religion and magic evaporates here. Only in the case of violent Catholics may it be suggested that a withdrawal of their clergy from the discourse seriously hampered access to the Catholic collection of counter-magic. So, if we still want to understand violent behaviour in the course of unwitchment as a sign of a decline of the discourse, then we have at least to consider the religious context in which it was acted out. This leads to the conclusion that only in very specific, transitional circumstances was violence connected with witchcraft's demise.

But again we need to be cautious and refrain from hasty conclusions. For why should we suppose a steady decline of the witchcraft discourse over the centuries? Indeed it seems more accurate to consider fluctuations. That is to say, as far as the peaks and troughs that have been found in the witch trial statistics were related to changes in the occurrence of bewitchments then there is no reason why this should have stopped when bewitchments ceased to be considered as criminal by the authorities. Specific ways of dealing with bewitchment, and even the diagnosis of bewitchment itself, may have been related to either the dearth or abundance of the witchcraft discourse in a certain period. This makes every current conclusion about decline premature, given the state of research into nineteenth- and twentieth-century witchcraft. For at present we can argue that witchcraft was still a relevant force in modern western society and so counter broad and imprecise notions of disenchantment. As Enrique Perdiguero puts it in this volume, we are interested in whether 'magic' was still an 'essential part of cultural repertoires', a significant element in the conception and treatment of illness, and also seek to extend this to misfortune in general. But before it is even possible to show fluctuations in its occurrence it is necessary to differentiate between kinds of magic and single out witchcraft. Statistical methods are unproductive in this endeavour, which becomes especially clear when the kind of information is correlated to the kind of source and the depth of research. A good example of this is provided by Henningsen in his attempt to establish the basic rules of Danish witchcraft discourse, the so-called 'witchcraft catechism'. 'We can read through hundreds of folklore or witch trial records without ever finding these articles of faith', he observes.[5]

Witchcraft's transformations and their importance in relation to other means of addressing misfortune need to be identified in several important ways. To start with, subtle changes in the content of local witchcraft discourses may be observed when considering the perceived objects of bewitchments. Signs of decline may, for instance, be indicated when industrial products stop being targeted. On the other hand, there are also instances of bewitched engines, which indicate adaptation rather than diminution. As well as content, participants can also be subject to change. In the course of time one social group after another has left the discourse and in some places men seem to have dropped out altogether. Next, unwitchment experts were not always the same kind of people. As already shown, Catholic clergy sometimes refused to answer to the demands of their clientele and in some instances their position was taken over by laymen. Witches themselves have been diminished from being notorious throughout whole villages to being more private personal evil-doers. Sometimes witchcraft even became completely depersonalized as human agents were no longer considered, as in cases where cunning-folk suggested general counter-measures rather than provided the means to identify the witch. Together the participants constitute the witchcraft triangle of bewitched, unwitcher and witch, and changes in its composition reflects on each. Again, witchcraft's resilience is shown in the counter-examples of people starting to apply the discourse anew where earlier they apparently had not done so, as twentieth-century cases from France and Germany reveal. More fundamentally, changes in the 'catechism' need to be revealed, in the ways bewitchments are thought to work, in the ways witches can be identified, and in the ways the capacity to bewitch is deemed to be transmitted from one generation to the next. As this differs from country to country, indeed from region to region or even from place to place, we first have to find out the geographical, temporal and social boundaries of clusters of basic rules and basic contents, so as to avoid, among other things, the danger of mistaking regional differences for indicators of change.

Yet another sign of changes in the witchcraft discourse, if not of its actual decline, is presented when witchcraft accusations become mixed up with other supernatural phenomena. Possession is a borderline case in this respect, as its link to witchcraft hinges on local traditions which blame humans rather than the Devil directly for the affliction. When this tradition is not present, witch-inspired possession may be considered as an alteration of the discourse. In a more general sense this applies to most instances in which the Devil is involved, since the theological interpretations that formed the official justification for most of the witch trials were hardly absorbed by the general populace. Nineteenth- or twentieth-century incidences where the Devil is promoted as an evil force behind the witch may very well be recent additions, inspired by the orthodox Christian climate in which accusations were then beginning to concentrate. Again, these distinctions can sometimes be hard to see and in any case have to be based on a thorough knowledge of all the available local source material. It is perhaps easier to recognize the blurring of witchcraft motifs, therefore, when they concern an obvious nineteenth-century phenomenon such as spirit rapping, as in a mid nineteenth-century French case in Davies's contribution, or when poltergeist manifestations are ascribed to a witch, as in Hoyle's case from Stratford-upon-Avon. However, as witchcraft discourses are known to have incorporated local traditions while gaining in strength, to take the above instances as examples of decline involves taking account of overall changes in their tradition. This further underlines that we may surmise a certain interpretation of particular modern cases but that we can be far from sure about it.

To complicate matters further, vague boundaries of witchcraft also occur in relation to the particular time and place chosen for study, or they can be part of the research strategy selected by present-day students. As this is the case in a number of contributions to this volume, we want to draw the readers' attention to the various fields that can be involved, especially healing, religion, 'magic' and its counterpart 'superstition'. Concerning the latter, Nils Freytag remarks in his recent book that it is a 'stigmatizing assignment from outside'.[6] It always involves others, people of another denomination, of another usually lower social class or of another gender, who somehow do not think in the dominant way and exhibit 'irrational' behaviour. We can better consider 'superstition' as part of the outlook of those who are ascribing it to others, rather than as some genuine, free-floating kind of 'world-view'. In this it resembles a witchcraft accusation (although the latter usually involves 'others' outside the household), which also concerns more a process of ascription than the observation of a practice. More often than not what is presented as a certainty is guided by selection within the framework of the ascription. 'Superstition' more than 'witchcraft', however, can be used as an overall category and it is questionable whether its various constituents have any relation to each other in any way different than this. That is to say, witchcraft, mesmerism, astrology or pilgrimages may be connected in the mind of

Protestant authorities, for example, but probably not for those directly involved. Ultimately, then, the label 'superstition' may reveal more about those applying it than about those to whom it is applied.

Magic, on the other hand, has become a much more neutral overall denominator for anything 'supernatural' that cannot be designated to either science or religion (we disregard professional magicians here). But as magic as a category can sometimes be seen as a reification of the former 'superstition' – at least the two exhibit a considerable overlap – we have to take into account that historically magic may not be as neutral as we would like it to be. What we clearly need is a cultural history of the concept of 'magic' alongside 'superstition', and to examine them as something that is specific to particular historical situations.[7] Furthermore, different parts of magic may have their own temporality. 'Magical beliefs were not all bound up with each other like some monumental cultural artefact', Owen Davies has written. 'Specific magical practices declined, continued or even advanced depending on different and often localised social trends'.[8] And like 'superstition', magic appears as something to tell tales about as well as to practise. How do we assess the place of witchcraft in all this? Some aspects of the answer have already been mentioned: witches are only related to other 'magical' or 'superstitious' beings when their stories start to interfere, or when they are pressed into the same overarching pigeon-hole. This makes it more attractive to widen the category beyond magic and to consider religion and medicine.

Although it is often reported by people who position themselves outside the discourse, who do not believe in it, witchcraft can only be reasonably studied from 'below', as part of the mental outlook and the actions of the people constituting the witchcraft triangle. This is not to say that the parts that make up this outlook are necessarily combined in such a way that they make an impregnable whole. Even witchcraft narratives may not always form a 'unified system'.[9] Different discourses and different repertoires can be applied in different contexts by the same people. When a particular situation calls for using one particular kind of speech or action, then another may require something totally different. From the perspective of actual historical actors it may be perfectly understandable to appear religious or scientific at one moment and 'superstitious' at another. Separating these fields beforehand, because a Church has decreed that religion stands apart from magic, or has outgrown it, or because science has decided magic to be nonsense, may thus hamper understanding on the level of those who are immediately involved in it. Seen from the people bewitched, or from the point of view of an unwitcher, a diagnosis of witchcraft is a choice to interpret events in a particular way and to resolve misfortune. Religion and medicine come in at this level, for it may very well have been considered that the affliction had a natural cause, or that resorting to a particular saint, or just praying and trusting in God would have brought relief. As Susan Hoyle argues in her chapter, the end of witchcraft may set in when the witchcraft story was replaced by a rational one. In other words, when a scientifically medical or agricultural solution was chosen to tackle problems previously ascribed to witchcraft. Witchcraft, however, has been too little studied as the result of a process of selecting options and answers, which can, of course, be blamed on the sources, since they usually stem from the moment when the choice has already been made.

When it concerns choices, witchcraft, medicine and religion may be mutually exclusive in the end. On a different level, however, they may be integrated. This is especially the case with religion, which is more often than not such an essential facet of the life of the bewitched, that it also informs the witchcraft discourse and presents justifications for it. Lay unwitchers often call upon the help of God or the Holy Trinity. Religious artefacts are applied as prophylactics against witches. Lines from the Bible, such as St John's Gospel, are used as counter-magic or used as evidence for the existence of witches – Exodus for example. It thus makes perfect sense, as Sabina Magliocco stresses in her chapter, to see witchcraft within the context of 'vernacular religion' and to study its 'entire range'. It is also evident that people from different religious denominations have a different outlook on witchcraft, but precisely how remains largely a matter for future enquiry. Catholicism with its focus on ritual presentation probably provides for a kind of witchcraft that is more actively practised. Protestantism, as noticed above, can invite its adherents to violence, although both observations are possibly too broad and in need of precision. Even more interesting is the interplay between denominations, as when an occasional Protestant resorts to Catholic 'magic' to counter witches, or, as Éva Pócs relates in her chapter on Transylvania, when Roman Catholics seek the help of Orthodox priests. Similar positions can be ascribed to medicine, although we will have to look primarily to psychiatry or to medicine's 'irregular' variants. Adherents of animal magnetism, for instance, acknowledged witchcraft, if only to usurp the martyrs of the prosecutions for their own cause, while some psychiatrists claimed to 'understand' witchcraft. As in the case of religion, patients may very well have related to this to strengthen their use of the witchcraft discourse. Or to descend to the practical level once more, unwitching is in most cases only one of the possible cures a healer has to offer. Having an overview of the supply side of the medical market can help us to uncover the extent to which witchcraft as a diagnosis is favoured over other explanations. This is abundantly stressed by Enrique Perdiguero in the case of Spain, but it also applies to any other European country or region.

Transformations or fluctuations in local witchcraft discourses can be seen as the result of the sum of the choices people made when confronted with misfortune. The choices, in their turn, may have been governed by changes in available options and by changes in the religious or ideological outlook.

The little discussion that has taken place, however, has concentrated on witchcraft's decline rather than on its transformations, and has been related primarily to changing economic circumstances. At the moment we have not proceeded beyond the question why witchcraft disappeared earlier in one area of Europe than in another, and how this is possibly linked to the rationalization of infrastructure. This was, according to Nils Freytag, exactly what the Prussian government already suggested in the mid nineteenth century: improved education, better distribution of scientific medical knowledge and better communications would lift the remote parts of the country where superstition was linked to isolation. When we compare the situation in France with England it is evident that industrialization took an earlier hold in the latter country, and that the countryside emptied there much sooner. If witchcraft is intrinsically tied up with agriculture and foreign to urbanization, and there is evidence that it is not, this may explain why accusations have disappeared in England and are still much alive in France. The counter-example is presented by the western Netherlands, a much smaller region, but one that experienced urbanization and industrialization back in the seventeenth century, and where agricultural communities were far from self-sufficient. It therefore remains theoretically possible that witchcraft also survived in Britain, but that it is just poorly recorded or not at all. The witchcraft chronology of the western Netherlands is actually akin to England, as in both areas the last known cases happened before the Second World War. The eastern parts of the Netherlands, with traces of witchcraft accusations in the 1950s and 1960s, bears more resemblance to Germany and Denmark. There is too little substantial information about the rest of Europe to extend this map.[10]

A new element in this discussion is presented by Owen Davies in this volume when he supersedes the economic explanation by focusing on the typically French *mentalité paysan*. Witchcraft accusations are convincingly presented as belonging to a lifestyle that clings to traditional values and a regional rather than national identity. This may have wider relevance for the rest of Europe, that is, if a similar kind of lifestyle can be identified in nineteenth-century England or in mid-twentieth-century Germany for instance. Again we lack the research to answer these musings. Another question is whether these kind of comparisons have any relevance. They presume general rules on a European level,[11] while it may very well be the case that different explanations apply to different situations or different geographical entities. If the content of a witchcraft accusation and the repertoire of counter-measures are in any way related to the more encompassing ideologies that help inform them, then we should indeed expect one explanation to be valuable in only one locality. But how, for instance, a typically English custom such as scratching witches to draw blood relates to a specific regional rural economy and English identity has yet to be discovered. Comparisons can serve both to find out basic rules – if there are any, and to understand local particularities. To minimize complications they can better be kept between neighbouring countries or within the broad umbrella of Christianity in the case of Europe.

As already hinted, we also have to take the kind of source into account when trying to formulate provisional conclusions. If available, a different source does not immediately undermine findings, but rather puts them into perspective. In itself a case of witch assault taken from newspaper reports would not become less violent when a rare folklore account or an even rarer diary entry has transmitted other aspects of it. But other sources may indicate the presence of other cases with less violent endings. Laura Stark makes a remark to this extent about the folklore records she used as the basis for her chapter on Finnish witchcraft. Retribution in cases of bewitchment 'tended to assume the form of counter-sorcery rather than physical violence'. There was 'no need' to cause bodily harm. Elsewhere, folklore material does occasionally reveal violent unwitchments, but the bulk, however, show non-violent reactions. This material concerns not so much narratives, stories with a clear structure such as fairy tales, but legends, narrated memories inter-viewees had heard from others or even experienced themselves. These kind of texts are, on the whole, to be found more in twentieth-century collections than in nineteenth-century ones. The earlier witchcraft stories are usually too much selected and polished and published as autonomous examples of 'folk' narrative art. Only in the twentieth century did folklorists really begin to note down in shorthand most of what their informants told them, and even then not everything was published. As a result, the general image of the folk narrative text has remained one that resembles more a fairy tale than a fragment of daily speech. Folklore archives all over Europe, though not in England, are waiting to be explored to adjust this image. And as Willem de Blécourt shows in the case of the western Netherlands, it may be useful to consult a variety of local publications to counteract the geographically coincidental and thus limited range of folklore interviews, even though they did produce hundreds of texts for the places that were covered.

Next to this, much more use can be made of trial material, whether it concerns cruelty to animals, slander, assault, unlicensed medical practice, fraud, manslaughter or other misdemeanours and crimes. When almost a hundred cases featuring witchcraft can be collected in Germany for the thirty years between 1925 and 1956, then this provides promising prospects for other areas where the discourse was still vibrant, or for that matter for nineteenth-century Germany. And most of the German cases still await analysis. Furthermore, novels and movies have hardly been used as sources for nineteenth- and twentieth-century representations of witches. Like the pagan witches, the fairy-tale witches depicted in various forms of fiction may have little to do with the kind of witches accused of causing misfortune, but they are still part of the overall picture. On the basis of television series, for instance, we may even question whether witchcraft has really declined.

The contrast between stories and images on the one hand, and real-life witchcraft accusations or even practices on the other, can also be found on an everyday level. It is, in fact, in different ways one of the main themes of this volume. When we describe the witchcraft discourse as 'thinking and acting in terms of witchcraft' it refers to the process from formulating an event as witchcraft to witnessing the outcome of counter-measures. More abstract forms of the discourse are bound by specific geographical or social clusters, like any language or dialect. Although this implies the priority of the accusation, the ascription of someone as a witch, which is, in itself, a speech act, also includes other actions such as threatening a witch or ostracizing him or her. Other active forms of witchcraft, such as love magic, constitute the pendant of an accusation. They are, however, not always easy to establish and often stay within the realm of speech. People talk about putting pins in a doll or putting menstruation blood in coffee but the act itself may remain hidden, if it is ever performed at all. Witchcraft is more often than not restricted to texts, to stories, rather than put into practice. This applies to the participants in the witchcraft triangle as well as it does to the historian. Field work by Éva Pócs and her students also revealed, 'not so much practice as the narratives about it'. As long as we do not linger on historical 'facts', such as acts of violence, but also concentrate on what Laura Stark calls 'the narrative field which encoded and transmitted cultural think-ing about magical harm', this should be an advantage rather than a hindrance.

The tension between narrative and practice is also noticeable within the discourse. Sabina Magliocco suggests using the label 'folkloric witch' for those that figure primarily in stories: 'many activities attributed to witches were folkloric in nature', she writes in her chapter on Italy; 'that is, no living member of any community, even traditional magic-workers, practised them'. As she indicates, the problem is that this 'folkloric witch' and the ascribed or practising witch 'overlapped considerably in people's minds'. Stories, for example, about flying or animal metamorphosis could easily become attached to a member of the community. How then should we evaluate the principle of ostention which is central to Stephen Mitchell's interpretation of the 1808 Izzard case? This principle refers to the possibility of people acting out stories, but how did they perform broomstick riding or change into an animal? A very special example of making stories into physical reality is provided by Richard Jenkins in the case of Northern Ireland, where 'evidence' of black magic rituals was fabricated. Here, however, the meaning of the relics was based on movies and novels rather than on an indigenous Irish tradition, and the effects they produced were, in their turn, also narratives. As Mitchell demonstrates, ostention can be very useful if one wants to argue that when a 'doable' story circulates it may well be put into practice by someone, even when it concerns merely a suggestion of a practice. But it has to be used with caution. To see witchcraft stories as simply guides for violent action amounts to the denial of a previous process in which choices have been made and implies that what is narrated is also feasible. It thus undermines the position of the story on the one hand and the possibility of historical change on the other. It still does not follow that when only a story survives, it necessarily points to a past event and it does not make witchcraft less subject to ascription.

In witchcraft, stories and actions may be indiscernible from each other in the sense that the story can be the main observable action. As Jonathan Barry commented regarding the early modern period: 'the line between fact and fiction, history telling and storytelling, will be blurred, not just for the subsequent historian but also for the contemporary participant, above all when dealing with as elusive a subject as witchcraft. This very circumstance is itself of crucial importance to an understanding of witchcraft's history.' [12] What needs to be elaborated is the distinction between kinds of story, inside and outside the discourse. Susan Hoyle's chapter stresses the replacement of witchcraft by non-witchcraft stories and considers different interpretations of a witchcraft event as competitive. We can also ponder the difference between accounts of fully remembered events and vague reminiscences, between narratives about bewitchments and unwitchments and those about mere shape-shifting, for the vaguer stories may be a sign of the decline of the discourse. As Owen Davies concluded, 'the witch figure disappeared before the belief in witchcraft', that is, the practice of accusing someone of witchcraft dwindled earlier than the circulation of witchcraft stories.[13] But as long as the stories remain, witchcraft has not disappeared.

Notes

1 See the seminal articles by Marijke Gijswijt-Hofstra, 'Witchcraft after the Witch-Trials', in Willem de Blécourt, Ronald Hutton and Jean La Fontaine, *Witchcraft and Magic in Europe: The Twentieth Century* (London, 1999), pp. 95–189; Willem de Blécourt, 'The Witch, her Victim, the Unwitcher and the Researcher: The Continued Existence of Traditional Witchcraft', in Willem de Blécourt, Ronald Hutton and Jean La Fontaine, *Witchcraft in Twentieth-Century Europe* (London, 1999), pp. 141–219.

2 See Owen Davies, *Witchcraft, Magic and Culture 1736–1951* (Manchester, 1999); Owen Davies, *A People Bewitched: Witchcraft and Magic in Nineteenth Century Somerset* (Bruton, 1999). Two notable exceptions for other countries are, Judith Devlin, *The Superstitious Mind: French Peasants and the Supernatural in the Nineteenth Century* (New Haven and London, 1987); Christine D. Worobec, *Possessed: Women, Witches and Demons in Imperial Russia* (DeKalb, 2001).

3 Gustav Henningsen, 'Witchcraft', in Thomas A. Green (ed.), *Folklore: An Encyclopaedia of Beliefs, Customs, Tales, Music and Art* (Santa Barbara, 1997), p. 842. On modern pagan religion see, for example: Ronald Hutton, *The Triumph of the Moon: A History*

of Modern Pagan Witchcraft (Oxford, 1999); Susan Greenwood, *Magic, Witchcraft and the Otherworld: An Anthropology* (Oxford and New York, 2000).

4 Gijswijt-Hofstra, 'Witchcraft after the Witch-Trials', p. 183.

5 Gustav Henningsen, 'The Catechism of Witchlore in Twentieth-Century Denmark', in Jawaharial Handoo and Reimund Kvideland (eds), *Folklore in the Changing World* (Mysore, 1999), pp. 137–49.

6 Nils Freytag, *Aberglauben im 19. Jahrhundert. Preußen und seine Rheinprovinz zwischen Tradition und Moderne (1815–1918)* (Berlin, 2003), p. 363.

7 See Laura Stark-Arola, *Magic, Body and Social Order: The Construction of Gender Through Women's Private Rituals in Traditional Finland* (Helsinki, 1998).

8 Davies, *Witchcraft, Magic and Culture*, p. 271.

9 This appears, for instance, from Willem de Blécourt's work on metamorphosis narratives which refer partly to a sexual domain rather than to a witchcraft discourse. See, for example, his forthcoming book *Werewolves*, especially part 2.

10 See the references in de Blécourt, 'The Witch, her Victim, the Unwitcher and the Researcher'.

11 For a recent discussion with a global perspective see Ronald Hutton, 'The Global Context of the Scottish Witch-Hunt', in Julian Goodare (ed.), *The Scottish Witch-Hunt in Context* (Manchester, 2002), pp. 16–32.

12 Jonathan Barry, 'Keith Thomas and the Problem of Witchcraft', in Jonathan Barry, Marianne Hester and Gareth Roberts (eds), *Witchcraft in Early Modern Europe: Studies in Culture and Belief* (Cambridge, 1996), p. 44.

13 Davies, *Witchcraft, Magic and Culture*, p. 280. See also de Blécourt, 'The Witch, her Victim, the Unwitcher and the Researcher', p. 215.

1

A case of witchcraft assault in early nineteenth-century England as ostensive action

Stephen Mitchell

In his provocatively entitled *Cows, Pigs, Wars, and Witches: The Riddles of Culture*, anthropologist Marvin Harris suggests a one-dimensional explanation for the witch-hunts of early modern Europe, an all-encompassing theory of class warfare manipulated by elite culture, in effect, 'the magic bullet of society's privileged and powerful classes'. Of course, the case for the marriage of anthropology and history as a means of unravelling such mysteries as the European witch-hunts has been – and was already being in the early 1970s – made by a number of scholars, and usually, although not always, brought to this question a measure of subtle and helpful insights. Confidence was high that the lessons derived from fieldwork in living traditions of witchcraft might shed light on the seemingly irretrievable historical situation of early modern Europe. Throughout much of this century, functionalist interpretations of witchcraft in non-western contexts, for example, held that concepts of witchcraft are also theories of causation – and if there is causation, then there are agents of causation, and if there are agents of causation, then such agents can be identified. This view of witchcraft as a logical cultural construct was classically formulated by Evans-Pritchard in his study of Zande witchcraft,[1] in a conscious refutation of the views promoted by Lévy-Bruhl that regarded magic as unintelligible to logical thought.[2] Following Evans-Pritchard's monograph, several main trends in the anthropological interpretation of witchcraft accusations evolved, neatly categorized by Max Marwick as: (1) an outlet for repressed hostility, frustration, and anxiety; (2) the means for reaffirming social norms; (3) an index of social tension in society; and (4) a measure of tense personal relationships between accuser and accused.[3] While helpful, these four categories can and have been expanded and altered depending on the type of approach taken.[4] Following decades of study at the structural level of society, a more dynamic, incident-specific interpretive framework emerged in the 1960s. This approach is most closely associated with Victor Turner and did much to refine, and even revolutionize the anthropologist's understanding of witchcraft,[5] although not without criticism.[6]

It was at roughly this stage in the headily percolating ethnographic debate, that the observations of anthropologists were specifically turned to the historical European situation,[7] and with these important developments, the study of European witchcraft changed profoundly.[8]

The suitability of the analogical ethnographic argument to historical western European materials, although generally well regarded,[9] has not been without its difficulties. One obstacle has been the frequently insurmountable differences between the realities of highly localized observations within a small community and the uncertainties of reconstructed, region-wide events that present additional, special complications, such as the involvement of outside secular and religious authorities. An attendant difficulty has been the proliferation of theories looking to interpret the data, many of them exceedingly useful but almost always presented with a discernable quality of intellectual hegemony. Historians have certainly felt the pinch that comes with interpretations that are overly subtle or dare to rely on multiple theories for getting at some central truth, as Robin Briggs reminds us in his *Witches and Neighbours.*[10] One evolutionary pattern that has received a measure of approbation is implicit in the works of Kieckhefer, Cohn, Klaits and others. This runs along the following lines: popular (non-elite) fears and belief systems concerning individuals capable of harmful magic fuse in the later Middle Ages and in the early modern period with elite concerns, especially those of the Church, regarding heresy and other issues, resulting in a symbiosis between elite and non-elite views, the most apparent results of which were the witch trials between 1400 and 1700.[11] Following the so-called 'Enlightenment' in the eighteenth century, religious and secular authorities repudiate such belief systems, whereas non-elite views about witchcraft and evil continue into the contemporary world. Briggs accords a far smaller role to the interventions of elite culture and goes so far as to note that witchcraft beliefs may provide evidence of biologically conditioned fear of evil magic and its practitioners, and reminds us that, *contra* Harris and a host of others, the peasantry itself was by no means without its own active role in the process of the witch-hunts.[12] And yet after several decades of concentrated debate, Macfarlane's bipartite summary of the phenomena necessary for the formation of accusations in specific instances – 'firstly, the presence of some tension or anxiety or unexplained phenomenon; secondly, the directing of this energy into certain channels' – remains a useful reminder of the basic ingredients of an accusation.[13] It should be tempered though, as Ronald Hutton notes, by an 'emphasis on the need to reconstruct holistically the mental world of the participants in the trials, and a perception of the enhanced importance of folklore studies and psychology in the interpretation of the Hunt'.[14] Into this brief consideration of the theories of witchcraft, and with an eye towards a better understanding of theories of causation, the relevance of Hutton's perceptive observation concerning the 'mental world' of the participants in witch-hunts, and the folkloric dimensions that help create and define these activities – specifically the question of ostension – I would like to insert an incident from a village in the English countryside from long after the era of the witch-hunts.[15]

The case of Ann Izzard [16]

In 1808 Ann Izzard and her husband, of Great Paxton, Cambridgeshire, were attacked in their cottage by a mob of other villagers on two successive nights. The case has maintained a certain notoriety in local tradition, and forms part of – what was once in any event – a vigorous local belief system regarding witchcraft.[17] It was also a case that demanded the attention of contemporary legal authorities. According to the court documents, the case begins from this perspective when the accused residents of the village

> together with divers to wit fifty other persons to the Jurors at present unknown being rioters routers and disturbers of the public peace of our said Lord the King on the eighth day of May ... with force and arms in the parish of Great Paxton aforesaid in the County aforesaid unlawfully riotously and tumultuously did assemble and gather themselves together to disturb the Peace of our said Lord the King and being so assembled and gathered together the dwelling house of Wright Izzard situate and being in the parish of Great Paxton aforesaid in the County aforesaid then and there did unlawfully riotously and riotously break and enter and the Door of the said Wright Izzard of and belonging to the said dwelling house and then and there affixed thereto and then and there being shut bolted and fastened did then and there unlawfully riotously and riotously force and break open, break to pieces and destroy And that they the said Joseph Harper Thomas Braybrook James Staughton Mary Amey Frances Amey and Alice Brown and the several other persons to the Jurors aforesaid yet unknown then and there with force and arms riotously and tumultuously did make an assault on the said Wright Izzard and also on and upon the Ann the wife of the said Wright Izzard And them the said Wright Izzard and Ann his wife in the Peace of God and our said Lord the King then and there being did beat wound and ill-treat and her the said Ann then and there with force and arms did then and there seize and drag from the Bed in which she the said Ann then and there lying and being and with Pins and other Sharp Instruments did then and there lacerate and wound the said Ann in and upon the Neck Breasts Arms Sides and different parts of the body and then and there greatly terrify and affright the said Ann and put her in great fear of the loss of her life and other wrongs to the said Wright Izzard and Ann his wife.[18]

In addition to the court records, we are fortunate to have the detailed, published observations of these events by Isaac Nicholson, the curate of the parish that included Great Paxton.[19] The Rev. Nicholson's description of these assaults is much briefer than the Crown's, but also much clearer about the cause of it:

> A considerable number of people assembled together, as it grew dark on Sunday evening, the eighth of May, and taking with them the young women ridiculously supposed to be bewitched, and about ten o'clock; proceeded to the cottage of Wright Izzard, which stands alone, at some distance from the body of the village. When they arrived at this solitary spot, so favourable for the execution of their villainous designs, they broke into the poor man's house, dragged his wife out of bed, and threw her naked into the yard; where, her arms were torn with pins, her head was dashed against the large stones of the causeway – and her face, stomach, and breast were severely bruised with a thick stick that served as a bar to the door. Having thus satisfied themselves, the mob dispersed. The woman then crawled into her house, put her clothes on, and went to the constable, who said, 'he could not protect her, because he was not sworn'.[20]

On the evening of the following day, Izzard is assaulted a second time, with the result that, again according to the court papers, the attackers

> unlawfully violently and maliciously did seize and drag the said Ann from the bed in which she was then and there lying and being And with their fists did then and there strike the said Ann divers violent and grievous strokes and blows whereby the said Ann was then and there thrown and forced to and upon the ground and with certain Pins and other sharp Instruments which they the said Joseph Harper Thomas Braybrook James Staughton Mary Amey Frances Amey and Alice Brown then and there had and held in their hands unlawfully and maliciously did then and there lacerate and wound her the said Ann in and upon the Breasts and other parts of the body.[21]

It should be noted that neither the indictment nor the Rev. Nicholson's account appears to comprehend the reason for the violent assaults on Ann Izzard. Certainly, the Rev. Nicholson understood that it was connected with the supposed bewitchment of several young people, but would appear to believe that his flock has simply turned into a mob in order to avenge itself on Izzard. The court documents come closer when they specify that the attackers have come prepared with pins and other sharp objects with which they lacerate Izzard, 'whereby the said Ann then and there lost great quantities of Blood which ran and flowed from the breasts and body of her the said Ann and then and there suffered great pain smart and anguish'.[22] It is, I submit, on the intersection of interpretations about what takes place at this juncture that the case as a whole turns. The surviving contemporary evidence – our various testimonies from elite sources – are largely deaf on this issue, although the indictment's emphasis on 'Pins and sharp Instruments' reflects the understanding the villagers themselves, attackers and attacked alike, placed on events, as I argue below.

According to the Rev. Nicholson, the troubles of 1808 began when several young women, Alice Brown, Fanny Amey and Mary Fox, began *seriatim* to fall subject to 'convulsions', 'fits, weakness, and dejection' of an unknown origin and can no longer work. In an attempt to discover the cause of the troubles in the village, the father of one of the afflicted girls tries a charm. He does so on the advice of a stranger,[23] who, according to the Rev. Nicholson, relates the following story:

> 'As sure as you are alive, Sir,' continued a man, who stood by, 'she is bewitched, and so are two other girls that live near her. There is a man in the town I come from in Bedfordshire, who was exactly like Alice Brown – he could do no work, lost all his strength, and was wasting away very fast, when a person told him what was the matter with him, and how he might be cured. He filled a bottle with a particular kind of a fluid, stuffed the cork both top and bottom, with pins, set it carefully in an oven of a moderate heat, and then observed a profound silence. In a few minutes the charm succeeded; for, he saw a variety of forms flitting, before his eyes, and amongst the rest the perfect resemblance of an old woman who lived in the same parish. This was what he wanted – he was now satisfied who it was that had injured him, and that her reign would soon be over. The woman, whose figure he saw, died in a few days, and the man immediately recovered.'[24]

Later, Nicholson is told that the girl 'is under an ill tongue' and 'bewitched'. The following Sunday, Ann Izzard tells Nicholson that her neighbours claim to have discovered through various charms that she is a witch and blame her for the illness of the three young women. Despite Nicholson's best efforts, a frenzied state of panic eventually ripples through the parish, following a triggering event that in the minds of the villagers tips the scales in favour of the violence described by Nicholson and the court papers.

A year and three court proceedings later, nine villagers are found guilty of assaulting the couple.[25] Importantly, it should be noted that the attackers do not accept that their behaviour was wrong. According to the *Sussex Weekly Advertiser* of 27 November 1809, one of them, Joseph Harper, testified at his trial that Ann Izzard had cried out with a voice – 'the Old Note' – just as the girls had done when they were in their fits, and one of the fathers, Thomas Brown, claimed that once his daughter had drawn blood from Ann, her fits had come to an end.[26] Against this view from the participants in the attacks on the Izzards, I place part of the judge's pronouncement against the accused when they were found guilty and sentenced to various periods in gaol. It stands as an excellent reminder of just how at odds were elite and non-elite opinions about the case:

> But however such an assembling of persons and their committing such assault may excite our surprise, and call our indignation; the *pretence* for doing it is still *more* extraordinary and surprising; namely, that two of you, the defendants, were under the influence of the witchcraft of the prosecutrix

Ann Izzard, and that the torturing and drawing blood of this poor woman, was the only remedy for that witchcraft. – Such a pretence is so extraordinary, that it can hardly be used by any honest people in the present state of human knowledge in the community in which we live, when it is known by the most ignorant among us, that the law prohibits, and punishes severely, persons who shall pretend to possess the power of witchcraft, sorcery, or incantation … In fact, the wisdom of the Legislature has declared, that such a cause as that which you have pretended to have operated upon your mind, and led to your outrageous conduct on this occasion, does not exist, and therefore you cannot stand excused by your pretence of a deluded ignorance, and it is now held out to the world that the presence of the power of witchcraft is only founded in delusion, claimed to be exercised by none but *knaves*, and believed by none but *fools*. – It was to prevent the fraud of impudent impostors practising on the folly of others, that the statute was enacted. – Indeed there is a difficulty in believing that any of you could, seriously, conceive that this poor women you so cruelly assaulted, really possessed the power of witchcraft; but that you pretended that ignorance to excuse your malice; and when we reflect on the consequence which might have followed your misconduct, the power that might have been necessary to repel your riotous behaviour to protect the public and preserve the peace, or indeed to get this poor unfortunate woman out of your power, your offence becomes a very serious one, and the more I have turned the subject in my mind since the trial, the more I am disposed to think that the pretence of your believing in the witchcraft of this poor creature, was the effect only of your malice against this individual.[27]

The background of the assaults

Described in 1808 as 'a small mean village' at the time of the attacks, Great Paxton consisted of 217 inhabitants living mainly in mud-walled cottages.[28] Huntingdonshire was at this time in the midst of serious economic realignment, with factory labour becoming a growing source of income.[29] Adding to the sense of great economic changes, the process of enclosure was under discussion for Huntingdonshire, for which it would be authorized shortly after the events of the Izzard case. In addition to the economic situation of the villagers and the major cultural changes under way in the area, what best contextualizes the events of 1808 are the personal tragedies in Great Paxton in the preceding period, calamities that outline the tension, anxiety and unexplained phenomena – to paraphrase Macfarlane's useful remark – present in Great Paxton. According to the parish records, Mary Hook, one of those imprisoned for her part in the assaults on Izzard, had lost four of her seven children at early ages, mostly under eighteen months, by the time of the attacks, and one of her three surviving children died just months afterward on 21 July 1808.[30] In fact, the parish records suggest a series of unusual deaths among the villagers. In 1799, Thomas Russel, 'Died in a fit at the

bottom of the Hill, near the village'; in 1801, James Anvill accidentally
drowned; in 1803, James Staughton, the six-year-old son of James Staughton,
who will be one of those jailed for the attacks on the Izzards, 'accidentally
drowned in a Pond in the Street'. Especially meaningful, in the months
leading up to the assaults, we find that on 21 February 1808, Robert Emery
'aged 14: yr 3. mo. In a fit of lunacy hanged himself owing as it was thought
to the loss of his sight. He had been blind something more than two months
– this heavy affliction preyed upon his mind. He used to tell his father he
had more upon it than he could bear.' [31] It is in this context, in an atmosphere
of odd deaths in a village of some 200 inhabitants, and just weeks after a
young man commits suicide, that a number of other young people fall subject
to fits. To the residents of Great Paxton, some evil force no doubt seemed
to be abroad. For his part, the Rev. Nicholson mentions only the fits of the
young women (which he is inclined to attribute to natural causes) and takes
no note at all of these other factors, not even Emery's death.[32]

Collateral information about Izzard's reputation as a witch suggests that
it was in all likelihood strong before, and not merely after the events of 1808,
and although Izzard moved out of Great Paxton, she continued to be harassed
and stories about her magical powers continued to be told. One of the most
striking features of the Izzard case is its similarity to other, earlier accusations
of bewitchment; and as in many incidents of witchcraft accusation and
persecution, while the table for such accusations is set by long-simmering
troubles and reputations a lifetime in the making, the events in Great Paxton
are touched off by first one and eventually several young women behaving
oddly, oddly enough to bring the attention and concern of adult society to
bear on their collective condition.[33] When no normal medical remedy seems
to have an effect, popular opinion holds that the agents of causation can be
identified through special divination. It is at this point, however, that the
Great Paxton case differs so sharply from earlier cases: whereas in pre-En-
lightenment cases, ecclesiastical and judicial authorities joined, indeed,
directed subsequent prosecution of the accused, in the Huntingdonshire of
the nineteenth century, the church and the law stood firmly against belief in
witchcraft. But official reactions are not fully post-Enlightenment: it should
be remembered that the parish constable, an office typically held by a local
farmer or other community member, refuses to give relief to Izzard following
the attacks on her, with the excuse that he has not yet been sworn in. This
figure more than any other, perhaps, underscores the differences between elite
and non-elite assessments of the situation: despite having been chosen to
represent the courts in the village of Great Paxton, the constable, coming
from the village itself but importantly holding the confidence of elite society,
apparently sides with the villagers' interpretations of events.[34]

For the villagers of Great Paxton, causation is the immediate key to
solving their trouble, and they consequently undertake to find the individual

responsible for the malefic magic in their midst, identifying Ann Izzard as the cause of their problems. At this juncture the disintegration of the witch-hunting pact between elite and non-elite is most apparent. In essence, the dilemma over which Great Paxton found itself torn in 1808 – torn along class lines – is well described by an astute conclusion drawn from an observation from the field nearly forty years ago about attitudes toward the killing of a witch: does a popular response to witchcraft represent an act of public service, or is it an attack on the very foundation of society? [35] Precisely these conflicting interpretations were made of the events of 1808 by the various participants. To the villagers, the attacks on Izzard are neither illogical nor hysterical outbursts, but rather understood by the attackers to be acts of value to the community as a whole, in effect, a necessary cleansing rite. The fathers of the afflicted girls hail as a success their work to free their daughters from the evil in the village, yet the same behaviour causes the judiciary and the clergy to recoil in horror at the violence and injustice of the villagers' behaviour. To the Rev. Nicholson and the justice system, the attacks are nothing more than outrages committed against an innocent victim, acts which threaten social order as a whole, an order of which they are the most prominent representatives in the area. In the view of the elite class, the villagers are anything but pillars of society; they are nothing more than 'rioters routers and disturbers of the public peace'.[36] To follow the symbiotic model noted earlier, when the synergy of witchcraft beliefs held by the elite and popular segments of society ends, the two largely go their separate ways, as the two views about what happens in Great Paxton in 1808 underscores.

The assaults on Izzard as ostensive action [37]

To put the Izzard case into the sort of perspective in which non-European witchcraft traditions are often assayed, the villagers held to a 'magical world view', one that is perceived by elite society then as now to be inferior with respect to both religion and to science.[38] It is a world-view that does not recognize the possibility of accidents or randomness: in the 'magical world view' everything is logically connected in a chain of causation.[39] The 'magical world view' provides an important perspective on the case of Ann Izzard, as the villagers remain convinced that they have behaved properly: they identify the problem, confront it and fix it. Certainly this is the interpretation reflected in the testimony of one of the participants, Thomas Brown, who maintains at the trial that the village 'remedy' has worked. One important and helpful way to understand the events of 1808–9 is to view the collective behaviour of the villagers as acts of ostension, that is, the acting out of traditional narratives – what one folklorist describes as the dramatic extension of legend complexes into real life, a factor frequently cited in the context of contemporary rumour panics.[40] As has been noted of the reticulations between legendary beliefs, on one hand, and behaviour that helps constitute these phenomena, on the other, 'not only can facts be turned into narratives but narratives can also be turned into facts'.[41] In his discussion of contemporary satanic incidents in the US, Bill Ellis argues a point that has particular relevance for the Izzard case: 'Folklorists must acknowledge that traditional narratives ... are also maps for action, often violent actions.'[42] Among the villagers of Great Paxton, the assaults were considered neither violent outrages, revenge attacks nor irrational outbursts. Rather to the villagers, conditioned as they were by a unified system of witchcraft beliefs and supporting narratives, the attacks represented an appropriate remedy to their problems; their reaction was the enactment of an inherited script for a folk exorcism. It is for this reason they appeared outside the Izzard cottage armed with 'Pins and sharp Instruments', prepared to play out their parts in this serious drama by drawing blood from the person believed to be a witch. That the contours of this case were profoundly shaped, not only by the proximate events and social details within Great Paxton itself, but also by the larger native traditions of 'how to respond in the event of witchcraft', may be seen by the degree to which much of the story of 1808–9 and its subsequent life as oral history and lore in the village, is paralleled elsewhere in the corpus of English witchcraft traditions as represented in Baughman's *Type and Motif-Index of the Folktales of England and North America*.[43] Virtually all aspects of the Izzard case – the unusual events that take place in Great Paxton, the means used to discover the malefactor, the methods employed in countering the witch's charms, how Izzard herself responds when she realizes she is thought to be the witch – are conceived, interpreted and shaped by traditional rubrics about witchcraft.[44] Phatic and healing conversations using – indeed, dictated by – the narrative motifs which made up such scripts rippled through the village with the unfolding of each new event.[45] It is precisely in this sense that we must understand the following episode, one of a growing number of signs that something is amiss in the village just before the assaults, of which the Rev. Nicholson reports:

> On Thursday the fifth of May, Ann Izzard was at St. Neots market; and it so happened that her son, about sixteen years old, was sent the same day to St. Neots, by his master, a respectable farmer of Great Paxton, for a load of corn. When he returned, his mother and another woman accompanied him. Contrary to the better advice of her neighbour, the latter insisted upon putting a basket of grocery upon the top of the sacks of corn. One of the horses which drew the cart, was young and unmanageable, and in going down the hill which leads into the village of Paxton, by his plunging and restiveness, overturned it. By this unfortunate accident the shopkeeper's grocery was materially damaged; and, because Ann Izzard had repeatedly advised her not to put the basket upon the sacks, she charged her with overturning the cart by means of her infernal art, on purpose to spoil her

goods. It will scarcely be credited, that in an hour after, the whole parish was in an uproar: 'She has just overturned a loaded cart, with as much ease as if it had been a spinning wheel,' was echoed from one end of it to the other. Men, women and children raised their voices, and exclaimed, 'we have now proof positive of her guilt – this last act in open day speaks for itself – she is the person that does all the mischief, and if something is not done to put a stop to her baseness, there will be no living in the place.' [46]

In this account, we see how misfortune and physics are turned by the residents of Great Paxton into marvels and signs that conform to traditional motifs (*Witch bewitches wagon; Witch upsets loads of hay on level ground*), shaping the accusations that follow.[47] Macfarlane's model of pre-existing tensions being channelled in a certain direction in the aftermath of an incendiary event aptly accounts at one level for events in Great Paxton.[48] But that explanation is considerably enhanced when we recognize the degree to which this channelling represents a manifestation of complex traditional codes of behaviour concerning witchcraft.

Further evidence of the reticulation between (1) beliefs about appropriate responses to witchcraft, (2) witchcraft narratives in general, (3) the specific actions taken in the Izzard case and (4) the stories about this incident, is providentially provided for us through a competition for Huntingdonshire village stories organized by the Women's Institute in 1935. One entry in the resulting manuscript, offered by the wife of a descendant of one of Izzard's persecutors, gives us new insights into how the story has been remembered within the village.[49] Izzard is described as having 'a good knowledge of herbs and simples', making her a feared witch figure in the community. But the stories also associate Izzard with an array of behaviours we do not have knowledge of elsewhere, either in the Rev. Nicholson's reports or the court documents. All of these stories parallel aspects of English witchcraft tradition: Izzard is said, for example, to have bewitched the wife of her creditor, the innkeeper and grocer, 'making her go through all sorts of queer antics, even to dancing on the tea table among the cups and saucers' (*Magic dancing; Enchanted persons dance until released; Witch causes innkeeper to dance in revenge for overcharging; Witch torments person by making him act in a ridiculous manner*).[50] It sounds like a reworking of the wagon episode, in which the shopkeeper's groceries are ruined. 'Nanny' Izzard is also reported to have gone to local farmers, demanding butter, 'and if people refused to let her have it, she would put her hand in the churn so that it was "witched" and refused to turn any more. One day, the farmer, Mr Bidwell, put a red hot poker into the churn, so when poor old Nanny tried to do the bewitching she got badly burnt' (*Breaking spell on cream that refuses to become butter by putting hot iron in the cream, thus burning the witch; Breaking spell on cream by putting hot poker in the cream; Hot iron put into churn*).[51] Not only were the events of 1808 shaped by witchcraft narratives, but the subsequent 'defence' of the villagers' collective behaviour, specifically among the families of those most responsible, is similarly moulded by such motifs.

The case of Ann Izzard is hardly a particularly severe instance among post-Enlightenment witchcraft episodes. Yet had it taken place two hundred years earlier, elite English institutions might well have agreed with the villagers' understanding of their situation and joined them in the persecution. By the early nineteenth century, however, the symbiotic relationship between elite and non-elite sections of society where witchcraft is concerned has changed, and the differing views of magic, evil and causation held by the authorities and by those over whom they had dominion play out in significantly different ways. As Trevor-Roper noted, the eradication of such a belief system could not take place in isolation, but only when the total environment that supported it has changed.[52] Such a transformation had indeed occurred in elite society by the nineteenth century, as we are reminded when the judge berates the defendants at the trial by calling their defence – that the girls were 'under the influence, the sorcery and witchcraft of the prosecutrix' – 'absurd' and an 'impossible pretence'.[53] But a very different view was held among non-elites, as the behaviour of the villagers in the Izzard case usefully reminds us. The result of this hybridized situation, with institutional opinion totally transformed, but village-level perspectives largely unchanged, did not in the end spare Ann Izzard pain, humiliation and actual harm, although it very probably spared her life. Moreover, it is a case that highlights how profoundly ingrained traditional views remained among the populace as a whole, and how quickly such views could be turned into ostensive action.

Notes

1 I take this opportunity to express my heartfelt thanks to the many librarians, churchwardens, local historians and pub owners (and customers) in the Great Paxton area for their assistance in researching this essay; I am particularly obliged to Alan Akeroyd and his colleagues at the County Records Office, Huntingdon. E. E. Evans-Pritchard, *Witchcraft, Oracles and Magic Among the Azande* (Oxford, 1937), p. 387. See, however, Evans-Pritchard, *Theories of Primitive Religion* (Oxford, 1965), p. 114: 'The so-called functional method was too vague and too slick to persist, and also too much coloured by pragmatism and teleology. It rested too much on a rather flimsy biological analogy.' Nevertheless, it can be little doubted that Evans-Pritchard's *Witchcraft, Oracles, and Magic Among the Azande* came to be associated largely with such homeostatic concepts as the patterned expression of tension within the community, the normative effect of witchcraft beliefs on behaviour, and so on, and gave rise to a number of works on African witchcraft which took this view as a starting point.

2 In discussing sympathetic magic, for example, Lévy-Bruhl remarked, 'en créant entre eux et lui un lien, *inintelligible sans doute pour la pensée logique*, mais conforme à la loi de participation qui régit la mentalité prélogique et ses représentations collectives': Lucien Lévy-Bruhl, *Les fonctions mentales dans les sociétés inférieures* (3rd edn, Paris, 1918), p. 350. The italics are mine.

3 Max Marwick, 'The Study of Witchcraft', in A. L. Epstein (ed.), *The Craft of Social*

Anthropology (New York and London, 1967), pp. 237–40. See also Marwick, 'Witch-craft as a Social Strain-Gauge', in Max Marwick (ed.), *Witchcraft and Sorcery* (London, [1964] 1982), pp. 300–13.

4 Alan Macfarlane for example, categorized anthropological approaches as: (1) 'witch-craft as explanation', (2) 'the function of witchcraft as a release of tension', (3) 'witchcraft and the social structure', (4) 'witchcraft and social control' and (5) 'west-ernization and witchcraft': Macfarlane, *Witchcraft in Tudor and Stuart England: A Regional and Comparative Study* (London, [1970] and Prospect Heights, 1991), pp. 240–53. Tamara Multhaupt organizes these approaches to African witchcraft into historical and theoretical categories: missionary and other colonial views; Lévy-Bruhl's concern with rationality *versus* irrationality; and so on: Multhaupt, 'Sozialan-thropologische Theorien über Hexerei und Zauberei in Afrika', *Anthropos* 82 (1987) 445–56. To these approaches one would necessarily want to add emerging metho-dologies, such as the growing number of feminist and other gendered approaches. See, for example, Ingrid Ahrendt-Schulte, 'Hexenprozesse als Spiegel von Alltags-konflikten', in Sönke Lorenz and Dieter R. Bauer (eds), *Hexenverfolgung. Beiträge zur Forschung* (Würzburg, 1995), pp. 347–58; Diane Purkiss, *The Witch in History* (Lon-don, 1996); Marianne Hester, *Lewd Women and Wicked Witches* (London, 1992).

5 See Victor Turner, 'Witchcraft and Sorcery: Taxonomy Versus Dynamics', in idem, *Forest of Symbols* (Ithaca and London, [1964] 1967), pp. 112–27. Turner's review article of Middleton and Winter 1963, in which he pursues the question, 'What bearing has a method of sociological analysis on the study of witch beliefs?' (p. 118), argues in favour of social interactionism over a more static interpretation of witch-craft. See also Victor Turner, *Schism and Continuity in an African Society* (Manchester, [1957] 1972), pp. 148–53.

6 See William Arens, 'Taxonomy versus Dynamics Revisited: The Interpretation of Misfortune in a Poly-Ethnic Community', in Ivan Karp and Charles S. Bird (eds), *Explorations in African Systems of Thought* (Bloomington, 1980), pp. 165–80.

7 The most prominent signs of this new symbiosis were Keith Thomas's *Religion and the Decline of Magic* (London, 1971) and Macfarlane, *Witchcraft*. Mary Douglas also indicates this sea change: 'Historians and anthropologists have a common interest in the subject of witchcraft, but until very recently their outlooks have diverged … Now this difference is being narrowed: the historians who have contributed to this volume have succeeded in delving into material very comparable to that used by anthropo-logists and the latter are gradually improving the time-scale of their observation. The moment has come for a survey of the subject': Douglas (ed.), *Witchcraft Confessions and Accusations* (London, 1970), p. xiii.

8 This paradigm shift is neatly dated by Wolfgang Behringer to the change in 1974 in the *Encyclopaedia Britannica*: Behringer, 'Witchcraft Studies in Austria, Germany and Switzerland', in Jonathan Barry, Marianne Hester and Gareth Roberts (eds), *Witchcraft in Early Modern Europe* (Cambridge, 1996), pp. 66–7. See also the overviews offered by H. C. Erik Midelfort, 'Recent Witch Hunting Research, or Where Do We Go From Here?', *Paper of the Bibiliographical Society of America* 62 (1968) 373–420; Jens Christian and V. Johansen, 'Tavshed er guld … En historiografisk oversigt over amerikansk og europæisk heksetros-forskning 1966–81', *Historisk Tidsskrift* 81, 2 (1982) 401–23.

9 See the contributions in Douglas, *Witchcraft Confessions*.

10 See Robin Briggs, *Witches & Neighbours* (London, 1996), p. 397: 'There are indeed historians who claim that there is something illegitimate about offering multiple explanations for simultaneous occurrences.'

11 Joseph Klaits, *Servants of Satan: The Age of the Witch Hunts* (Bloomington, 1985);

Richard Kieckhefer, *European Witch Trials: Their Foundations in Popular and Learned Culture, 1300–1500* (Berkeley and Los Angeles, 1976); Norman Cohn, *Europe's Inner Demons: An Inquiry Inspired by the Great Witch-Hunt* (London, 1975).

12 See Briggs, *Witches*, p. 394: 'Witchcraft may therefore be a phenomenon we are predisposed to suspect, a psychic potential we cannot help carrying round within ourselves as part of our long-term inheritance.'

13 Macfarlane, *Witchcraft in Tudor and Stuart England*, p. 231.

14 Ronald Hutton, review of Diane Purkiss's *The Witch in History: Early Modern and Twentieth-Century Representations*. See 'Reviews in History', Institute of Historical Research website: www.history.ac.uk/reviews/paper/hutton.html.

15 The importance of post-Enlightenment cases has been highlighted in Gustav Henningsen, 'Witch Persecution after the Era of the Witch Trials: A Contribution to Danish Ethnography', *Arv* 44 (1988; first published in Danish in 1975) 103–53; Henningsen, 'Das Ende der Hexenprozesse und die Forsetzung der populären Hexenverfolgung', in Sönka Lorenz and Dieter R. Bauer (eds), *Das Ende der Hexenverfolgung* (Stuttgart, 1995), pp. 315–28; Willem de Blécourt, 'On the Continuation of Witchcraft', in Barry *et al.*, *Witchcraft in Early Modern Europe*, pp. 335–52; Owen Davies, *Witchcraft, Magic and Culture 1736–1951* (Manchester, 1999).

16 For a fuller treatment of the details of the case, its participants, and their situations see Stephen A. Mitchell, 'Witchcraft Persecutions in the Post-Craze Era: The Case of Ann Izzard of Great Paxton, 1808', *Western Folklore* 59 (2000) 304–28. The present article builds on and extends the arguments, especially the relationship between the historical events and the subsequent narratives about them. See also Davies, *Witchcraft, Magic and Culture*, pp. 49–50, 111–12 and 197–8.

17 The area is famously associated with witchcraft. For early modern examples see C. L'Estrange Ewen, *Witchcraft and Demonianism* (London, [1933] 1970), pp. 169–73, 454, 461. For more recent reports see Mitchell, 'Witchcraft Persecutions'.

18 Public Record Office (hereafter PRO), London, KB 11/66 (1), St Hilary 1809, #36'c'.

19 Isaac Nicholson, *A Sermon against Witchcraft: Preached in the Parish Church of Great Paxton, in the County of Huntingdon, July 17, 1808. With a Brief Account of the Circumstances which Led to Two Atrocious Attacks on the Person of Ann Izzard, as a Reputed Witch* (London, 1808); Nicholson, *An Abstract of the Proceedings had against Joseph Harper, James Staughton, Thomas Braybrook, Mary Amey, Fanny Amey, Alice Browne, Edward Briers, Mary Hook, and Mary Fox, for Assaulting Ann Izzard of Great Paxton, in the County of Huntington, on the 8th and 9th of May, 1808, under the Pretence of her being a Witch* (London, 1810).

20 Nicholson, *A Sermon Against Witchcraft*, pp. vii–viii.

21 PRO, KB 11/66 (1), St Hilary 1809, #36 'c'.

22 PRO, KB 11/66 (1), St Hilary 1809, #36 'c'.

23 The role this stranger plays suggests that he might have been a cunning-man brought in for the purpose of helping in precisely this way. See Davies, *Witchcraft*, pp. 214–29.

24 Nicholson, *A Sermon Against Witchcraft*, pp. ii–iii.

25 The cases are removed from the lower courts by writs of *certiorari* (PRO, KB 11/66 (1), St Hilary 1809, #36 'a' and #37 'a'), and kept within the purview of the King's Bench. The defendants are charged both there and in the indictments themselves with 'Riots and Misdemeanours'. Importantly, the facts presented by the Crown (PRO, KB 11/66 (1), St Hilary 1809, #36 'c' and #37 'c') tally neatly with the version given by the Rev. Nicholson, without mentioning witchcraft.

26 Quoted in Mike Stephenson, 'The Story of Ann Izzard – Retold', *The Huntsman: The Journal of the Huntingdonshire Family History Society* 16 (1993) 18.

27 Nicholson, *Abstract of the Proceedings*, pp. 9–10.

28 E. W. Brayley and John Britton, *Historical Description of the County of Huntingdon* (London, 1808), pp. 572–3.

29 Rose Young, *St Neots Past* (Chichester, 1996), p. 81.

30 The Register Book of Great Paxton 1702–1807 (County Record Office, Huntingdon, 2685/1/2).

31 The Register Book of Great Paxton 1702–1807 (County Record Office, Huntingdon, 2685/1/2).

32 The Rev. Nicholson's role in these events is complex, and I note that he may have pursued a personal agenda in his writings. Although I continue to regard his pamphlets as the most important testimony we have to events in Great Paxton, I recognize that they are anything but a mirror-like reflection of historical reality.

33 See Davies, *Witchcraft*, p. 197.

34 See Davies, *Witchcraft*, pp. 111–12, on the ambiguous and often conflicted situation of the constables.

35 'The problem of social order rests on the consensual meshing of public opinion about an act of violence which is either a favour to the society as a whole, or the most flagrant violation of its moral equilibrium': Manning Nash, 'Witchcraft as Social Process in a Tzeltal Community', in John Middleton (ed.), *Magic, Witchcraft and Curing* (Garden City, [1961] 1967), p. 128.

36 PRO, London, KB 11/66 (1), St. Hilary 1809, #36 'c'.

37 Within folklore, the term 'ostension' is most directly borrowed from the field of semiotics, notwithstanding its venerable use in other fields. The meaning of the word – 'the act of showing; manifestation; revealing; appearance; display; monstrance' – and its etymology (*ostendere* 'to show') underscore its relevance to the sort of situation under discussion.

38 See the encompassing and synthetic treatment of this thorny issue in Stanley Tambiah, *Magic, Science, Religion, and the Scope of Rationality* (Cambridge, 1990), pp. 1–15.

39 As Wax and Wax note, 'We think of ourselves as the believers in causal law and the primitive as dwelling in a world of happenstance. Yet, the actuality is to the contrary: It is we who accept the possibility and logic of pure chance, while for the dweller in the magical world, no event is "accidental" or "random," but each has its chain of causation in which Power, or its lack, was the decisive agency': Rosalie Wax and Murray Wax, 'The Magical World View', *Journal for the Scientific Study of Religion* 1 (1962) 183. It is, of course, exactly the exploration of this point that is at the heart of Evans-Pritchard, *Witchcraft, Oracles*.

40 Bill Ellis, *Aliens, Ghosts, and Cults: Legends We Live* (Jackson, Mississippi, 2001), p. 41. With respect to the applicability of 'ostension' and 'ostensive action' to folkloristics, see Linda Dégh and Andrew Vázsonyi, 'Does the Word "Dog" Bite? Ostensive Action: A Means of Legend-Telling', *Journal of Folklore Research* 20 (1983) 5–34; Gary Alan Fine, 'Redemption Rumors and the Power of Ostension', *Journal of American Folklore* 104 (1991) 179–81; Bill Ellis, 'Death by Folklore: Ostension, Contemporary Legend, and Murder', *Western Folklore* 48,1 (1989) 201–20; idem, *Raising the Devil: Satanism, New Religions and the Media* (Lexington, 2000), pp. 204, 226, 236, 286–7; idem, 'Ostension as Folk Drama', in *Aliens, Ghosts*, pp. 165–85.

41 Dégh and Vázsonyi, 'Does the Word "Dog" Bite?', 29.

42 Ellis, 'Death by Folklore', 218.

43 Ernest Warren Baughman (ed.), *Type and Motif-Index of the Folktales of England and North America*, Indiana University Publications, Folklore series 20 (The Hague, 1966).

44 Among the motifs connected with the Izzard case are the following: D1741.2.1 *Drawing witch's blood annuls her spells*; G263.4.2 *Witch causes victim to have fits*; G265.8.3.2 *Witch bewitches wagon*; G265.8.3.2(d) *Witch upsets loads of hay on level ground*;

G257.1(d) *Boiling needles or pins forces witch to reveal herself*; G271.4.1(h) *Breaking spell by boiling victim's urine*; G271.4.1(le) *Breaking spell on person by putting quart bottle of pins by the fire*; G273.6 *Witch rendered powerless by drawing blood from witch*; H234 *Weighing witch against Bible*. For a full and detailed list see Mitchell, 'Witchcraft Persecutions'.

45 The phrase 'phatic communion' was coined by Malinowski to describe language's role in promoting social solidarity and reinforcing the hierarchies within the group. See Bronislaw Malinowski, 'The Problem of Meaning in Primitive Languages', in C. K. Ogden, I. Richards anf J. Postgate (eds), *The Meaning of Meaning: A Study of the Influence of Language upon Thought and of the Science of Symbolism* (London and New York, 1923), pp. 451–510. The sense of 'phatic communion' has been extended to include, as I intend it here, a broad range of social, as opposed to directly informational communications.

46 Nicholson, *A Sermon Against Witchcraft*, pp. vi–vii.

47 Baughman, *Type and Motif-Index*, G265.8.3.2 and G265.8.3.2(d).

48 Macfarlane, *Witchcraft*, p. 231.

49 Huntingdonshire Federation of Women's Institutes, c. 1935, *Tales from Hunts. Villages* (bound, typed manuscript). See also C. F. Tebbutt, *Huntingdonshire Folklore* (St Neots, 1952), p. 32; and idem, *Huntingdonshire Folklore*, 2nd edn, Friends of the Norris Museum Occasional Publications 4 (St Ives, 1984), pp. 82–3.

50 Baughman, *Type and Motif-Index*, D2174, D2174(c) and G269.21.

51 Baughman, *Type and Motif-Index*, G271.4.1(k), G271.4.1(kc) and D2084.2(dd).

52 Trevor-Roper, *European Witch-Craze*, p. 105.

53 Nicholson, *Abstract of the Proceedings*, p. 7.

2

Witchcraft, witch doctors and the fight against 'superstition' in nineteenth-century Germany

Nils Freytag[1]

> The Most Esteemed Royal Government may commonly find these beliefs in witches and ghosts, in the devil and his supposed manifestations <u>everywhere</u> among the <u>educated</u> and the uneducated, in the province of Prussia and in <u>all others</u> of this state and all states. Even in most recent times, witch-hunts have occurred in the Regierungsbezirk [administrative sub-unit within a Prussian province] of Coeslin, in the area of Bütow and, before that, near Peplin and in the Marks, as documented examples of the difficulties of exterminating a madness perpetuated and continued by tradition.

The above quotation is taken from a lengthy report written by von Platen, the *Landrat* or administrative head of Neustadt district, West Prussia, to a government minister in 1836.[2] It concerned the murder of Christina Ceinowa, a mother of six, who had long been suspected of witchcraft by her neighbours. The widow had been drowned in the waters off the Prussian Baltic peninsula of Hela on 4 August 1836. She had received terrible mistreatment at the hands of eight fishermen from the small village of Ceinowo, led by the so-called witch doctor Stanislaus Kaminski, who had made them subject her to a water test. The fishermen were absolutely convinced that because of her bewitchment one of the villagers was actually possessed by the devil. Because of this, they had imprisoned Ceinowa, a lay healer, on the day before, beaten her with clubs, tied her up and thrown her into the Baltic Sea. When she stayed afloat for some time, probably because of her voluminous skirts, their suspicions were confirmed: Christina Ceinowa really was a witch, and obviously responsible for the grave illness of the fisherman Johann Konkel. The fishermen involved gave her a day and a night to take back the bewitchment. When the allotted time was up and Konkel was still no better, they once again threw her into the sea, where she finally drowned while Kaminski stabbed her.

It was the Prussian Minister of the Interior, Rochow, horrified at reading this, who underlined the words and phrases in the above quotation. Additionally, he marked the passage by a large question mark in the margins. He

also documented his astonishment at passages reporting widespread superstition throughout the Prussian realm – one was, after all, living in the
nineteenth century. In no way did the enlightened Rochow agree with the
Landrat's summary regarding the widespread and commonplace belief in
witchcraft, ghosts and the devil. Instead, he sought alternative explanations
for the gruesome murder. As will become evident, his responses to the
incident need to be seen within the context of the religious situation at the
time. Prussia had long been an officially Protestant state. Yet by 1836 a
sizeable minority (around 40 per cent) of the Prussian population was
Catholic, most of whom lived in Silesia and former Polish territories annexed
in the previous century, and in the provinces of Rhineland and Westphalia
annexed in 1815. Ceinowo, now part of Poland, was one such Catholic
community.

The measures taken by Rochow are fortunately documented in the files
of the Prussian Ministry of the Interior kept at the Berlin *Geheimes Staatsarchiv* (Prussian State Archive). This particular archival material complements
a wide range of sources aiding us in researching attitudes regarding the belief
in witchcraft during the nineteenth century. As well as examining the archival
material kept by the state administration and official church records, in which
administrators and clergy stated their opinions, it is also helpful to consider
the opinions of physicians and journalists regarding popular beliefs. After all,
it was a news report that initially made the Prussian Ministry of the Interior
aware of the Hela murder. Sources deriving from within the witch-believing
public are much rarer, but are still extant in written charms, petitions
addressed to the administration, and eyewitness accounts from patients
explaining the reason for their medical choices. One more class of material
needs to be considered: anti-superstition literature. Books and pamphlets
railing against popular beliefs were published throughout the nineteenth
century, and contain many useful pieces of information. As to their efficacy,
it appears more likely that rather than reducing the sum of 'superstition' they
kept public interest in its subject going – even among those sections of the
population who were the target of their 'improving' discourse.

Research on the continuation of witchcraft beliefs after the end of the
witch trials is still in its infancy among German historians. Recently, there
have been some innovative impulses in researching the persistence or re-
emergence of magic in the nineteenth century. Here, so-called superstitious
practices and beliefs are placed within their social and cultural context and
analysed according to modern patterns of interpretation.[3] However, the
results are, as a whole, quite meagre, a summary that can be repeated
regarding recent folklore research as well, even though the discipline has a
long and influential tradition of investigation into witchcraft and superstition.[4] Many nineteenth- and early twentieth-century German folklore and
antiquarian studies contain references to relevant contemporary occurrences.

Early folklorists interpreted 'superstition' mainly as a relic of pagan or medieval beliefs that were already widely submerged. Even in the twentieth century, folklorists were using their material to prove the timeless and mythical continuity of pre-modern ideas.[5]

All these various sources demonstrate that the belief in witchcraft remained widespread during the nineteenth century, and was consequently considered a virulent problem by the authorities. Since the age of Enlightenment, witchcraft had largely ceased to be considered a probable cause of misfortune in educated circles, but outside these circles it remained a common explanation for many incurable diseases and sufferings. Even if the religious understanding of disease was in all practical aspects supplanted by a medical and scientific one, we can severely doubt whether Heinz Dieter Kittsteiner's theory about the internalization of evil in the era of Enlightenment holds true outside educated society.[6] The Catholic Church and state administration were confronted time and again with petitions and queries regarding witchcraft and magic, which contain many differing views and interpretations. The opinions of the acting parties will be the subject of the following discussion, which analyses the intentions of the medical profession and the state administration, the reaction of the Catholic Church and clergy, and the views of the people at the heart of such events as the Ceinowa incident.

Superstition or illness? Interpretations by the state and the medical profession

The authorities' campaign for the enlightenment of the population continued far into the industrial era, often accompanied by journalistic efforts. The state administration subtly but consistently co-ordinated its campaigns against the belief in witchcraft, magic and ghosts with the Catholic Church authorities, assigning active roles to clergy, teachers and doctors. The Hela murder is a very good example of this. Although the eight fishermen involved and their ringleader, the lay healer Stanislaus Kaminski, who was known to the Prussian authorities from related incidents, were severely punished, the main concern in far-away Berlin was the extermination of the witchcraft superstitions that had governed the fishermen's actions. Although in the short term the preferred instrument of this fight was suppression by means of censorship, bans and medical intervention, the Prussian state would, in the long run, combat superstition by means of better education, religious instruction and the popularization of medical knowledge, especially among the younger generation. Mid-range efforts included the improvement of communications, among which the Prussian ministerial officials during the Vormärz era counted the construction of roads. These made remote villages like Ceinowo on the Baltic peninsula of Hela much more easily accessible and served to include them into the economy at large. Local government in the nearest administrative centre Danzig saw an important cause for the Ceinowa murder in the fact that the Ceinowo economy was precariously reliant on fishing. The economic situation in the village was said to be 'meagre and highly precarious. These unfortunate circumstances have much contributed to severely retarding civilisation, as people are far too impecunious to avail themselves of its blessings'.[7] The main consequences for the villagers consisted of an increased presence of the state in their midst. This was of primary importance for Rochow. In 1836 extra money was assigned to hire an additional constable as well as to improve schooling, which was perceived to be highly deficient.[8] The state representative in Ceinowo, the village mayor, Jacob Trendel, who believed in witchcraft, was replaced; the Prussian state would not tolerate unenlightened civil servants.[9] However, the correspondence between Rochow and his colleague Altenstein in the *Kultusministerium* (Ministry of Culture and Education), shows that increased policing took absolute precedence over improving education.[10]

Yet the overriding perception was still that education was the most powerful instrument for the containment of superstition alongside religious edification and admonition. Thus Altenstein insisted on urging the Catholic clergy to fight the 'delusional' beliefs in witchcraft. For a long time, the curriculum in Prussian schools had concentrated less on imparting progressive knowledge and education than on discipline and obedience. Again, it is no surprise that the typical laments about the lack of education as reason for the continued belief in witchcraft was repeated and confirmed again and again – a verdict that even the Catholic Church might have shared.[11]

In Ceinowo, things were out in the open. Those involved in the deadly water test were charged with murder. In most cases, however, manifestations of belief in witchcraft were not considered capital offences. In the opinion of Prussian legislation, superstition was mainly caused by stupidity and lack of education, so the state was more worried about the cynical exploitation of the superstitious by cunning-folk and the like. Criminal charges of fraud were the standard procedure in these cases, and suspects were, as a rule, found guilty. Additionally, the charge of *grober Unfug* or 'criminal mischief' (§360, no. 11 in the penal code of the German Reich from 1871) was also used to combat the practice of magic. The offence was initially primarily employed to suppress various Social Democrat political intrigues. It gained its relevance regarding magical practitioners from a decree issued by the Prussian Ministry of the Interior on 14 October 1873, which declared 'the encouragement of superstition' an offence punishable by a fine of 150 *Reichsmark* or imprisonment.[12]

Prussian medical authorities, and many doctors in their wake, tried to use their medical and scientific world-view to rationalize the irrational and to explain 'abnormal' beliefs increasingly in terms of mental illness. At least the same importance was accorded to keeping peace and order. Public security was the primary concern, for example, when in 1837 the somnambulistic visions of ten-year-old Peter Hennes of Koblenz came to the attention of the authorities. The boy had seen not only the apostles but also the Devil and drew large crowds in the city, which caused the Koblenz police sergeant to perceive him as a threat to *'Ruhe und Ordnung'* ('peace and order'). In order to get the bottom of these incidents and to control the crowds, the sergeant set about questioning numerous witnesses. One of them was the Koblenz doctor Richter, who diagnosed the boy as displaying 'artificial' somnambul-ism.[13] Yet the psychological interpretation of such beliefs in witchcraft and the Devil was cited increasingly often throughout the century and had its roots among the first mesmerists, who sought to explain everything – even early modern witch-hunts – in terms of animal magnetism.[14]

Throughout the nineteenth century, as the medical profession established itself, religious healers were increasingly relegated merely to consoling and comforting the sick rather than actually diagnosing and curing.[15] A central decree for the Rhine province dated 29 September 1827, which the Prussian civil servants were subsequently admonished to strictly enforce, banned all forms of pastoral medical therapy. Clergymen in violation of this law were threatened with severe punishment.[16] However, the practice of following and administering this decree was discontinued after some time. In 1841, the chaplain of the Siegburg mental institution, Reverend Löhr, had to ask the Cologne *Generalvikar* to intercede against the practice of exorcising mentally ill women who thought themselves witches, and to have them immediately consigned to the lunatic asylum.[17] This is proof of the well-aimed efforts by the medical administration and individual doctors to disassociate illness from its interpretation within the context of Christian religion. Using the charge of superstition in this context demonstrated the advance of secularization and modernization in the understanding of 'superstition'. The incident is addi-tional proof of the many-faceted use of this term, the use of which helped Prussian civil servants and physicians to repeatedly reassure themselves of its consistent definition and their shared point of view. From this perspective, belief in miracles and witchcraft gave reason to repeatedly classify these incidents among similar occurrences, thus providing them with a semblance of a historical context and divesting them of their religious significance.[18]

Quite obviously, the administrative and medical view of the closely connected belief in witchcraft and the Devil changed visibly during the nineteenth century. While at the beginning of the century, exorcism caused official concern only when it became a public spectacle, at the end even its tacit toleration was frowned upon. While earlier the high number of possessed or spiritually healed people gave cause for scandal, later on even the mere fact of an incident of exorcism or *Überlesen* ('reading over'; the reading of religious text in order to cure illness or possession) would cause public offence and ridicule.[19] Such activities were perceived as a sign of rural Catholic retardation in the eyes of the liberal bourgeoisie. With the beginning of the

Prussian and German *Kulturkampf* this ostracizing discrimination joined
wider controversies regarding *Weltanschauung.* This point of view was widely
accepted among Prussian civil servants and led to many conflicts with the
Catholic Church. Denominational motives were certainly behind some of
these attacks. Members of the *Evangelischer Bund zur Wahrung der deutsch-
protestantischen Interessen* (Evangelic Association for the Realization of German
Protestant Interests) and journalists associated with them often accused the
Papacy and the Jesuits of concertedly promoting the belief in witchcraft. This
propaganda may lie at the root of the persistent legend that early modern
witch-hunts and the belief in witchcraft had been an almost exclusively
Catholic phenomenon.

Between secret investigation and toleration: variants in the attitude of the Catholic Church

The persistence of traditional forms of piety, like the belief in witchcraft and
the Devil, which were sporadically highlighted and lamented by the enlightened press forced church authorities into action.[20] Banning religious 'heresies'
and their scandalous consequences was an important issue for the Catholic
Church throughout the century. The Cologne *Generalvikariat* in particular
took careful note of any breaches of Catholic norms, labelling them *'religiöse
Mißbräuche und Umtriebe'* ('religious abuses and subversive activities'). This
blanket term was used to describe and denounce religious activities as varied
as the reading of supposedly superstitious tracts, the use of spiritual therapies
like exorcism and miracle cures, and the belief in witchcraft, hauntings,
stigmatizations and other so-called false pieties.[21] While all ideas and practices
associated with these beliefs were frowned upon as violations of the norms
and ideas of the official Catholic Church, on their own they were not usually
serious enough to draw the interest of the archbishopric. More important to
the Cologne *Generalvikariat* than the violations themselves were instances
when the local clergy supported or even instigated these incidents, or when
the events drew conspicuously large crowds.[22] It is important to note that
the definition of what were legitimate and illegitimate activities was never
clearly stated in the first place and varied widely, depending on time and
circumstance.

The difficulties of explaining the distinction between miracles and superstitions were quite apparent in the practical handling of the belief in
witchcraft. Outside the Catholic Church itself, all efforts to distinguish clearly
the two fields of belief met with failure.[23] The Church and the Rhineland
clergy were constrained by the demands for peace and order from the
Prussian authoritarian state, which insisted on the medical and scientific
interpretation of illness on the one hand, and the needs of many practising
Catholics who still adhered to traditional religious ideas on the other. For

the Catholic Church, this meant constant rivalry in its relations with medical science and state-approved physicians and, at the same time, a loss of its normative function. An understanding of natural science lowered the probability of a miracle – even if it was, in principle, still possible – and incited general doubts about the truth of religious teachings. In addition, pressure from the press, which was extremely critical of any religious deviation, further constricted the radius of action for the Catholic Church. Nevertheless, the leadership of the diocese did possess several instruments with which to react to religious deviations and miraculous incidents. For example, secret investigations of odd occurrences and miraculous manifestations were conducted – 'at first quietly and without causing a stir' as Church sources repeated time and again.[24] Public investigations ran the risk of attracting the attention of the newspapers, which the church wanted to avoid at all cost. The diocese tried to quell public perception that official recognition of the strange and miraculous was certain and imminent.

The usual practice throughout the nineteenth century was to select expert clergy to investigate miraculous affairs.[25] In difficult cases, when several of the local clergy had already stated their agreement on the reality of events, the leadership of the diocese itself decided to intercede. This occurred in Giesenkirchen in 1890 when the visions of the probably epileptic 33-year-old Gertrud Püllen attracted the strong backing of the local clergy. The case interwove the belief in miracles, diabolism and witchcraft. She experienced apparitions of both the Virgin Mary and the Devil, who took regular turns to communicate with or through her. While possessed by the Devil she would blaspheme, as the embarrassed author of a report on these events put it, against 'the present clerics, the dirty Nazarene and, in a way that doesn't bear repeating, the Mother of God'. This was often accompanied by the vomiting of coins, needles and steel nibs in addition to the more usual bloody bile.[26] A local mystic, whose visions confirmed Püllen's ecstatic outpourings, bolstered her credibility and intensified her influence on the population.[27] The local clergy composed a joint petition to the Cologne Archbishop, urging his consent to exorcise her. However, the woman died before the canon, suffragan bishop and later Archbishop of Cologne, Antonius Hubert Fischer, who had speedily hurried to Giesenkirchen, could complete his report.[28] Even if such occurrences were imbued with an aura of the extraordinary that caused public scandal in some sections of the population, they also served to prove the interconnection between Christian belief in miracles and the certainty of Evil that extended even into the rank and file of the Catholic clergy. Still, there were phases when the Catholic Church reacted with caution and restraint, leaving things to run their natural course, especially during the German-Prussian *Kulturkampf*, when the toleration of miraculous apparitions of the Virgin Mary may certainly have been motivated by denominational politics.[29]

Although many of the local clergymen tried to avoid exorcism, they were repeatedly forced to appeal to the church authorities. They were regularly confronted with pleas for help from their parishioners to aid with curing people and animals by *Überlesen* or 'reading over' the patient when orthodox medical alternatives proved inadequate.[30] This highly popular religious therapy was used against both possession and bewitchment, and was not only employed by the clergy. In 1825, in the small village of Walldorf (Kreis Bonn), a witch doctor named Heinrich Küchen stood in for the parish priest, Jacob Schmidt, who had refused to treat an allegedly bewitched child.[31] Owing to the popularity of such spiritual therapies, and because of a particular query by the Neukirchen parish priest Friedrich Christian Philipps, in 1831 the Cologne *Generalvikariat* was forced to outline its own views about the use of exorcism in cases of bewitchment. Under the condition that the *Kreisphysikus* (district medical doctor) was consulted, the *Generalvikariat* defined exorcism 'as a psychological measure perhaps not without its successes, but contrary to the declared intentions of the church, as they would hand justified cause for censure and ridicule to the unbelievers and heretics of our enlightened times'.[32] In his answer, the epochal change towards favouring medical explanations is also present, as mental therapy in the Siegburg asylum (founded in 1825) was ultimately advocated.[33] Nevertheless, sometimes when patients, who believed themselves bewitched, were discharged from the asylum as incurable, their families once again sought the clergy to 'read over' their relatives.[34]

The position taken by the *Generalvikariat* assured the unquestioning acceptance of medical authorities and their responsibilities in order to avoid immediate interference from the Prussian state in internal Church affairs. Yet when clergymen clearly and unmistakably denounced the belief in witchcraft and miracles, they had to expect problems from below. When, for example, the priest of the Aachen parish of St Foilan, preached from the pulpit against a miracle healer, the next morning he found himself confronted with a graphic reprimand in the shape of a dead cat nailed to his house.[35] As this clergyman was the widely known and highly important Aachen city dean and arch-canon Johann Theodor Mürckens, this incident serves to prove the fact that the anger of the population was not tempered in the face of high-ranking personages within the Church.

The demand of the state authorities for the immediate removal of superstitious clergymen from their parish duties put Church authorities in a precarious situation, as large parts of the clergy evidently tolerated or even encouraged such ideas and practices. The archival sources from the Cologne *Generalvikariat* show that some clergy actively participated in the popular discourse on witchcraft, possession and mystical phenomena, especially monastic clerics like Jesuits, Capucins, Redemptorists, and, in the Rhine province, Franciscans.[36] Parish priests in the diocese who did not toe the official line and publicly voiced their belief in such phenomena were subject to severe punishment from the Church authorities.[37] It is important to note that such clergy understood that the belief in witchcraft and miracles served to nourish traditional piety, which could be channelled into other popular expressions of faith such as the veneration of the Sacred Heart.

Education and admonition were primary among the preventative measures pursued by the Church. While thorough studies constituted the basis for a well-educated parish clergy, later additional education within the dioceses served to build upon these foundations.[38] Numerous sources from parish archives show how far into the century the fear of the uncertainties of everyday life was expressed in terms of magic and witchcraft. As a consequence Catholic Church admonitions were rather common. In the autumn of 1837, for example, the wife of the bargeman Goswin Schneider of Remagen was ostracized as a witch and physically abused. The Remagen population accused the woman of having bewitched a sick child. To resolve the tensions in the town the Prussian authorities relied on the admonishing influence of the experienced parish priest of Remagen, Johann Joseph Windeck, who was told to calm his parishioners down. Windeck's role was all the more important because the representative of local authority in the shape of police constable Klein had utterly failed his official duties by taking part in the persecution of Schneider.[39]

Did the official Ultramontane Church succeed in controlling and directing divergent Catholic practices and beliefs? This is an important question, not only for current research, but also to help contextualize the claims of nineteenth-century commentators who accused the Catholic Church of reinvigorating the belief in witchcraft.[40] It is absolutely necessary to remind oneself of the difference between traditional Catholicism and Ultramontanism. Even if Ultramontanism supported traditional forms of piety, its utopian goals were ultimately anything but traditional. Of course, its intentions were nurtured by the retroactive utopia of re-establishing old balances of power by modern means. Even beyond the middle of the century it was still obvious how narrow the radius of action was for clergymen trying to contain and suppress traditional forms of piety, as in conflicting situations they frequently had no choice but to accede to the wishes of their parishioners.

Internal views: warding off fear, illness and crises

Historians' attempts to understand the internal perspective of those who believed in witchcraft and the Devil during the nineteenth century are fraught with several problems. In the first place, there is the issue of source material. There are relatively few sources that derive directly from the pen of those actually involved in witchcraft disputes. Much research is still needed in this area. What we find in Catholic Church archives are numerous statements on the subject by those clergy who played secondary roles in disputes. Miracle healers and lay exorcists certainly publicized testimonies from grateful patients to document their success rate, but we rarely hear directly from those patients. Some sources, however, do bring us closer to the 'popular' voice. There are, for example, documents in which people apply for dispensation from the bishopric to conduct exorcisms for family members. Investigations by the official Church against clergymen charged with exorcism would also quite frequently contain testimonies from parish members stating their belief in witchcraft and the Devil.

During the first decades of the Prussian rule in the Rhine province from 1815 onwards, the cultural distance of many civil servants from the many customs of the Rhine area help explain the reason for numerous bans and prejudices. Lack of cultural comprehension could culminate in accusations of superstition by the new rulers.[41] They were not at all used to such Rhineland and Westphalian customs as the *Gänsereiten* or *Gänsehauen*, which concerned the ritual clubbing to death of live geese from horseback, a custom reserved exclusively for servants using their masters' horses in a classic reversal of social roles. Neither did they look favourably on the lavish wakes called *Reuessen und –trinken*, the *Gebehochzeiten* – sumptuous weddings that often brought the participating families close to ruin, and the wedding custom known as *Brautfangen* ('bride-catching'). Attempts were made to suppress such 'unenlightened' practices.[42] Further considerations of medical policy and public order as well as the enlightening intentions of the Prussian administration led to frequent bans of such customs by the authorities. However, cultural and denominational distance must have played a prominent role and should not be underestimated, especially as it was used for auxiliary argumentation culminating in the handy and catchy accusation of superstition. Even if exorcists and witch doctors who spread the belief in witchcraft were seen as damaging, superstitious and dangerous in the official verdict, this view only prevailed very haltingly among the local population.

When, in 1818, a letter bearing a false address was passed to the Cologne *Oberpräsident*, Solms-Laubach, denouncing the 'superstitious' ringing of church bells to turn away thunderstorms in the municipality of Wichterich, the chief administrator reacted immediately in having the abuse investigated and banned.[43] The *Oberpräsident* correctly connected this custom of '*Gewitter- oder Wetterläuten*' with traditional methods of warding off lightning, demons and witches that were banned in the archbishopric of Trier around 1783 by the last Trier Elector and Archbishop, Clemens Wenzeslaus.[44] Despite such prohibitions it should come as no surprise that church bells continued to be rung in the Rhine province during the nineteenth century to ward off witches as well as thunderstorms.

Behind such beliefs, which were widely denounced as expressions of irrationality and pre-modern thinking, we may find far more rationality than is evident at first sight. Consulting a witch doctor after numerous medical professionals had been consulted and failed to offer a solution can be seen as a rational act if we assume health to be a forward-looking value, in so far as it helps assure a better future.[45] Additionally, it is of course an active and independent act to undertake a journey by one's own choice in order to find relief for a disease deemed incurable. This is a quite rational decision – an attribute of 'superstition' denied by all enlightened administrative statements. The Hela case from 1836 demonstrates the point. The sick fisherman, Johann Konkel, had little choice but to consult the cunning-man Kaminski for his help as no doctor had yet settled near the remote village. Only when Kaminski's therapeutic means did not meet with success did the suspicion of witchcraft lead to an act of 'superstitious' physical violence. It is interesting, though, that the brute force of the highly inebriated villagers was enacted against none other than a potential rival of the lay healer Kaminski.[46] The questioning of some villagers and the 23-year-old village mayor, Trendel, turned up the fact that everyone thought the influence of witches on the weather, fishing catches and the health of the villagers a self-evident truth. In addition, everyone thought that the easily excitable Christina Ceinowa was a witch who could induce as well as cure all kinds of illness.[47]

Belief in witchcraft and in warding off evil personified was not only rooted in a long and varied tradition of medical diagnosis and cure, it also remained a common source of resolving a multitude of fears and personal and communal crises.[48] Emotions of fear and guilt were part of everyday life for Catholic men and women, as research on contemporary autobiographical sources has suggested. These emotions culminated in the fear of hell as punishment for religious and moral misbehaviour.[49] Trying to find a deeper meaning behind events strengthened the idea of illness as a punishment from God. But new fears were also integrated into traditional patterns of interpretation. An overt expression of this phenomenon was the common refusal to use the increasingly ubiquitous steam trains. Popular prejudices against the railways, contemporary symbol of progress and facilitators of industrialization sometimes culminated in actual phobia. The trains, spewing sparks and steam, were thought by some to be a fiendish manifestation. In Baden, for example, it was said that people believed that the Devil took one passenger at each station as his reward.[50]

Protection from the evil influences of the Devil, ghosts and witches, or the warding off of general bad luck remained important to a significant section of the population throughout the century and beyond, as the impressive collection of scrapbooks and loose papers from the vicarage of Konfeld (Trier Diocese) shows.[51] This anthology, which contains numerous prophylactic charm formulae, was probably confiscated and kept safe by the parish priest around the beginning of the nineteenth century. It seems to have been compiled by several literate authors from different early modern magical

texts. One protective formula repeatedly found in this collection is entitled,
'To banish evil spirits and evil people from the house and the stables':

> Bethzairle and all evil spirits, spirits human and airy, watery, seeds of fire
> and earth and all ghosts, I, N. forbid you my bed and the beds of my children,
> I forbid you in the name of God my house, stables, barns, the flesh and blood
> of myself, my wife and my children, our bodies and souls; I, N., forbid you
> all holes, even nail holes, in my house, stables, barns, everywhere around my
> house, until you … all the little hills and empty all the little brooks, count
> all the little leaves on the trees and all the stars in the heavens, until the
> dear day comes unto us when the Blessed Virgin Mary bears her second son.
> +++ These I forbid you in the name of the most holy trinity God Father +
> Son + and Holy Ghost + Amen.[52]

It is remarkable that this formula aims to put witches, ghosts or devils to
never-ending work in order to keep them eternally busy and unable to fulfil
their evil intentions. The formula was not meant to defeat evil but merely to
keep it at bay, while the speaker asked for divine support and warding off of
evil by calling it by its name. The continuity of such ideas is proven by the
existence of *Schutzbriefe*, protective letters purporting to be written by Jesus,
the Virgin Mary, or various saints, which were supposed to protect their
bearer by their mere presence. They were enormously popular during the
First World War.[53] Frightening or miraculous events like stigmatizations,
ecstatic visions or accidents of fate not only strengthened the belief in the
work of personified evil but also the willingness to use exorcism to banish
it. It was not just in rural areas that such beliefs found expression, but also
in towns and cities such as Berlin, where, in 1849, the satanic visions of
eleven-year-old child prodigy Luise Braun electrified the populace as much
as the revolutionary instability gripping the place.[54]

Only a few of the social and societal functions of witch-hunts were still
extant in the nineteenth century. In Ceinowo a medical rival and outsider was
reinterpreted as a witch and destroyed with the help of several villagers,
although state and Catholic Church had already considerably narrowed the
radius for magical interpretations of personal crises and threats. Historians
of the French *Annales* School have shown us the importance of 'long-persistent
structures' in society. These structures have been found especially in the context of pre-industrial rural culture and manifested in the belief in witchcraft.
This supposition of 'long persistence' corresponds partially with folkloristic
research into superstition during the nineteenth and early twentieth centuries,
which sought to identify the belief in witchcraft as a relic of Germanic and
pagan practices. This notion is also hinted at in the concept of the '*Überhang
traditioneller Normen*' ('overhang of traditional norms') applied to the rural
world of the *Kaiserreich* (1871–1918).[55] However, this interpretation is only
one potential perspective on the practices that contemporaries subsumed as
superstitious. The extent to which this was an exclusively rural phenomenon

remains to be assessed by means of extensive surveying of sources relating to urban societies such as newspapers. Beside the continuity and the extension of presumably pre-modern ideas into modern times, the question of change in these ideas is important, especially as an evolution of the belief in witchcraft can be proven when traditional ideas mingled widely and variously with the realities of modern life. A profound change in dealing with the belief in witchcraft, however, cannot be discerned for the nineteenth century. Instead of the public and judicial fight against witchcraft typical of the early modern age, a private and predominately rural struggle against alleged witches prevailed during the nineteenth century. After the secular and ecclesiastical authorities penalized these ways of dealing with witch-inspired misfortune, its crises and its conflicts, and while scientific medicine constantly gained influence, only extraordinary eruptions of these beliefs can be found in the sources so far studied, while the probably much more common suspicions and slanders of witchcraft only rarely found their way into the public sphere.

Notes

1 The following is based on Nils Freytag, *Aberglauben im 19. Jahrhundert. Preußen und seine Rheinprovinz zwischen Tradition und Moderne (1815–1918)* (Berlin, 2003). The following abbreviations are used: LHAK (Landeshauptarchiv Koblenz), HAEK (Historisches Archiv des Erzbistums Köln), HStAD (Hauptstaatsarchiv Düsseldorf), BAT (Bistumsarchiv Trier), GStAPK (Geheimes Staatsarchiv Preußischer Kulturbesitz Berlin), AmrhKG (Archiv für mittelrheinische Kirchengeschichte). Contemporary spelling is kept in all quotes. Unless page numbers are mentioned, the archival material lacked pagination. In the use of 'superstition' in the following pages, no judgement of value is intended. Superstition is not meant as an instrument of historical analysis, merely as a rendition of contemporary positions.

2 Copy by Landrat von Platen to the Danzig provincial government of 10 Sep. 1836 [emphasis extant in the original], in GStAPK, I. HA, Rep. 77, Tit. 415, Nr. 39. A detailed summary of the Hela occurences can be found in Wilhelm Mannhardt, *Die praktischen Folgen des Aberglaubens, mit besonderer Berücksichtigung der Provinz Preußen* (Berlin, 1878), pp. 62–75.

3 See Judith Devlin, *The Superstitious Mind: French Peasants and the Supernatural in the Nineteenth Century* (New Haven and London, 1987); Eloïse Mozzani, *Magie et superstitions de la fin de l'Ancien Régime à la Restauration* (Paris, 1988); the review of these books by Eugen Weber, 'Religion and Superstition in Nineteenth Century France', *Historical Journal* 31 (1988) 399–423; Eva Labouvie, *Verbotene Künste. Volksmagie und ländlicher Aberglaube in den Dorfgemeinden des Saarraumes (16. –19. century)* (St Ingbert, 1992); Owen Davies, *Witchcraft, Magic and Culture 1736–1951* (Manchester, 1999); Davies, *A People Bewitched: Witchcraft and Magic in Nineteenth-Century Somerset* (Bruton, 1999).

4 Recent research on superstition can be found in: Wolfgang Brückner, 'Zu den modernen Konstrukten "Volksfrömmigkeit" und "Aberglauben"', *Jahrbuch für Volkskunde* 16 (1993) 215–22; Christoph Daxelmüller, *Zauberpraktiken. Eine Ideengeschichte der Magie* (Zurich, 1993); Dieter Harmening, 'Superstition – "Aberglaube"', in Dietz-Rüdiger Moser (ed.), *Glaube im Abseits. Beiträge zur Erforschung des Aberglaubens* (Darmstadt, 1992), pp. 368–401. A compilation of the literature is given in Martin Stute, *Hauptzüge*

wissenschaftlicher Erforschung des Aberglaubens und seiner populärwissenschaftlichen Dar-stellungen der Zeit von 1800 bis in die Gegenwart. Eine Literaturanalyse (Frankfurt am Main, Berlin and Bern, 1997). Less recent, but still worth reading is Hermann Bausinger, 'Aufklärung und Aberglaube', *Deutsche Vierteljahrsschrift für Literaturwis-senschaft und Geistesgeschichte* 37 (1963) 345–62.

5 As a rule, these publications merely described 'pre-modern' ideas, culminating in the most comprehensive folkloristic collection of superstitious ideas and practices, the *Handwörterbuch des Deutschen Aberglaubens* (HDA). See Hanns Bächtold-Stäubli (ed.), *Handwörterbuch des deutschen Aberglaubens, unter besonderer Mitwirkung von Eduard Hoffmann-Krayer,* 10 vols (Berlin and New York, 1987). Its most important precursor is Adolf Wuttke, *Der deutsche Volksaberglaube der Gegenwart* (3rd edn, Berlin, [1860] 1900).

6 Heinz Dieter Kittsteiner, 'Die Abschaffung des Teufels im 18. Jahrhundert. Ein kulturhistorisches Ereignis und seine Folgen', in Alexander Schuller and Wolfert von Rahden (eds), *Die andere Kraft. Zur Renaissance des Bösen* (Berlin, 1993), pp. 55–92.

7 Regierung Danzig to Rochow vom 7 Sep. 1836, in GStAPK, I. HA, Rep. 77, Tit. 415, Nr. 39.

8 Regierung Danzig to Rochow vom 4 Feb. 1837, in GStAPK, I. HA, Rep. 77, Tit. 415, Nr. 39.

9 Regierung Danzig to Rochow vom 30 Sep. 1836, in GStAPK, I. HA, Rep. 77, Tit. 415, Nr. 39.

10 Altenstein to Rochow vom 3 Dec. 1836, in GStAPK, I. HA, Rep. 77, Tit. 415, Nr. 39.

11 Generalvikariat Münster to Regierung Düsseldorf vom 27 Dec. 1836, in HStAD,Best. Regierung Düsseldorf, Nr. 226, Blatt 11 (Hexenglauben auf der Bönningharder Heide).

12 Justus von Olshausen, Kommentar zum Strafgesetzbuch für das Deutsche Reich. Nebst einem Anhang, enthaltend die Strafbestimmungen der Konkursordnung, 2 Bände, 10., umgearbeitete Aufl., Berlin 1916, hier Bd. 2, S. 1431–5. Innenministerium to Regierung Koblenz vom 14 Oct. 1873, in LHAK, Best. 441, Nr. 9481. Emphasis extant in the original.

13 Court protocol from 30 May 1837, in LHAK, Best. 441, Nr. 2858.

14 Compare Nils Freytag, 'Praxis zwischen "Wissenschaft" und "Aberglauben". Animali-scher Magnetismus in Preußen in der ersten Hälfte des 19. Jahrhunderts', *Medizin, Gesellschaft und Geschichte* 15 (1996) 141–66.

15 An example from Württemberg of the continued coexistence of medical and spiritual therapy, as well as the medical and theological patterns of interpretation for illnesses in the first half of the nineteenth century, can be found in Doris Kaufmann, *Aufklärung, bürgerliche Selbsterfahrung und die 'Erfindung' der Psychiatrie in Deutschland, 1770–1850* (Göttingen, 1995), pp. 78–89.

16 Copy by Oberpräsident Ingersleben to Regierung Koblenz, 29 Sep. 1827, in LHAK, Best. 491, Nr. 274.

17 Löhr to Hüsgen, 18 Jan. 1841, in HAEK, Generalia I 31, 4.

18 See several examples in Friedrich Everhard von Mering and Ludwig Reichert, *Historische Nachrichten über Teufelsbanner, Wahrsager, Wundermenschen, Geisterseher und andere dergleichen ausserordentliche Erscheinungen in den Rheinlanden und Westfalen seit Beginn diesen Jahrhunderts. Bei Gelegenheit des Auftretens des Wunderdoctors Heinrich Mohren zu Niederempt nach meist noch unbenutzten und zuverlässigen Quellen bearbeitet* (Cologne, 1843).

19 See *Wahre Geschichte der Befreiung eines vom Teufel Besessenen. Ein sensationelles Ereigniß aus unsern Tagen. Ausführlich berichtet von einem Augenzeugen,* 2. Aufl. (Aachen, 1887).

20 Jürgen Scheffler, 'Hexenglaube in der ländlichen Gesellschaft. Lippe im 19. und 20. Jahrhundert', in Gisela Wilbertz, Gerd Schwerhoff and Jürgen Scheffler (eds),

Hexenverfolgung und Regionalgeschichte. Die Grafschaft Lippe im Vergleich (Bielefeld, 1994), pp. 263–96, evaluated newspapers and calendars containing several local examples from the county of Lippe. Danish examples from the eighteenth and nineteenth century are found in Gustav Henningsen, 'Das Ende der Hexenprozesse und die Fortsetzung der populären Hexenverfolgung', in Sönke Lorenz and Dieter R. Bauer (eds), *Das Ende der Hexenverfolgung* (Stuttgart, 1995), pp. 315–28. Examples from England can be found in Owen Davies, 'Methodism, the Clergy, and the Popular Belief in Witchcraft and Magic', *History* 82 (1997) 252–65.

21 The material of the Cologne *Generalvikariat* survives in HAEK, Generalia I 31.
22 Violations against the norms are to be understood as offences against informal as well as canonical precepts of varied importance for proper Catholic behaviour. See Irmtraud Götz von Olenhusen, *Klerus und abweichendes Verhalten. Zur Sozialgeschichte katholischer Priester im 19. Jahrhundert. Die Erzdiözese Freiburg* (Göttingen, 1994), pp. 143–5.
23 Extensively documented in Freytag, *Aberglauben*, pp. 57–65. Some examples from the theoretical literature are Hubert Theophil Simar, *Der Aberglaube* (Cologne, 1877); Franz Walter, *Aberglaube und Seelsorge mit besonderer Berücksichtigung des Hypnotismus und Spiritismus* (Paderborn, 1904); Joseph Fehr, *Der Aberglaube und die katholische Kirche des Mittelalters. Ein Beitrag zur Kultur- und Sittengeschichte* (Stuttgart, 1857).
24 As, for example, in Generalvikariat Köln to Landdechant Peter Bono (Erkelenz) vom 2 Dec. 1842, in HAEK, Generalia I 31, 5.
25 This method was also used, for example, in the case of the stigmatized Karoline Beller in Lüttgeneder in Westphalia, when the Paderborn diocese responsible for the village sent an episcopal commissioner. Compare Rudolf Muhs, 'Die Stigmata der Karoline Beller: Ein katholisches Frauenschicksal des Vormärz im Spannungsfeld von Volksreligiosität, Kirche, Staat und Medizin', in Irmtraud Götz von Olenhusen (ed.), *Wunderbare Erscheinungen. Frauen und katholische Frömmigkeit im 19. und 20. Jahrhundert* (Paderborn, 1995), pp. 83–130, especially pp. 109–21.
26 These quotes can be found in a letter from Amtgerichtsrates Granderat from Mettmann to Archbishop Philippus Krementz, 28 Jan. 1890; the letter from the clergymen Karl Löwing, Heinrich Hubert Hansen and Johann Wilhelm Otten of 21 Dec. 1889, in HAEK, Generalia I 31, 6, 1. The objects vomited by the woman were generally regarded as a manifestation of evil.
27 Dechant Heinrich Hubert Giersberg (Bedburdyck) to Generalvikariat Köln vom 23 Feb. 1889, in HAEK, Generalia I 31, 6, 1.
28 Compare Fischer's protocol of 20 Feb. 1890. Especially his remark of having been unable to distinguish whether 'he was dealing with conscious fraud or self-deception' is interesting; from this, we can conclude that an exorcism of the woman was not very likely to have been allowed.
29 Compare David Blackbourn, *Wenn ihr sie wieder seht, fragt wer sie sei. Marienerscheinungen in Marpingen – Aufstieg und Fall des deutschen Lourdes* (Reinbek bei Hamburg, 1997), pp. 324–33; original English edition, *Marpingen: Apparitions of the Virgin Mary in Bismarkian Germany* (Oxford, 1993).
30 Dechant Johann Franz Antwerpen (Deutz) to Generalvikar Johann Jacob Iven (Cologne) vom 1 March 1841, in HAEK, Generalia I 31, 4.
31 Copy by Bürgermeister Walldorf to Landrat Eberhard von Hymmen (Bonn) vom 4 Jan. 1826, in HAEK, Generalia I 31, 2.
32 Generalvikariat Köln to Philipps vom 12 March 1831, in HAEK, Generalia I 31,4.
33 On the Siegburg Asylum see Dirk Blasius, *'Einfache Seelenstörung'. Geschichte der deutschen Psychiatrie 1800–1945* (Frankfurt am Main, 1994), pp. 24–40; Christian Bradl, *Anfänge der Anstaltsfürsorge für Menschen mit geistiger Behinderung ('Idiotenanstaltswesen').*

Ein Beitrag zur Sozial- und Ideengeschichte des Behindertenbetreuungswesens am Beispiel des Rheinlands im 19. Jahrhundert (Frankfurt am Main, 1991).

34 Pfarrer Friedrich Friederici to Generalvikariat Köln vom 21 Aug. 1860, in HAEK, Generalia I 31, 4.

35 Compare Franz Bertrams, Heinrich Mohr, genannt 'der hl. Schäfer von Niederembt', masch. Manuskript, Niederembt 1925. In this compilation, details from the Dekanatsarchiv Bergheim and the parish archive of Niederembt that are no longer extant or findable have been evaluated.

36 The example of Bavarian Redemptorists can be found in Otto Weiss, 'Die Redemptoristen in Bayern (1790–1909). Ein Beitrag zur Geschichte des Ultramontanismus', phil. Diss. masch., 3 Bde., Munich 1977, 971–80 and 1170–88. More concisely: Ders., Seherinnen und Stigmatisierte, in Götz von Olenhusen, *Wunderbare Erscheinungen*, S. 51–82.

37 See Dechant Franz Alexander Halm to Generalvikariat Köln vom 7 May 1852, in HAEK, Generalia I 31, 6, 1.

38 For this compare Michael Felix Langenfeld, *Bischöfliche Bemühungen um Weiterbildung und Kooperation des Seelsorgeklerus. Pastoralkonferenzen im deutschen Sprachraum des 19. Jahrhunderts* (Rome, Freiburg and Vienna, 1997), pp. 442–58. Furthermore see Bernhard Schneider, 'Lesegesellschaften des Klerus im frühen 19. Jahrhundert. Ein Beitrag zur historischen Kommunikationsforschung', *AmrhKG* 49 (1997) 155–77; Rudolf Schlögl, *Glaube und Religion in der Säkularisierung. Die katholische Stadt – Köln, Aachen, Münster – 1700–1840* (Munich, 1995), pp. 153–5.

39 Copy by Landrat Carl Gerhard von Gärtner (Ahrweiler) to Windeck vom 20 Sep. 1837, in LHAK, Best. 635, Nr. 407. Draft Regierung Koblenz to Gärtner vom 1 Sep. 1837, in LHAK, Best. 441, Nr. 9481.

40 See, for example, Friedrich Nippold, *Die gegenwärtige Wiederbelebung des Hexenglaubens. Mit einem literarisch-kritischen Anhang über die Quellen und Bearbeitungen der Hexenprozesse* (Berlin, 1875).

41 This reasoning, however, can no longer be considered valid for the time of the Prussian-German *Kulturkampf* in the *Kaiserreich* of 1871. Blackbourn, *Wenn ihr sie wieder seht*, p. 373, explains the excessive reactions of some local officials by stating that the Catholic belief in miracles was '*zutiefst wesensfremd*' ('deeply contrary to the nature') of the Prussians.

42 About *Gänsereiten*: copy by Regierung Aachen to Polizeidirektor Coels vom 15 Dec. 1820, in HStAD, Best. Landratsamt Erkelenz, Nr. 208. Reuessen und -trinken: Regierung Aachen to Ingersleben vom 30 May 1823, in LHAK, Best. 403, Nr. 953, S. 1–7. See also Gunther Hirschfelder, 'Reu- und Trauertrinken im Regierungsbezirk Aachen. Das Beispiel einer entgleisten Totenfeier im Jahre 1823', in Hildegard Mannheims, Georg Kehren and Peter Oberem (eds), *Volkskundliche Grenzgänge. Festgabe der Schülerinnen und Schüler H. L. Cox zum 60 Geburtstag* (Erkelenz, 1995), pp. 205–19. To learn about the *Gebehochzeiten* the Prussian administration consulted extensive material compiled by French officials between 1794 and 1814: Beilage E Unterpräfekt Arrondissement Hamm to Präfekt Ruhrdepartement vom 24 Jan. 1810, in GStA PK, I. HA, Rep. 77, Tit. 435, Nr. 7, Vol. I. About *Brautfangen*: Landrat Georg Bärsch (Prüm) to Regierung Trier vom 4 June 1830, in LHAK, Best. 442, Nr. 3768, Bl. 5.

43 Solms-Laubach to Landrat Joseph Freiherr von Weichs vom 24 July 1818; Weichs to Solms-Laubach vom 13 Aug. 1818, in HStAD, Best. Oberpräsidium Köln, Nr. 804, Bl. 3 und Bl. 4r–5v. An *Oberpräsident* is the official in charge of a *Regierungsbezirk*.

44 See article 'Gewitter', in HDA, vol. 3, col. 815–33 Nikolaus Kyll, 'Die Glocke im Wetterglauben und Wetterbrauch des Trierer Landes', *Rheinisches Jahrbuch für Volkskunde* 9 (1958) 130–79. About the change in the perception of thunderstorms see Heinz Dieter Kittsteiner, *Die Entstehung des modernen Gewissens* (Frankfurt am Main,

[1991] 1995), pp. 55–79. About the measures taken in the electorate of Trier see Andreas Heinz, 'Das Ende der "figurierten" Karfreitagsprozessionen im Kurfürstentum Trier unter Erzbischof Clemens Wenzeslaus (1768–1802)', *AmrhKG* 44 (1992) 177–88.

45 See Roy Porter, 'The Patient's View: Doing Medical History From Below', *Theory and Society* 14 (1985) 175–98.

46 Beilage der *Allgemeinen Zeitung* vom 24 Aug. 1836, in GStAPK, I. HA, Rep. 77, Tit. 415, Nr. 39.

47 Questioning of the village mayor from 28 Aug. 1836. Beilage Nr. 5 zum Schreiben des Landrats Platen to Regierung Danzig vom 10 Sep. 1836, in GStAPK, I. HA, Rep. 77, Tit. 415, Nr. 39.

48 From the perspective of medical history, exorcism is seen as an early form of therapy for neurotics and hysterics. In the present context, the main part of our attention is with the more varied contemporary views. See Robert Jütte, *Geschichte der Alternativen Medizin. Von der Volksmedizin zu den unkonventionellen Therapien von heute* (Munich, 1996), pp. 78–90. Still important is the study by Gustav Roskoff, *Geschichte des Teufels*, 2 vols (Leipzig, [1869] 1967). About the following, also compare Alfonso di Nola, *Der Teufel. Wesen, Wirkung, Geschichte* (Munich, 1990), pp. 329–57.

49 Andreas Heller, '"Du kommst in die Hölle …". Katholizismus als Weltanschauung in lebensgeschichtlichen Aufzeichnungen', in Therese Weber and Olivia Wiebel-Fanderl (eds), *Religion und Alltag. Interdisziplinäre Beiträge zu einer Sozialgeschichte des Katholizismus in lebensgeschichtlichen Aufzeichnungen* (Vienna and Cologne, 1990), pp. 28–54.

50 Compare Wilhelm Heinrich Riehl, *Land und Leute*, 5. Aufl., Stuttgart/Augsburg 1861, S. 78f. On hostility towards technology during the nineteenth century see Rolf Peter Sieferle, *Fortschrittsfeinde? Opposition gegen Technik und Industrie von der Romantik bis zur Gegenwart* (Munich, 1984), pp. 87–117.

51 This collection, the provenance of which appears to be uncertain, cannot be dated precisely, although there appears to be a barely legible letter dated Pellingen, 6 June 1824 among the loose papers. In BAT, Best. 71, 43, Nr. 8, 8. Zitierte Beschwörungsformel. The omission is illegible in the original.

52 'Bethzairle, und allen bösen Geister, Menschengeister Luft, Wasser, Feuer Samen, Erd und alle Geister, ich N. verbiethe euch mein und meiner Kinder Bettstädte, ich verbiethe euch im Namen Gottes mein Haus Ställe Scheuer, mein, meiner Frau und meinen Kindern Blut und Fleisch, unser Leiber und Seelen, ich N. verbiete euch alle Löcher, ja gar Nägellöcher in meinem Haus, Ställen, Scheuer, überall meines Hauses, bis alle Berglein … und alle Wässerlein wattelt, alle Blättlein, an den Bäumen zehlet, und alle Sterne am Himmel zehlet, bis, uns kommt der liebe Tag, wo die Hl. Maria Mutter Gottes ihren zweiten Sohn gebähret +++ Diese verbiethe ich euch im Namen der allerheiligsten Dreyfaltigkeit Gott Vater + Sohn + und Hl. Geist + Amen.'

53 See Benjamin Ziemann, 'Katholische Religiosität und die Bewältigung des Krieges. Soldaten und Militärseelsorger in der deutschen Armee 1914–1918', *Jahrbuch für Friedensforschung* 6 (1997) 116–36, especially 123–5.

54 See A. Mielay, *Das Berliner Wunderkind. Ein Beitrag zur Tagesgeschichte nach vierzehntägigen genauesten Beobachtungen* (Berlin, 1849), p. 12; Rudolf Leubuscher, 'Das Wunderkind in der Schifferstrasse', in Robert Jütte (ed.), *Wege der Alternativen Medizin. Eine Lesebuch* (Munich, 1996), pp. 97–100. See also Manfred Gailus, *Strasse und Brot. Sozialer Protest in den deutschen Staaten unter besonderer Berücksichtigung Preußens 1847–1849* (Göttingen, 1990), p. 136; Rüdiger Hachtmann, *Berlin 1848. Eine Politik- und Gesellschaftsgeschichte der Revolution* (Bonn, 1997), p. 838f.

55 Compare Thomas Nipperdey, *Deutsche Geschichte 1866–1918, Erster Bd.: Arbeitswelt und Bürgergeist* (Munich, 1990), p. 225.

3

The witch and the detective: mid–Victorian stories and beliefs

Susan Hoyle

Why did the witchcraft-beliefs of the English non-urban working class go into decline during the course of the nineteenth century?[1] I want to argue that it is the *kind of story* that believers and non-believers told that eventually made science and rationality (narrated here by forensic witnesses) more attractive than magic (narrated here by witchcraft-believers). Thus the decline in witchcraft-belief was not due to an increasing respect for the claims of science and a matching retreat from irrationality, but to a falling off in the acceptability of the traditional witchcraft narrative, and an attendant rise in the acceptability of a forensic narrative based on the demonstration of detective skills – in particular the skills of policemen, doctors and lawyers. My analysis can be seen as just part of a tale that others have been telling, others much longer in the field than I, and in different corners.[2] They have shown that the essentially Whig story of the triumph of rationality over superstition does not account for what historians find in the record. Despite being presented with the evidence of decades of scientific advance and even revelling in those advances, people persist in believing 'weird things', however 'weirdness' is defined.[3]

I am not arguing that all that changed over this period was the popularity of this or that kind of story. Real changes can be traced – for example the profound shift in the status of the 'expert' in the eyes of the court and of the public in the courtroom.[4] My point is that such changes can be traced and largely explained through the changes in the stories the courts heard: as the contrasting styles of the various witnesses' narratives examined below illustrate well. Nor am I claiming that the social and economic background of my storytellers is irrelevant or unproblematic. Rather I am saying that the influence of those factors is more readily discernible through narratological lenses than through an analysis of content that seeks to divorce it from matters of style. By 'narrative', I mean both the 'how' and 'what' of the stories which victims and witnesses told about their experiences and allegations of witchcraft. Much recent narratology is concerned with distinguishing between the 'narrative' (as told) and the 'story' (its essence), but here I want to avoid the paradoxes, infinite regresses and ultimate privileging of some version or other of any particular story which the story/narrative distinction seems to involve. As Barbara Herrnstein Smith puts it, 'for any particular narrative, there is no single *basically* basic story subsisting beneath it but, rather, an unlimited number of other narratives that can be *constructed in response* to it or *perceived as related* to it'.[5] Thus each of these 'witchcraft' narratives will be regarded, not as a version of the true story discoverable by sifting through all possible versions (whatever that might mean), but as one of the many diverse accounts that could be given. This will not prevent me, or anyone else, from believing some narratives rather than others, but it does discourage a stereotyped privileging of one narrative over another.

The best source for the study of Victorian witchcraft is newspapers. The reports in the local press of what were usually if erroneously called 'witchcraft trials' are often our only indicator of the depth and range of such practices and beliefs. With nice irony, as witchcraft-belief declined and newspapers became more common, reports of cases of witchcraft-belief are easier to find. At the same time, court papers relating to these cases seem to have had no better chance of survival than any others.[6] So it is to the newspapers that one must turn in the great majority of instances to discover anything at all about the evidence. There are two different kinds of story which can be unearthed from the files of newsprint – but although there are occasional letters to the editor which cast interesting light on the matter, the actual opposition (such as it may turn out to be) between the witch-believers' and the forensic detectives'[7] stories was repeatedly made real somewhere else: in the courtroom. Somewhere between those two are found the stories of the cunning-folk, who did most to keep the old beliefs alive. Their stories were rarely if ever recorded, in the courtroom or anywhere else, and unfortunately there is not room here for any reconstructions.[8]

Witnesses and lawyers, in their various statements to the court, used widely different kinds of narrative. It is important to understand what the court would accept – including the laws of evidence – as this obviously influenced what was allowed to be said in fundamental ways. The accused, for example, were almost never permitted to speak, so their stories are even more imperfectly known than those of the accusers, witnesses and 'detectives'; and what medical witnesses were expected to say and do was not only changing, but was a matter of deep division.[9] However, I am only interested in court procedures in so far as I have to be in order to understand the evidence. In seeking to trace changes in the acceptability of this or that narrative tradition, I am trying to make the 'ordinary person's' rules central. By 'ordinary person' I mean the person who at the start of the nineteenth century would have routinely considered witchcraft as an explanation for unpleasant experiences, but whose descendant at its end rarely if ever did.

My suspicion is that this shift is accounted for by the increasing fascination which detective narratives held for this 'ordinary person'. The fascination was exemplified not just in fiction (perhaps hardly at all in fiction, given the poor to non-existent literacy of many witch-believers), but also in their experience of the local police station, magistrate's court and assizes, and in their experience of forensic science (typified by the policeman and physician).

Keith Thomas noticed that the decline of witchcraft-belief amongst the educated classes in England in the late seventeenth century preceded the rise of empirical science and of modern technology.[10] I am suggesting that the decline of such beliefs amongst the scarcely-educated two hundred years later was similar, in that popular belief and interest in the power of forensic science seems to have been ahead of its actual development. The fascination with forensic evidence seems to have been due more to the lure of its associated narrative – the perceived strength of its storytelling – than to a collapse of peasant credulity in the face of irrefutable science. Peasant credulity may simply have switched its allegiance.

This chapter is an outline of the case for this thesis. I will be looking at two instances of alleged witchcraft, both of which attracted much notoriety in their day. The charges usually laid in these cases were obtaining money or goods by false pretences and various degrees of assault.[11] The assault usually arose because of the persistent belief, going back at least three hundred years, that to cut a witch (typically, but not necessarily, on the face) removed the power of the witch over the assailant (and by implication over his or her family). The particular case I shall deal with here, from Stratford-on-Avon in 1867, was a straightforward witch-cutting of this kind. False-pretences charges in 'witchcraft trials' were against cunning-folk, always after they had accepted cash or payment-in-kind for their services, and usually after they had failed to achieve what they had promised. Payment was necessary for the transaction to be accounted fraudulent, while failure was frequently the real cause of complaint. The case I will be referring to here was more serious than most: James Tunnicliff, prosecuted for false pretences at Rugeley in 1857, was lucky not to have been on a murder charge. First, however, in order to create a clearer context for my treatment of these cases, I want to discuss the power of narrative.

The power of narrative

Narrative is very powerful in our lives; it is a prime way of making sense of the world.[12] It is a major provider (for some people the only provider) of intelligibility; its rhetoric, carefully used, is a major persuader. Acquiring the skills needed to tell and understand stories is an early and vital aspect of a child's socialization: it is not instinctive. We learn to use 'symbols ... to talk about absent things as though they were present (that is, imagining), making use of the concept of time, and, of course, participation in social life'.[13] Also critical to oral storytelling is dramatic skill: emphases, pauses, glances and gestures. In the courtroom, from a lawyer, this is a good part of what is sometimes called 'forensic eloquence', but theatrical skills of this kind are not foreign to any successful witness, expert or otherwise. But beyond agreeing that narrative is 'a recounting of events'[14] which, in effect, follows the form 'And then ... and then ...', there is no consensus about what a narrative is, or what makes it work well, or badly. Attempts to establish rules have only created opportunities for others to find narratives where the rules have been successfully broken.[15] At the same time, it is demonstrably possible to write lucidly about narrative, and to conduct meaningful arguments about it – not so much in general as in and across specific instances or genres. Much that has been written about narrative and the novel is illuminating when considering, for example, narrative in the courtroom. Even though the distinction between fact and fiction (problematic in other settings) is of prime importance to the court, studies of narrative suggest that either the narrator or her listeners, or both, deeply feel the narrative itself to be a prime guarantor of its 'truth'.

Numerous studies in different societies suggest that sequences that conform to our idea of a good story are easier to remember, and that if something is missing from a story, we tend to supply it. Indeed, it has been said that 'almost anyone who speaks any language can understand the story grammar of almost every other person'.[16] Narrative is central not only to how we explain external reality; it provides the shape for accounts of our own and others' lives. When stories of any kind are successful, they are coherent and plausible accounts of how and why things happened as they did.[17] There is much to suggest that 'coherence' and 'plausibility' depend crucially upon sequence, and upon the causality thereby implied: the bald sequence 'And then ... and then ...' of the narrative draws on 'a miscellany of conventions'[18] which alerts everyone – narrator and listeners – to the *likelihood* of a causal statement. 'He loved her. He stabbed her': we are likely to read that as causal, and in this way, much nonsense is passed off as sober fact. 'He drank a glass of water. He stabbed her': here we want to be told the connection – to be given the cause (was it something in the water?) – otherwise we may assume that we are being told of its absence. 'Coherence' and 'plausibility' depend also, in Frank Kermode's elegant phrase, on a 'sense of an ending'.[19] This is distinct from the need for the narrative to conclude with justice done (or not), or a life fulfilled (or not): the 'sense of an ending' pre-dates, so to speak, the end, and provides some at least of the rules by which the right 'facts' are selected from the infinity of facts available, and by which those facts are then related one to another. Selection is not automatic, not merely a matter of rejecting the irrelevant (which is not a straightforward matter either): even from amongst the relevant facts, however determined, few are chosen. 'To tell everything would be pathologically tedious.'[20] Selection is thus fundamental to narrative, and relies critically upon a common understanding and acceptance of that shadowy, shape-shifting 'miscellany of conventions' which is the closest we have to narrative rules. Depending on context, there is agreement (of a sort) that certain things need explanation, and agreement (of a sort) as to what counts as explanation.

The criticality of selection applies as much to what is *not* said as to what is said; from time to time and place to place and person to person, and in this or that narrative, there are things which cannot be said. They may be true, but they are thought to be trivial, private, obscene and partial. To have uttered such words, to have selected these facts, could cast doubt on the narrative by casting doubt on the narrator: if she does not know not to say that, what else does she not know? If he cannot distinguish truth which is fit to be uttered from the unutterable truth, how do we know that he can recognize the truth at all? How can such people be trusted? The person of the narrator is also important, and in a sense a matter of selection; what counts as lending authority to their narrative also changes over time. For the narrator simply to have 'been there' may not be enough (even in the case of the author of an avowedly fictional work): a slave may be supposed not to be fully human; an uneducated man may be thought incapable of following an argument; a non-Christian may be held to be blind to any truth. If we want 'here' and 'now' to understand what a narrative constructed 'there' and 'then' meant, we need *inter alia* to know what, and in which contexts, was thought to be trivial, private, obscene or partial, as well as who was expected or allowed or forbidden to speak.[21] Then we may know something of what was left out. The Victorian novel is by no means the only place where truth is no defence.

Implicit in selection is secrecy. Complicit with the narrator are the listeners, who understand that not everything can be said, and not just for reasons of time, or decorum. Secrets carry the narrative forward. One vital secret is what happens next, and perhaps the biggest secret is how the narrator knows what happens next – how the selection proceeds. And if the selection works, and continues to work throughout the tale, then the story is a good story and 'truth', of a factual or fictional kind, is deemed to have been served. The competent narrator knows what happens next for several reasons, amongst them the afore-mentioned externally conferred authority so to do: we as listeners are inclined to allow, for example, that the witch knows the power of her spells and the detective the meaning of his clues. There are, however, ineffectual witches (though these will be rare, since a witch is known precisely by the efficacy of her spells) and, more commonly, stupid detectives. The right rhetoric is vital – it can of itself provide explanation: 'Once upon a time ...' foreshadows one sort of story; 'I was proceeding in a north-easterly direction ...' quite another; and as the narrative moves on, the correct use of the proper rhetoric not only bolsters the narrator's authority, but helps to select and reject the facts of the narrative.

In short, one could agree with Sarbin and others as to 'the universality of the story as a guide to living and as a vehicle for understanding the conduct of others', and believe with them that 'human beings think, perceive, imagine, and make moral choices according to narrative structures'.[22] The search for 'rules' of narrative may have been frustrating for narratologists, but for the world at large it is liberating that we apparently nevertheless all know a story when we hear one. This fact (if it is a fact) implies that the construction and understanding of a narrative is a collective act: that the project of uttering successful narratives requires not only suitably inspired speakers, but also suitably inspired listeners. And we do seem to be inspired. We find stories even where they do not pre-exist: people shown films of randomly created shapes making randomly created movements will make up narratives to account for what they see. 'It matters not whether historian, novelist, or student: a person tries to make sense of the world with limited epistemic and linguistic skills. Where there are no firm connections between empirical events, the individual organizes them into an imaginative formulation that meets one or more tests of coherence.'[23] In the courtroom, it is the judge who, in agreement with legal precedent and statute, says what narratives are acceptable: who may say what when. But the public audience may well have different ideas about what is worth listening to.

So now I turn to a couple of mid-nineteenth-century 'witchcraft' cases. In both, desperate people used ancient and respected conventions to create stories that helped them to make sense of their lives. In both, those stories were countered in court by forensic stories. I begin with witch-cutting in Stratford-on-Avon in the late 1860s.

The cutting of Jane Ward (1867)

The newspaper narratives

For some time past, a family named Davis, residing in Emms-court, Sheep-street, Stratford-on-Avon, have laboured under the most extraordinary delusions. They have persisted in a belief that visits have been made to them in various shapes by individuals in a bodily form – some after the manner of the patron saint of Paris, who carried his head under his arm, 'as a gentleman carries his cane'; others have come down the chimney bereft of their caput, and when landed in the room they have gone through a variety of capers – seizing the inmates, tossing them in the air, throwing the furniture about the apartment, pulling the bed-clothes off, and playing 'such fantastic tricks' as to be absolutely incredible. One young girl, who happened to be an invalid, and obliged to recline on a sofa, has declared her positive knowledge that a man and woman came down the chimney a few days since, both persons headless, and seized her by the body, cast her violently on the ground, and then tossed her in the air, after which they took up the sofa she had used and went through a similar feat with it. Although Police-Superintendent Richardson showed that the accumulated dust around the legs of the furniture proved that no such thing could have happened, the entire family confirmed their belief that the witches had been there, and also that the only way to break the spell they were under was to draw blood from the person they supposed to be the witch. This was, unfortunately, attributed to a neighbour named Jane Ward, who lived two doors away, and on Friday, the man John Davis carried out his delusion by suddenly pouncing on the poor creature, and, seizing her firmly, he inflicted a frightful gash in her cheek, fully three inches long. Having done this, the whole family felt relieved and assured that 'the spell was broken', for they told the superintendent that the following day they had all slept well and undisturbed, which they had not done while the witch was left unexorcised. The man, John Davis, was brought before the magistrates – the mayor (Mr. C. F. Loggin) and Alderman Kendal – at the Town Hall, Stratford-on-Avon, on Thursday, charged with wounding the said Jane Ward with a knife, with the intent of doing grievous bodily harm. Mr. J. E. H. Greaves, solicitor, appeared for the prosecution; and the hearing, which lasted some time, ended with the prisoner being committed to take his trial at the next Warwick Assizes.[24]

The press reports are the only surviving accounts of the relevant narratives and are plainly defective. Our reporter may have been a professional journalist, or perhaps just a local observer who thought to turn a quick penny, and he is playing it for laughs as well as for sensation. Moreover, much has been left out – this hearing, after all, 'lasted some time' – only some of which is supplied by the rather different account published in the *Stratford Herald*:

It will hardly be credited that in this year of grace, in a country which boasts of its education and common sense, that anyone can be silly enough to believe in 'witchcraft', but so it is.

John Davis, a great strapping fellow, who had been a soldier, was charged with cutting and wounding one Jane Ward, widow, with intent to do her bodily harm, on Friday, the 25th of October ...

Mr. J. E. H. Greves [*sic*] appeared for the prosecution, and Mr. J. Warden for the prisoner.

Mrs. Jane Ward, widow, 4 Emm's Court, Sheep-street, Stratford-upon-Avon, said on Friday night last she was putting up her window shutters when two women named Stanley came up to her and used bad language; they called her a 'witch'. The prisoner then made his appearance; he was going in the direction of his house in the same court in which she lived. He placed himself between the two women and struck her with a knife on the left cheek. It was dusk when he struck her; he called her a 'd—d old witch' and said 'I've done for you now; I can do anything with you.' She had known Davis since he was a boy, and never had any words with him until lately. She hooted 'murder' and ran up to Mrs. Timm's. The prisoner went to his own house; the Stanleys went away and she gave information to the police. Mr. Stewart, surgeon, dressed the wound. During the last five months the prisoner had threatened to take her life; he had often called her an 'old witch', and said 'if he could draw blood of her he would be satisfied.' She had forbidden the prisoner her house. Mr. Richardson had taken the apron and shawl she wore at the time off her. (The blood-stained garments were produced in Court.) – Cross-examined by Mr. Warden: It was between six and seven o'clock when Davis struck her; she could not see what he had in his hand; she felt something sharp go into her face; she said nothing to the prisoner to provoke him; she had never 'be-called' him; both day and night she had no rest from him; when she forbade the prisoner her house he was interfering with herself and family; when he struck her Friday last they had no words.

Mr. Wm. Stewart, assistant to Mr. H. Lane, surgeon, said that on Friday night last, about seven o'clock he was called to see Mrs. Ward at Superintendent Richardson's. She had an incised wound on the left cheek, half an inch deep in one part, from the upper part of the face downward. The knife (produced by Supt. Richardson) would inflict the wound, which was more of a cut than a stab. Under certain circumstances it might have been a dangerous wound. – Cross-examined by Mr. Warden: The wound could not have been caused by the finger nails. He had tested the stain on the knife and found it was from blood.

Supt. Richardson said that on the 25th October Mrs. Ward came to him crying very much and bleeding; she seemed in a fainting state, holding her handkerchief up to her face, which was smothered in blood. He washed the wound and then went for the surgeon. Afterwards himself and p. c. Hitchcox apprehended the prisoner; he charged Davis with wounding Mrs. Ward, and told him it might turn out a serious case. Prisoner said 'he was obliged to do it; he could get no rest!' He (witness) said 'you might have taken her life.' The prisoner said 'and a good job too.' He found a knife, and some money on Davis; the weapon appeared to have fresh blood on it. The prisoner said nothing when he took the knife from him. On the following morning when Davis's sister brought the prisoner's breakfast, he accompanied her to the cell. She asked Davis 'how he had slept?' He said 'he never had a better night's rest in his life; she (Ward) had no power over him now!' – Cross-examined by Mr. Warden: He cautioned the prisoner twice when he apprehended him.

There were no witnesses called for the defence. The usual caution was read to the prisoner.

Davis said he had no wish to say anything now.

The charge is a serious one, and the prisoner is liable to penal servitude for life. The magistrates committed him to take his trial at the Assizes, and commented on the folly and wickedness of his dastardly act.[25]

This, the local newspaper's account, is both longer and, not surprisingly, less interested in the laughs to be had at the expense of denizens of their town; but we have to read the other papers to know *why* Davis believed his family to have been bewitched. The accounts of the trial a few weeks later add little. The Stanleys, we find, are Davis's sister and sister-in-law or niece; and although the surgeon, Mr Williams, was able to identify the substance on Davis's knife as blood, he was unable to say whether it was human blood. While John Davis had a regular and responsible job at the local brewery (E. F. Flower gave him an excellent character), Jane Ward was less respectable. She described herself in court as earning her living by 'going out nursing',[26] her son had been transported for an unspecified crime, and she had to deny that she had spent two months in prison for assault. Nevertheless, throughout, the sympathy of the newspapers was with her as the victim of an ignorant and vicious attack. The court took the same view, and sentenced Davis to eighteen months' hard labour.

Dust and the detective's narrative

Despite the limited data on what was actually said in and out of court, it is possible to make several important points about these narratives. To begin with, it is clear that John Davis and his extended family on the one hand ('the Davises') and the policeman, the medical man and the lawyers on the other ('the forensic team') were talking right past each other. The narrative pursued by the witch-believers had nothing to do with what the forensic team was talking about, and the evidence of the forensic team meant nothing to the Davis clan. If Superintendent Richardson had not noticed the dust still gathered around the legs of the sofa, the court would still not have believed the Davis family's tale, because dust or no dust, the court did not believe in witchcraft. If the court had been disposed to believe that the Davises had been bewitched, then the undisturbed dust could have been explained as part of the enchantment (which is presumably what the Davises told themselves after Supt. Richardson pointed it out) or, even more likely, it would simply not have been noticed in the first place. If the Davises had had the advantage of today's detective novels and films, they might have realized that the policeman would pounce on such things, and without necessarily prejudicing their own belief in the witchcraft, might have removed the dust. Finally, the dust is actually irrelevant to the case. It was the cutting of Jane Ward that was illegal, not the witchcraft, and John Davis did not deny cutting her.

Something other than science *versus* magic is going on here. If Superintendent Richardson was using a scientific approach, it was not 'pure' science. In fact, the policeman's adduction of the dust as clinching his case was not as far removed from the way the Davises viewed the world as the forensic team and the court would have liked to think. Helpful here is Carlo Ginzburg's discussion of 'conjectural science,' under which head he includes medicine, psychoanalysis and detection.[27] Within what he calls an 'evidential paradigm' the dust can be shown to have been merely a clue, a sign; it was taken as indicating that some things were highly probable (such as that Mrs Davis, or whoever was in charge of these things, was a negligent housewife) and the nigh impossibility of others (such as that the sofa had danced around the room), but it was not proof, and it was not the event itself. Its status in court depended upon a world-view of orderly Newtonian cause-and-effect, but its evocation partook of ritual. The facts about the dust only work as evidence if it is accepted *a priori* that there is no such thing as witchcraft – in which case, the evidence of the dust is not needed anyway. But the court allowed it and the papers were only too delighted to print it (as we still are to read it). We like hearing about the dust not least because it shows Richardson to have been a good detective; his particular application of such skills may have been neither here nor there in this case, but could well have been crucial in another matter. Accepting this account was also one of the ways in which the court stressed its disbelief in witchcraft and, perhaps, sought to educate others in how to think about such matters.

The Davises for their part were not ignorant about clues. That was how they 'knew' who had bewitched them. The clues they followed were not the ones to which the forensic team or the court paid attention, of course (and no one bothered to ask the Davises what those clues were, which is why we do not know either), but in privileging some clues and disallowing others, the court was not using any explicit rules. It is not enough to say that the law did not require the Davises to prove witchcraft; it did not require Superintendent Richardson to disprove it either, since the case was not about whether there had been any witchcraft; but Richardson tried to disprove it anyway, and the court respected his clues, and did not even enquire into theirs. Nor is this the only such example even within this small trial: the evidence of William Stewart, the surgeon's assistant, regarding the blood on the knife is similarly tantalizing.[28] New forensic techniques enable him to say that it is indeed blood, but not whether it is human blood, let alone Jane Ward's blood.[29] His evidence in this matter thus adds little to the case, but he is nevertheless positively invited to announce the findings.

The witchcraft narrative

The point is not to demonstrate that these narratives – the forensic team's and the witchcraft-believers' – employ equally valid hypotheses. Superintendent Richardson represents the world in which I want to live, and indeed in which I believe I do live. The ignorance, superstition and reliance on casual violence which drove John Davis to attack Jane Ward is deplorable, but I cannot deny Davis's sincerity. The point is rather to call attention to the deployment in this case of at least two narrative traditions. As this example from Stratford shows, a belief in witchcraft can create cracking good stories: 'a man and woman came down the chimney a few days since, both persons headless, and seized her by the body, cast her violently on the ground, and then tossed her in the air, after which they took up the sofa she had used and went through a similar feat with it.' [30] It is not the kind of narrative I seek out myself, but it is undeniably in an ancient, popular and still-enduring tradition. What has endured is its power as a story. Neither the storyteller nor his or her audience has to believe in witches or sorcery in order for the cracking good story to be told and enjoyed; admittedly *someone* has to believe in witches and their powers, if only in the universe of the story itself, in order for the tale to work, but that someone does not have to be the teller or the listener. Or we can all suspend our disbelief and *pretend* to believe. If only fleetingly, the witchcraft narrative may create a faith in spells and a longing to be granted just three wishes.[31] This may have been what some of the public did in this case. We need to understand the appeal of this esoteric knowledge: the assurance that life and the world can be understood and controlled by ritual and cunning; the temptation of hidden, meet and utter revenge on one's enemies. In so far as some people in Stratford-upon-Avon in 1867 believed it, the Davis's witchcraft narrative had great power.

The gulling of the Charlesworths (1856–57)

The cunning-man's story

The tale of how a cunning-man called James Tunnicliff duped the newly-married Thomas and Elizabeth Charlesworth is complex, and this section will be only as long as it needs to be to provide a bare context for the forensic narrative.[32] The partial failure of the forensic case attempted against Tunnicliff highlights the success of the forensic men in Stratford-on-Avon. In April 1856, the Charlesworths, four months married and already with a baby in the house, became convinced that they had been cursed by Thomas's widowed mother, who had moved out a month earlier. The cheese would not set, and the dairymaid was ill. Charlesworth was advised to go to see James Tunnicliff 'to take off the witchcraft'. Tunnicliff was in his mid-sixties, a beerhouse-keeper and agricultural labourer who lived a scant three miles north of Bromley Hurst, where the Charlesworths farmed. The involvement of most cunning-people with their clients was brief – perhaps only a single consultation per query – and that was probably Tunnicliff's usual *modus operandi* too. But this time was different. The Charlesworths were not rich, but their resources were certainly far more than Tunnicliff was used to, and they were frightened and credulous. The cunning-man may well have known what the problem was before they opened their mouths. Even if he did not know the family well, the mother's acrimonious departure must have set tongues wagging. Despite his wife's opposition, Tunnicliff agreed to help the young couple.

He seems to have done several things to 'help'. He diagnosed widespread witchcraft, extracted a hefty preliminary fee, and at his request Charlesworth 'wrote a letter for him to a man named Conway, in London, but whose address I forget, for a spell-book'. Tunnicliff probably engineered a 'fearful' night, when there was a terrible howling heard at the farm; he almost certainly also began a long course of poisoning the family. But they had no suspicions about him on that or any other account. He explained the 'fearful' night as a by-blow of his magical battle with one of old Mrs Charlesworth's wizards. The Charlesworths decided to employ him full-time, ostensibly as a labourer, but in fact to counter the bewitching. He moved in ten days later, and stayed for nine months.

On at least one occasion, as part of the treatment, Tunnicliff slept in the same room as the Charlesworths. One of Tunnicliff's daughters stayed at Bromley Hurst for a period too, adding to the expense, and maybe also the dignity of the treatment; but one day she had a fit, and said: 'Oh, they are doing wrong to Mr. C; they will kill him.' In early February, Tunnicliff and Elizabeth went to Derby. Thomas accompanied them as far as Burton, on some business to counter the witchcraft. For the most part, however, Tunnicliff stayed in or around the farmhouse. Whenever anyone came to the farm, he hid. At some point, a bottle filled with a strange liquid was found in the cowhouse thatch, but we don't know whether Tunnicliff said that this was old Mrs Charlesworth's witchcraft or his cunning. Everyone in the household (which also included a housekeeper, a nursemaid and a maid) was ill some of the time and, in hindsight, they realized that they were often ill after Tunnicliff had fixed their meal. Charlesworth had several severe attacks over the months, taken as continuing evidence of his mother's ill-wishing – the widow's curse, as the indictment against Tunnicliff called it. The animals fared no better with seven cows slipping their calves and one horse her foal. Even worse, Elizabeth Charlesworth had two miscarriages while Tunnicliff was on the farm, and in September the baby Elizabeth died of convulsions.

Tunnicliff's downfall was sudden. After months of fear and horror, on 10 February there was another 'awful night'. Thomas Charlesworth lost consciousness and it was thought that he was dying. The Charlesworths, who had depended upon the cunning-man so utterly for nigh on a year, suddenly called in the surgeon and the lawyer – the latter so that Thomas could make his will. Tunnicliff had gone too far, although there is little evidence as to why the worm turned when it did. The servants had gradually taken against him, which cannot have helped, but the Charlesworths had ignored their servants' fears before, as when they had dismissed a sceptical dairymaid at Tunnicliff's bidding. This time, however, they dismissed Tunnicliff, and very quickly brought charges against him.

Bryony and the doctor's narrative

A fortnight later, on 25 February, Tunnicliff was arrested by Ellis Crisp, the police superintendent, on charges of obtaining money under false pretences and of having drugged Thomas Charlesworth. The police searched Tunnicliff's house and took away a root and some powder, but it is not clear whether the arrest came before or after the search. It is tempting to say that Mr Higgins the surgeon suspected poisoning when he examined Thomas Charlesworth early in the morning of 11 February, and that this, together perhaps with suspicions voiced by Mr Higgins the lawyer,[33] at last prompted the Charlesworths to call in the police and set in train the legal process. It may not, however, have been as straightforward as that. It may all have been suspicion. Indeed, in the end, the drugging charge did not stick. The medical witness at the committal hearing was a Dr Monckton.[34] There is no explanation of why Mr Higgins the surgeon was not called, and there is no sign that Monckton had been involved at an earlier point in the investigation; nor is there any mention of his having special knowledge of poisons.[35] His involvement moreover was curiously informal. He sat to one side during the proceedings, taking notes about the Charlesworths' medical condition, 'it being considered not improbable that their health had in some way been affected by the conduct of the prisoner'.[36] There is no record of his asking any questions. He identified the root found in the search of Tunnicliff's house as *bryonia dioica*, which may mean that he had seen the evidence before or he may have recognized it at first glance in the courtroom. *Bryonia dioica* is white bryony, a fairly common hedgerow plant and well known to herbalists.[37] Monckton testified that *bryonia dioica* was 'not used in legitimate medicine'. It could kill people, and cause cows to abort and was also used to stop barrenness in cattle. But such severe symptoms as Charlesworth described were, he said, 'unlikely' to have been caused by it.[38] Thus the charge of drugging was dropped. The trial was long at eleven hours, and at the end the jury did not hesitate to find Tunnicliff guilty of obtaining money by false pretences. He was sentenced to one year's hard labour.

Cunning-folk and forensic skill

Although no one said so (or not in print), Tunnicliff had surely been very close to getting away with it altogether. As it was, he got away with a great deal. Presumably the police had considered charging him with the murder of the baby – there is no mention of this [39] – but either the death was too long before (six months) or the evidence of convulsions too ambiguous. Perhaps it was simply that babies were dying all the time in the 1850s, and there was no reason to regard baby Elizabeth's death as out-of-the-way. All the same, the prosecution clearly suspected that Tunnicliff, systematically and over many months, had been poisoning a number of people and farm animals, and may well have been responsible for Elizabeth's two miscarriages, if not the death of her child, but they could not prove it. This lack of proof was only partly a failure of forensic science. Tests for the presence in dead human tissue of vegetable poisons had been developed a few years before,[40] but this was not a murder enquiry and there was no dead body, just the Charlesworths and their servants. There were steps which Monckton, or someone else, could nonetheless have taken, but did not, like eliminating other possible causes of ill-health at Bromley Hurst, examining vomit traces for signs of poison, or questioning members of the Charlesworths' household about the food they had eaten over the months. Alfred Swaine Taylor's *Medical Jurisprudence* was in its fifth edition by this time, and in it Monckton – and the magistrates – could have read simple and comprehensive rules on how to proceed in cases of suspected poisoning: but if they did read them, they did not follow them.[41] This neglect of good practice was not unusual, however, if the complaints of men like Thomas Wakley and Alfred Taylor are true,[42] and we should not make too much of it. The newspapers at the time did not. It is more to the point that the prosecution for drugging failed because it did not have the services of someone who could tell a good forensic story. Better use of existing science might have given the prosecution sufficient evidence of poisoning to allow the drugging charge to go forward to the trial, but its definite value to Charlesworth's team would have been a vastly improved narrative. Witchcraft, as we saw in Stratford, can tell some great stories, but it is weak on cause-and-effect. There are no *symptoms* of witchcraft: its effects are the witchcraft. What you see is what you get. The thrill of hearing of such powers is undeniable, but when directly countered with a forensic story that promises to provide a radically different explanation, its authority is suddenly in danger. Of course, if you believe in witchcraft, science will not change your mind, though if you are interested in a good story you will at least listen to what the forensic man says.

With hindsight Dr Monckton does not inspire confidence, however, and my lack of confidence is rooted in more than a recognition of his ignorance – my reaction to his evidence certainly pre-dated knowledge of the extent of his ignorance, and my knowledge that he had not long qualified at the time of the trial. What he said and how he appears to have said it (and it is central to my approach to these narratives that it is scarcely possible to divide one from the other) did not seem to come from extensive knowledge or experience. On the one hand, he said that *bryonia dioica* could kill people and could cause cows to abort; on the other, he thought Thomas Charlesworth's symptoms too severe to have been caused by it. Of course this impression of slipshod ineptitude may have been the fault of the journalist, whose report is not *verbatim*, but the rest of the piece has a varied tone which suggests that he was being reasonably true to what he heard. Dr Monckton sounds arrogant, ignorant and incompetent: perhaps he was just a nervous young man. The Stas test was available to him, and there is no sign that he knew of it, if only to explain why he was unable to carry it out; he was crucially poorly informed about the effects of bryony poisoning – possibly because of a hasty reading of Orfila's textbook.[43] This is not to argue that he should have found it in himself to assert that the bryony was very likely to have been the agent of the havoc that had hit the Charlesworths, but that a better forensic witness would have made more of whatever he was able to say and would have told a better story. William Stewart in Stratford was much more impressive with just as little to go on.

The charge that remained was false pretences. It is not quite clear what was involved in proving this. Certainly, the prosecution had to prove that James Tunnicliff had solicited and received payment for unwitching the Charlesworths. At least one court, however, deemed it necessary also to show that the client had believed that the cunning-person was able to do what she or he claimed.[44] If this was the usual attitude, then the prosecution must have been rather embarrassed when Thomas Charlesworth changed his evidence so radically between the hearing and the assizes. At the hearing, he had been quite open about his belief that his mother had bewitched him, and about his trust in Tunnicliff's ability to undo the magic. Presumably it was the 'great laughter' which greeted his naïve pronouncements on the first occasion which led to his denying his beliefs at the trial.

It may have been because of gaps like this that the prosecution went to such great lengths to show that none of the people alleged to have been 'put on' Thomas Charlesworth and his family by his mother actually existed. In fact, it was irrelevant whether they existed or not. Witchcraft was not illegal, and even if every one of the named men had been found alive and well – even if people had come forward to say that the named men were all well-known cunning-folk – it would have made no difference. Nonetheless, for example, a policeman came at some expense all the way from Burton-upon-Trent to state that no man called Plimmer lived there.[45] The main ploy of the prosecution, however, was to tell a quite different kind of story – a comic tale. The reaction of the crowd at the hearing had made it clear that most people found the case very funny ('The room was crowded with a much-amused audience,' said the *Staffordshire Advertiser*[46]), and it was not James Tunnicliff at whom they laughed. It was poor Thomas Charlesworth, who with his wife had suffered so much, and now had to suffer this. The judge eventually told Thomas that he did not have to answer questions which exposed him to ridicule, but by then the damage was done. The Charlesworths had had to listen to their own counsel tell the court that,

> in your own country there are persons weak enough – credulous enough – to believe in the existence of charms or spells or in what is usually termed

witchcraft, and that there are also designing persons, not far from your own dwellings, who avail themselves of this weakness and credulity to perpetrate frauds greatly to the injury of those unfortunate persons.[47]

This was the story that won the day for the Charlesworths who, 'weak' and 'credulous' as they undoubtedly were, may never have understood what had happened to them.

An unanswered question is what would have happened if the best story of all – James Tunnicliff's – had been told? As far as we know, James Tunnicliff never told his tale to anyone, though one can picture his wife telling it to him when he came back from prison. Did Tunnicliff know the risks he was running for himself and others? Had he ever imagined he wouldbe living at the farm for nine months? How had he thought it would end? Did he have any faith at all in the magical power of what he did, or professed to do? The other untold story is the witch's. It is not impossible that old Mrs Charlesworth thought she was a witch. Her son thought she was, and she had said some rather witch-like things such as 'may your cheese never take' and 'may you rot in your bed'. It is also the case that a wronged mother might say such things as she stormed out of the door. Thomas's is a typical witch-accusation: someone asks you a favour, you refuse, something unpleasant happens to you, and you accuse the person you refused to help of being a witch. As Keith Thomas put it, we have 'the same old pattern of charity evaded, followed by misfortune incurred'.[48] However, the 'witch' was not on trial and no evidence of witchcraft was needed. Thus much is left out of the witchcraft stories, so much that they sometimes hardly make sense. Evidence is often nonetheless offered, and is generally greatly appreciated (more laughter in court), but it is not relevant, often to the enduring mystification of the complainants. More than one remarked that when 'they' abolished witchcraft, they should also have abolished witches.[49] How many people who were present at the Stafford Assizes muttered it as they went home? Did Thomas Charlesworth say it to his wife the night after the trial?

The challenge of science and the law

So narrative is powerful, but it has competitors.[50] Highly relevant here is what is loosely called 'scientific method', which in the courtroom was typically the realm of the 'expert witness'. This figure was reasonably well known to the Victorian court[51] and, as we have seen, these gentlemen were there, commenting (Monckton) and reporting (Stewart). Such evidence was admissible only in so far as the court perceived it as contributing to the testing of the 'coherence' and 'plausibility' of the narrative they had been invited to support, but for the public gathered there (and it is their beliefs with which

I am concerned), the expert's reports were understood as narrative, and it is that narrative which increasingly held their attention.

In Victorian England the laws of evidence were in a state of flux and far from clear. Over the eighteenth and nineteenth centuries, and even into the early twentieth century, there was a slow and unsteady shift: from a preference for a confession by the accused, to a preference for strong corroboration by reliable witnesses, to a preference for the establishment of clear chains of forensic evidence. Foucault describes this as a movement from 'the exposition of the facts or the confession to the slow process of discovery'.[52] The process of justice can thus be seen as moving from domination by judges when the hearing of confessions was the point of the trial, to domination by witnesses when witnesses were the fount of truth, and finally domination by lawyers when what was at stake was 'the professional management of a mixture of evidence'.[53] The mid-Victorian period is at an interesting juncture in this turmoil. Much contemporary jurisprudence was concerned with what constituted a 'competent' witness – Christopher Allen looks at the perceived defects of the Victorian witness: religious principle, infamy, interest and, above all, the fact of being the accused.[54] The reason we never hear directly from the accused is that until 1898 they were barred from speaking, largely for their own protection. The overriding fear of the lawmakers was that a bullying prosecutor or judge could, by putting the accused 'to a species of moral torture',[55] betray them into incriminating themselves. Over the same period the slow rise of the 'expert witness' introduced other problems. Although this trend was vital to the rise of lawyers' courtroom power, they did not make common cause with the 'experts'. Their approaches to the court-process were fundamentally different, and in many ways they competed rather than co-operated with each other. Forensic scientists offer a pre-eminently objective stance, and have striven to be treated as focused guides to indisputable truth, while lawyers remain locked in the adversarial process. The police detective was somewhere betwixt and between these groups: a leading member of the prosecution team, and, if not a scientist, a man whose forensic skill was his chief qualification for his job and the chief reason he was listened to in court.

Detectives, fiction and the uncanny

It is a tradition of witchcraft narratives, as with ghost stories, to present them as 'told', even in their written form. Although aspects of this tradition – the listeners gathered around the storyteller by the fire – were in decline even then, orality remains very powerful elsewhere in our culture, in spheres apparently far removed from this, in the courtroom for example. Given the hostility of modern policemen, lawyers and forensic scientists to pretensions to magical powers, their storytelling activities take on added interest. Good evidence in the courtroom is not the result of a scientific experiment, it is a story that the courts will accept. How rational is detection? How irrational is witchcraft?

A great deal of attention has been paid to the development in this period of the detective novel, particularly to the work of Poe, Dickens and Collins.[56] This work has value for my enquiry for two reasons. First, because it is widely agreed that fictional representations of detectives and detective work were in many respects in advance of what real detectives actually did, and indeed that many detectives learned from these novels. Second, because much of what is known about real detectives at this time relies on what Poe, Dickens, Collins and their like wrote. It was a symbiotic relationship. While Dickens's Inspector Bucket in *Bleak House* was drawn in part from the real-life Inspector Field, for example, Inspector Bucket (and his literary counterparts) may have inspired Mr Field's counterparts (if not Mr Field himself), and helped prepare the public for them. There are also, however, the stories written by detectives themselves. The granddaddy of the genre is the memoirs published in 1828 by the once-and-future criminal Vidocq. This unreliable account of his extraordinary career with the French *Sûreté*, which he founded, was translated into English that same year and has rarely been out of print since.[57] He attracted imitations, for example the two volumes published in 1861 by the Edinburgh policeman James M'Levy (*Curiosities of Crime in Edinburgh* and *The Sliding Scale of Life*) and William Henderson's *Clues* (1889).[58] In the work of both men, it is notable that the police catch their man (or, occasionally, woman) because they plan carefully, because they share knowledge with one another, even across the country, because sometimes they break the law themselves (illegally detaining people, searching them without warrants, breaking into premises), and above all because they know the criminals and their ways of working. Extraordinary feats of detection are rare in these books, as they assuredly were in real life. At the same time, both M'Levy and Henderson are keen to be recognized as having uncanny skills. One of Henderson's cases involved concealing himself at a vintner's, where he was able to observe how some thieves operated. He writes with evident satisfaction of their reaction to his knowledge: 'there seemed to have arisen the feeling that some supernatural influence had been brought to bear to detect them.'[59] Similarly, M'Levy is not averse to our thinking him possessed of extraordinary powers:

> In nine cases out of ten there is something mysterious in the way of Providence towards the discovery of crime. Just run up the history of any detective you please, and you will come to the semblance of a trace so very minute that you may view it as a natural or a mysterious thing, just according to your temperament and your point of view. As a philosopher, and a little hardened against the supernatural, you may treat my credulity as you think proper. I don't complain, provided that you admit that I am entitled to my

weakness; but bearing in mind at the same time, that there are always working powers which make considerable fools of our reasoning.[60]

To revert to my opening question: why did the witchcraft beliefs of the English non-urban working class go into decline in the course of the nineteenth century? This seems to me the most interesting enquiry to make of nineteenth-century magic-beliefs, apart perhaps from the historiographical question of why historians neglected those beliefs for so long. The well-told forensic story is very close to the story that cunning-folk would have told had they been willing or able to do so. The witchcraft stories were not heard in the courtroom, as (a) witchcraft was not a crime and so evidence of it was not sought and (b) when cunning-folk were there as the accused they were not heard either. The forensic men moved into that space, but they were not bound to 'win', any more than the cunning-folk and witches had been in their day. Dr Monckton, relying (or so it seems) on the old, informal accounts both of the case and himself, did not advance the cause of the forensic scientist as expert witness. Mr Stewart, with his largely irrelevant but formal and scientific account, did.

As Levack suggests in looking at the decriminalization of witchcraft in the previous century, intellectual history may not be the place to look for an explanation of changing attitudes to magic and witches.[61] There is increasing evidence that the advance of science and of scientific attitudes makes little difference to what we believe. A glance at any newspaper will confirm that people are as willing now as they were when Lewis Carroll wrote it to believe six impossible things before breakfast; and Keith Thomas was only the first to notice that the persecution of supposed witches ended before any appreciable influence of scientific ideas can be traced. What people believe does change, that much is clear, but why is far less so. I suggest that it has something to do with fashions in stories and storytelling. If it is a good story, then people will believe it until a better story comes along: what is good and what is better is the moot point.

Notes

1 I am grateful to Dr Katherine D. Watson, Wolfson College Oxford; Dr Lesley Hall, Senior Archivist (Outreach), the Wellcome Library for the History and Understanding of Medicine; and Dr Norah Rudin (see n. 29 below) for their help and guidance on some finer points; and to the staffs of the Wellcome Library, the London Library and the Morrab Library, Penzance, for their assistance. This may be the place to state that in an obvious but still important sense I am the only storyteller in this chapter, using what narrative skills I have to keep the reader's trust and attention; and in the absence of sufficient space to argue my way out of that, I shall merely assert that that trust depends to a substantial degree upon my convincing readers that in extracting these narratives from contemporary newspaper reports, I am not obscuring the stories that were first told some 150 years ago.

2 For example, Stephen Shapin, *The Scientific Revolution* (Chicago, 1996); Barbara
  Shapiro, *A Culture of Fact: England 1550–1720* (Ithaca and London, 2000); and Ian
  A. Burney, *Bodies of Evidence: Medicine and the Politics of the English Inquest 1830–1926*
  (London, 2000). Specifically on witchcraft narratives, see for example Marian Gibson,
  Reading Witchcraft: Stories of Early English Witches (London, 1999) and Malcolm
  Gaskill, *Crime and Mentalities in Early Modern England* (Cambridge, 2000).
3 To use Michael Shermer's phrase *Why People Believe Weird Things: Pseudoscience,*
  Superstition, and Other Confusions of Our Time (New York, 1997)) – although not to
  adopt his answer – that people who believe 'weird things' simply do not think straight.
4 For an absorbing account of the medicalization of the inquest, which has clear
  implications for cases such as mine, see Burney, *Bodies of Evidence*, pp. 8–12, 107–36.
5 Barbara Herrnstein Smith, 'Narrative Versions, Narrative Theories', reprinted in
  Martin McQuillan (ed.), *The Narrative Reader* (London, 2000), p. 144 (her italics).
6 See for example Owen Davies, 'Newspapers and the Popular Belief in Magic', *Journal*
  of British Studies 37 (1998) 139–65. Davies's researches in Somerset, however, suggest
  that there may be untapped riches awaiting researchers in other counties too: Davies,
  A People Bewitched: Witchcraft and Magic in Nineteenth-Century Somerset (Bruton, 1999).
7 None of my policemen was a detective by title. The only such detectives at that time
  were in the Metropolitan Police. My policemen were all ordinary police inspectors
  and superintendents, but since it is their evidence-gathering and -presenting activities
  that interest me, it is useful to call them detectives.
8 But see n. 32 below.
9 Burney, *Bodies of Evidence*, pp. 108–9.
10 Keith Thomas, *Religion and the Decline of Magic* (London, 1971), e.g. pp. 789, 791.
11 Witchcraft itself had ceased to be a crime in England in 1736, and thus nineteenth-
   century newspapers' delight in reporting 'witchcraft trials' employed a serious mis-
   nomer. See Owen Davies, *Witchcraft, Magic and Culture 1736–1951* (Manchester, 1999),
   pp. 1ff. The 1736 Act created the offence of pretending 'to exercise or use any kind
   of witchcraft, sorcery, enchantment, or conjuration, or [undertaking] to tell fortunes'.
12 For much of the argument in this section, see especially McQuillan, *The Narrative*
   Reader and the essays cited below from Theodor Sarbin (ed.), *Narrative Psychology:*
   The Storied Nature of Human Conduct (New York, 1986); also Philip J. M. Sturgess,
   Narrativity: Theory and Practice (Oxford, 1992).
13 Theodor Sarbin, 'Narrative as a Root Metaphor', in Sarbin, *Narrative Psychology*,
   pp. 14–15. See also Brian Sutton-Smith, 'Children's Fiction-Making', in Sarbin, *Nar-*
   rative Psychology, pp. 67–90.
14 Sturgess, *Narrativity*, p. 18.
15 McQuillan, *The Narrative Reader*, *passim*.
16 James C. Mancuso, 'The Acquisition and Use of Narrative Grammar Structure', in
   Sarbin, *Narrative Psychology*, p. 104.
17 Ernest Keen, 'Paranoia and Cataclysmic Narratives', in Sarbin, *Narrative Psychology*,
   pp. 174–5; John A. Robinson and Linda Hawpe, 'Narrative Thinking', in Sarbin,
   Narrative Psychology, pp. 111–12.
18 Sturgess, *Narrativity*, p. 11.
19 Frank Kermode, *The Sense of an Ending: Studies in the Theory of Fiction with a New*
   Epilogue (Oxford, [1966] 2000).
20 Frank Kermode, *Poetry, Narrative, History* (Oxford, 1990), p. 35.
21 For example, Shapin in *The Scientific Revolution* discusses the importance of class (in
   the shape of 'gentility') to the acceptability of 'facts' to an educated audience a century
   or two earlier. How far this applied to the courtroom, especially by the period I am
   investigating, is moot. Shapiro, *A Culture of Fact*, has a robust attack on at least part

of Shapin's thesis: 'whatever the courtroom was, it was certainly not a place of shared, gentlemanly trust' (p. 5).

22 Sarbin, 'Introduction and Overview', p. x; 'Narrative as a Root Metaphor', pp. 3, 8, 9, both in Sarbin, *Narrative Psychology.*

23 Sarbin, 'Narrative as a Root Metaphor', in Sarbin, *Narrative Psychology*, pp. 12–144.

24 The *Warwick and Warwickshire Advertiser, Birmingham Post* and *The Times* carried an identical account. *Warwick and Warwickshire Advertiser and Leamington Gazette*, 2 Nov. and 7 Dec. 1867; *The Times*, 4 Nov. and 2 Dec. 1867. I have not seen the *Birmingham Post*; but *The Times* acknowledges it as the source of its article.

25 *Stratford Herald*, 1 Nov. and 2 Dec. 1867.

26 She was described as a washerwoman in the 1861 census, and as a charwoman in the 1871 census.

27 Carlo Ginzburg, 'Clues: Roots of an Evidential Paradigm', in Ginzburg, *Clues, Myths and the Historical Method*, trans. John and Anne Tedeschi (Baltimore, [1979] 1992), pp. 96–125.

28 Stewart seems to have been an apprentice or assistant to the surgeon Mr Lane, who was also the medical officer to the Stratford Poor Law Institution. He does not appear ever to have qualified. Thanks to Dr Hall of the Wellcome Library for this information (see n. 1 above).

29 In 1862 the Dutchman Izaak Van Deen had developed a presumptive test for blood using guaiac, a West Indian shrub, but the discovery a year later of Schönbein's hydrogen peroxide test seems to have carried the day. Stewart may have used Van Deen's guaiac test, although hydrogen peroxide was probably easier to find in Stratford-upon-Avon. See 'Forensic Science Timeline' (www.forensicdna.com/Timeline.htm); Keith Inman and Norah Rudin, *Principles and Practice of Criminalistics: The Profession of Forensic Science* (Boca Raton, 2000).

30 *The Times*, 4 Nov. 1867.

31 J. K. Rowling, the author of the *Harry Potter* stories, said on *Desert Island Discs* that adults at book-signings sometimes solemnly whisper to her that 'they are trying out her spells'. Kingsley Amis's supernatural novel *The Green Man* (1969) was greeted as a true tale by many readers.

32 A fuller account is in my unpublished paper 'James Tunnicliff's Story: The Narrative of a Cunning-Man'. The main source for the case is the *Staffordshire Advertiser*, 7 and 21 March 1857, which reported the committal hearing and the assizes trial respectively. See also Public Record Office (hereafter PRO), ASSI 5 177/17 f. 44, and also *The Times*, 7 and 24 March 1857.

33 According to the newspaper both men were called Higgins.

34 David Henry Monckton (MS London 1849, MD 1855, MRCS and LSA 1849), practised in Rugeley, and was associated with King's College London. He had continuing connections with the Royal College of Surgeons, in which he later held office, and contributed several articles to the *Medical Times and Gazette* (Information from Medical Directories kindly provided by Dr Hall of the Wellcome Library).

35 The Medical Witnesses Act 1836 applied only to the investigation of suspicious deaths in coroners' courts, but its provisions might have been taken as laying down best practice for situations such as this. In particular, the Act stipulated that the medical witness should preferably be the man who had attended the deceased; failing that, it should be a medical man who saw the deceased soon after death; failing that, 'any qualified man practicing in the vicinity': Burney, *Bodies of Evidence*, pp. 108–9. *Mutatis mutandis*, Monckton would seem to have qualified under the last rubric, if indeed they were respected here at all.

36 *Staffordshire Advertiser*, 7 March 1857.

37 Richard Mabey, *Flora Britannica* (London, 1997), pp. 131–3, who records that it is
   also called mandrake (which it is not) and wild vine. Mabey refers to Anne Pratt's
   Poisonous, Noxious, and Suspected Plants of Our Fields and Woods (London, 1857),
   pp. 107–9, but she seems to have confused white bryony (*bryony dioica*, family Cucur-
   bitaceæ) and black bryony (*Tamis communis*, family Dioscoreacæ). Her source may
   well be Alfred Swaine Taylor's influential *On Poisons, in Relation to Medical Jurisprudence and Medicine* (London 1848), p. 511, which, surprisingly, has the same con-
   fusion.

38 That bryony is a poison was known to Orfila, author of the first great manual on
   poisons, *A Treatise on Mineral, Vegetable and Animal Poisons, Considered in Their Relation
   with Physiology, Pathology, and Medical Jurisprudence*, trans. from the French by
   J. A. Waller, 2 vols (London, 1818), vol. 2, pp. 11–14, and his British followers such
   as Robert Christison, *On Poisons* (London, 1845), pp. 459–60, and Taylor, *On Poisons*,
   p. 511. In recent times, cattle have died from eating bryony root (see Mabey, *Flora
   Britannica*, p. 132).

39 No police records survive.

40 In 1851 the Belgian chemist Jean Servais Stas had devised a brilliant method for
   demonstrating the presence of vegetable poisons in human tissue – in this case
   nicotine. What is now called the Stas Otto method remains the basic test for alkaline
   poisons. For an account of the method, and of the murder which Stas thus helped to
   prove, see Linda Stratmann, *Linda's Crime Notes*, 'Tobacco and Crime' at www.
   parmaq. com/truecrime/Tobacco. htm (last checked 21 May 2002).

41 A. S. Taylor, *Medical Jurisprudence* (5th edn, London, 1854), pp. 26–34. The fourth
   edition (1852), if that was the latest to hand, was identical in this respect.

42 For Wakley's campaigns to reform the law of inquests to allow more scope for medical
   expertise, see Burney, *Bodies of Evidence*, e.g. pp. 56–7. For Taylor's attitude and
   evidence, see his *Medical Jurisprudence*, p. 27: 'there is no person so well fitted to
   observe these points as a medical man; but it unfortunately happens, that many facts
   important as evidence are often overlooked. The necessity for observing and recording them is not perhaps generally known.'

43 At one point Orfila reports that dogs poisoned with bryony die without distress, and
   he could be understood to aver that the same is true for humans, except that he goes
   on to say: 'A number of observers have attested that the administration of bryony
   has been followed by violent vomitings, accompanied with faintings, sharp pains,
   alvine [sc. 'of the intestines or belly'] evacuations profuse, and of a serious nature,
   great thirst, &c.' (*Treatise*, p. 13.) Monckton was probably right about the use of
   bryony in legitimate medicine. Christison, *On Poisons*, pp. 459–60, refers to its having
   been 'expelled from medical practice', but it has always been part of the herbalists'
   pharmacopæia. The earliest use of 'bryony' as recorded in the *Oxford English Dic-
   tionary* (2nd edn, 1989) is at least eleventh century: 'Genim as wyrte ð man bryonia
   nemnð' ('Pluck the plants which people call bryonia'). Thanks to Rod Griffin for the
   translation from Anglo-Saxon.

44 Davies relates an 1881 case from Somerset which failed when the accuser said he
   had never believed in the cunning-man's power to cure his wife, but had gone along
   with it for her sake. On another occasion, the same cunning-man was found not guilty
   when it was shown that he had cautioned his client not to pay him unless it was of
   her own free will: Davies, *A People Bewitched*, pp. 67–8.

45 John Anderson from Burton-upon-Trent was amongst the witnesses who were paid
   to attend for six and a half days (List showing 'Circuits of the Judges' for Stafford,
   on the Oxford Circuit, opening Friday 13 March 1857, PRO, ASSI 4/32).

46 *Staffordshire Advertiser*, 7 March 1857.

47 *Staffordshire Advertiser*, 21 March 1857.

48 Thomas, *Religion and the Decline of Magic*, p. 696.

49 The first mention of this that I have seen is in *The Times*, 16 Sep. 1830, purportedly from Ireland, but it recurs over the years.

50 For example, painting, sculpture and music can represent experience in non-narrative, non-verbal ways (although they all have narrative forms available to them, and perhaps even have their origins in narrative).

51 According to Tal Golan, 'The History of Scientific Expert Testimony in the English Courtroom', *Science in Context* 12 (1999) 7–32, the term was understood by the late eighteenth century: 'The 1795 edition of Lord Gilbert's seminal *Law of Evidence* was the first legal text to dedicate a distinct discussion to proof by expert testimony. In a new section titled "Of Proof by Experts," the editor, an English barrister named Capel Lofft, discussed the station of expert opinion on the legal continuum between fact and speculation' (p. 14). I am most grateful to Dr Watson for pointing me to this source.

52 Michel Foucault, *Discipline and Punish*, quoted, without page reference, in Ronald R. Thomas, *Detective Fiction and the Rise of Forensic Science* (Cambridge, 1999), p. 1. Also relevant, but not pursued here, is the debate about the 'culture of fact' (to use Shapiro's phrase) exemplified by the relevant work of Shapin, *The Scientific Revolution*; Lorraine Daston, *Wonders and the Order of Nature 1650–1750* (New York, 1998); Shapiro, *A Culture of Fact*. But see above, n. 22.

53 Quoted, p. 34, in Thomas, *Detective Fiction and the Rise of Forensic Science* from Alexander Welsh, *Strong Representations: Narrative and Circumstantial Evidence in England* (Baltimore, 1992), p. 35.

54 C. J. W. Allen, *The Law of Evidence in Victorian England*, Cambridge Studies in English Legal History (Cambridge, 1997), *passim*.

55 Quoted in Allen, *Law of Evidence*, p. 153, from *Parliamentary Debates*, 3rd series, clii, 762–3 (24 Feb. 1859) [Lord Campbell's speech].

56 Thomas, *Detective Fiction and the Rise of Forensic Science* is the latest, and his bibliography is an excellent guide to earlier studies.

57 Eugène François Vidocq, *Mémoires de Vidocq: chef de la police de sûreté, jusqu'en 1827, aujourd'hui propriétaire et fabricant de papiers à Saint-Mandé*, translated 1828 by H. T. Riley and published as *Memoirs of Vidocq, written by himself* (according to the Bodleian entry [last accessed 26 May 2002]).

58 James M'Levy, *The Casebook of a Victorian Detective*, ed. George Scott-Moncrieff (Edinburgh, 1975) [this reprints both *Curiosities* and *The Sliding Scale*]; William Henderson, *Clues, or Leaves from a Chief Constable's Notebook* (Edinburgh, 1889).

59 Henderson, *Clues*, p. 123.

60 M'Levy, 'The Bluebells of Scotland', in *Casebook*, p. 141.

61 Brian Levack, 'The Decline and End of Witchcraft Prosecutions', in Marijke Gijswijt-Hofstra, Brian P. Levack and Roy Porter, *Witchcraft and Magic in Europe: The Eighteenth and Nineteenth Centuries* (London, 1999), pp. 3–30.

4

Narrative and the social dynamics of magical harm in late nineteenth- and early twentieth-century Finland

Laura Stark

Suspicions of witchcraft in Finland did not die out with the witch trials.[1] Traditional forms of magic and sorcery [2] continued to be not only suspected, but also practised in the Finnish countryside some two hundred years after the last witchcraft prosecutions in Finland, if we are to believe dozens of eyewitness accounts from farmers and labourers in the early twentieth century.[3] Although descriptions of sorcery and magic practices from the late nineteenth and twentieth centuries rarely entered the historical record, folklore collectors encountered them in their efforts to preserve folk beliefs, which were considered an important national heritage. Perhaps the longest-lived sorcery practices were those in which household witches (*trulli*) visited their neighbours' cowsheds or sheep pens on the eve of certain holidays such as Easter, Shrovetide and the New Year, in order to milk their neighbours' cows or shear bits of wool from their sheep. The aim of this activity was in some cases the stealing or ruining of their neighbours' 'cow-luck' or 'sheep-luck', but it was also believed that if the witch sheared wool from a magical number of different farms, then she could weave from this wool a cloak which would render the wearer invisible. As late as the early decades of the twentieth century, reports of such acts were sent to local newspapers and to the Finnish Literature Society Folklore Archives. For instance Hugo Hörtsänä, a farmer from Western Finland, reported to the Archives that in 1934 a witch had visited the cowsheds in the village of Hirsilä in Orivesi parish. The sheep of one small farm owner had been sheared of the wool on their heads, under their necks, on their tails, and from the front of their chests.[4] The same collector also recorded the following account of how such 'witches' were punished:[5]

> Circa 1913 on a farm in Orivesi, one night near Easter an itinerant labourer residing on the farm stayed up late at the window of the farmhouse. He noticed someone going into the cattle shed. After waking the master of the farm, they went together to take a look, and there was Emma, the daughter of the neighbouring Onnela farm. They took her out and put a long pole

through the sleeves of her coat and sent her home along the main road with her arms thus outstretched. Her sister Saima, who was on lookout some distance away, freed Emma from this awkward position. Emma had not yet time to do her magic in the cowshed.[6]

The events described in these stories represent the tail-end of an iceberg, namely the final decades of a rich and long-standing tradition of sorcery in rural Finland. It is a striking fact of agrarian Finnish culture that it managed to preserve magic practices, beliefs and incantations in traditional poetic metre (certain motifs of which probably date back several millennia) until the early decades of the twentieth century. The tenacity of this historically-layered traditional world-view can be seen from the tens of thousands of descriptions of magic rites and over 52,000 recorded variants of magic incantations recorded in the nineteenth and early twentieth centuries from the agrarian populations of Finland and neighbouring Karelia.[7] These descriptions and incantations were first recorded by educated collectors in the 1830s, and later also by tradition enthusiasts coming from the ranks of the rural population (1890s onward). These latter collectors from the 'writing folk' sent their written recollections and those of their neighbours and kin directly to the Finnish Literature Society Folklore Archives in Helsinki.

For the narrator, and often the collector as well, the social context of sorcery was so familiar and taken for granted that it was rarely considered necessary to verbalize it. Yet for today's folklorist or oral historian, this context represents unknown territory. Without information concerning their social setting and underlying motivations, practices aimed at magical harm may appear as dark, mysterious, anti-social events completely divorced from normal, everyday social interaction and experience, or opposed to social integration and cohesion. In this chapter I draw upon over 300 narratives recorded in rural Finland in the late nineteenth and early twentieth centuries that provide information concerning the social relations, tensions and strategies that framed sorcery and the counter-magic employed against it. Folklore is an important source for the study of these magic practices, because even if we are dubious of a source narrative's accuracy in all details, the communicative content of folklore, the fact that it was intended to be intelligible to others in the community, means that it can illuminate the background knowledge regarding sorcery's place in social life which is not always available from historical documentation. Although folklore often falls short of meeting the historian's standards for precision in form and chronology, and often lacks support from other documentation,[8] these shortcomings become less relevant when what we seek from folklore is not necessarily verifiable historical fact but the semantic field of cultural thinking about magical harm.

Since members of the rural populace rarely wrote down their own feelings or experiences, descriptions of magical self-protection and aggressive sorcery provide rare insights into the kinds of social pressures and tensions people experienced in their everyday lives. By looking at what people strove to gain by working magic and how magical acts were justified through different types of discourse, we learn much about early modern notions of personhood. The desires and impulses expressed through sorcery were framed within historical and culturally-specific ideas concerning legitimacy, entitlement and rights of the individual, the ways in which ego identified with others, the boundaries of the body and self, and how the violation of the self was experienced through the cultural filter of normative emotional expression. One fact which is clearly revealed from the folklore is that magic was a form of social currency, an instrument in power struggles and socio-economic strategizing. Magical knowledge and practice can be seen both as a *tactic*,[9] and as units of *symbolic cultural capital*[10] which could be exchanged for prestige, recognition, or material goods.

Yet the role of the emotional, irrational or unconscious cannot be overlooked here. Finnish folk narratives speak volumes on hostility, quarrels and violence, the lack of empathy towards enemies who suffer appalling fates, and the value of anger as a personal resource, both in daily life and in the cultural imagination. One may speculate that if Keith Thomas had been able to include folk narratives of witchcraft in his data, he might have been less inclined to emphasize the prevalence of harmony and conformity in sixteenth- and seventeenth-century English village life.[11]

Sorcery and social tensions

Although cultural representations existing in the memories of informants and expressed in folklore do not directly reflect social reality, such representations nonetheless originate within the context of real-life conditions and reflect, moreover, what the informants themselves saw as relevant. Memorates and anecdotes concerning sorcery can thus provide glimpses into the social structures and behind-the-scenes power struggles which operated in rural Finnish life. The ways in which human relationships were organized and manipulated through sorcery point to some of the most serious tensions plaguing this society, supporting the notion of 'witchcraft as a social strain-gauge'.[12] Although all manner of disputes and conflicts could give rise to sorcery, generally speaking the majority of stories depict farming or crofting households in ongoing competition with each other, although cases in which beggars went away empty-handed and muttering a curse[13] comprise their own clear sub-category of sorcery narratives. The reputations of 'witches' (*noita*) were thus rooted in tensions which were both vertical and horizontal with regard to social class structure.

Sorcery and magical harm practised by neighbouring farm households against each other can be understood in part as a result of resource scarcity and the notion of 'limited good',[14] in which it was assumed that the good fortune available to a community was of a fixed amount, so that a person prospered only at the expense of others. The concept of 'limited good' in Finnish and Karelian folk belief was already identified in 1960 by Toivo Vuorela.[15] This cognitive orientation was expressed in the Finnish-Karelian culture area through the concept of 'luck' (*onni*), which was thought to exist in finite quantity, as well as the 'stealing', 'spoiling', or 'breaking' of this luck. If a cattle owner's *onni* decreased (the cows became sick or stopped giving milk, for example), then it was assumed that the cattle-luck of a competitor had correspondingly been increased through unnatural means. Suspicions of sorcery were not merely a figment of farmers' imaginations: there is ample evidence that farmwomen, in particular, actually carried out harmful magic rites against their neighbours' livestock.

Finnish folk narratives regarding sorcery address (1) how the landless poor used their magical knowledge as a medium of exchange or barter to gain material goods; (2) how, as a last resort, the landless poor could receive negative respect and coerce material benefits from landowning farmers by cultivating a reputation for magical harm; (3) the use of sorcery in maintaining group cohesion and defining the symbolic boundaries of the farm household; (4) the key role of counter-sorcery in defusing aggression and providing an alternative to physical violence; and (5) the ways in which magical harm was collectively categorized as either legitimate or illegitimate.

Knowledge as social capital in the magical marketplace

Rapid population growth throughout the nineteenth century and especially famine in the 1860s gave rise to large numbers of itinerant labourers and beggars roaming the Finnish countryside, seeking room and board in exchange for performing menial labour such as chopping wood or bathing household members in the sauna. Such dependent lodgers were allowed to sleep in a corner of the main farmhouse or in an outbuilding. Although they might settle on a farm for decades if treated well, most itinerant labourers, and women who wandered the countryside in the capacities of masseuse or 'cupper',[16] were highly mobile, and thus able to pick up all manner of useful information.

Those who were most restricted to the domestic sphere, on the other hand, were farm mistresses, who were responsible for food preparation, cleaning, livestock husbandry, spinning, weaving, sewing and childcare, among other tasks. This contrast between the relative immobility of married women in the landowning classes and the much greater freedom of landless men and women gave rise to an information network operating behind the scenes of formal public power. Through this network, farm mistresses used the services of lower-class men and women in order to extend their own power and influence beyond the limits of the domestic sphere.

A farm mistress might send landless women on errands of either strategic information gathering or dissemination of information, in order to find a suitable bride for her son, sing her daughter's praises when visiting certain farms, spread false rumours in order to break up a liaison between her son and an undesirable young woman, or discredit a rival of her daughter.[17] Such errands furthered the farm mistress's own goals, and the messenger was repaid with food or even a bit of cash from the farm household, often without the knowledge of the farm master.

The information provided by the ranks of the landless poor also included knowledge of magic and sorcery. In some narratives, feuding farm households could use the magic knowledge possessed by the landless poor against each other:

> There lived two families, the Kekkonens and the Kestiläs. The farms were near each other, but in the middle was a patch of unused forest. The two farms quarrelled often with each other and tried in all ways to torment one another. One evening an old wandering beggar happened to come to Kestilä farm, and asked to spend the night. The farm master asked whether the stranger had in his power any 'wizardry', that is, the ability to harm others through magical means. The stranger answered in the affirmative. The farm master asked the stranger to stay the night, but at the same time urged him to summon a bear to attack the cattle of Kekkonens' farm. The stranger said he would do it, but announced that for that he would need a heated sauna, in which he could bathe. The sauna was heated, the stranger bathed and in all respects enjoyed the hospitality of his hosts.[18]

Itinerant labourers and beggars could also assist in healing illness or solving a theft, and they were, moreover, called upon to give advice on sorcery so that members of the landowning classes, especially farm mistresses, could advance their long-term socio-economic interests within the farm household. According to informants, those landless women who provided the farm mistresses with gossip or news of a prospective bride were also the same women who gave them advice about love magic or performed magic for them 'so that young lovers would stop seeing each other or so that an objectionable daughter-in-law or son-in-law would not come to the farm'.[19]

The women of the farm household had to work closely with each other in their various daily tasks, and were therefore greatly concerned about who shared the domestic sphere with them. This explains why farm mistresses occasionally performed sorcery to 'break' or 'ruin' the relationships their sons had formed with girls from poor families or those considered lazy, ill-tempered, sickly or unskilled. In a three-generational household, a new bride was also an important determinant of her mother-in-law's future well-being. It was the daughter-in-law who would eventually usurp the older woman's power and become mistress as the latter grew ill or frail, and whose kindness or ill-treatment would determine the quality of the mother-in-law's final years.[20] The adult women of the household were often those with the least official 'say' in matters of matchmaking. And because marriage was a socially-approved goal and the 'breaking' of a married or betrothed couple was disapproved of, the farm mistress could not in this case turn to a *tietäjä* for help.

Knowledge of magic and sorcery was an especially valued form of cultural capital because it was *secret*. Tanya Luhrmann, who has conducted fieldwork among modern magic-users in England, argues that secrecy is the key to the power of magic, because through restriction and concealment, knowledge becomes valuable, and its possession differentiates the possessor from other persons.[21] Knowledge of magic thus becomes a resource that others would like to obtain for themselves. Although secrecy was the *apparent* aim of magic rites in nineteenth- and early twentieth-century Finland, in reality the lack of privacy in Finnish rural life meant that very little escaped the attention of other household members and neighbours. The more secret the knowledge, the more it aroused interest among non-participants who tried to gain access to it through secretly listening at doors and peering through peepholes, or watching magic rites while hidden in the forest.[22] The circulation of information was, in fact, the deliberate goal of the magic-user in many cases. By threatening one's enemy openly with future sorcery, ensuring that a witness 'accidentally' saw the sorcery being carried out, or whispering to select confidantes of the possibility that 'secret' rites would be carried out on a given day or at a given time, the performer could guarantee that the act of magical harm would be witnessed or at least guessed at, and reports of it be circulated widely. Because persons were eager to demonstrate to others their possession of exclusive knowledge, both eyewitness accounts and narrative descriptions of magic were routinely broadcast by word of mouth. This in itself apparently led to concrete results, particularly in the case of unsolved theft: according to several accounts, stolen goods were secretly returned or confessions made as soon as the thief heard that a powerful *tietäjä* was on the case and preparing to either identify him or cause him harm through sorcery.[23]

Some persons made a career of the possession of secret knowledge. The *tietäjä* (lit. 'one who knows') was a seer, healer and sorcerer with shaman-like features[24] who possessed the most elaborate and structured knowledge regarding the supernatural. Most *tietäjäs* were men, although some were women, particularly in the northern parts of the country. Well-known *tietäjäs* were accorded respect just as were master craftsmen such as blacksmiths, carpenters, masons, bricklayers, fiddlers and castrators. *Tietäjäs* cured illness, retrieved stolen property, and performed *lempi*-bathing rituals on young women in order to increase their sex appeal to suitors, among other things. Like master craftsmen, *tietäjäs* were usually not paid in money but in kind, with a bottle of alcohol being the most usual gift.[25] To underpay a master craftsman meant that one did not respect his work, and it was common knowledge that in this case the 'master' might leave an intentional flaw in his work which would then be repaired or removed if shown the proper appreciation through an appropriate gift. In the same way, *tietäjäs* who were not appropriately compensated could turn magical protection into a curse.

Reputations for magical harm

Those whose magical knowledge was not necessarily in demand at a given moment could still coerce assistance from farm households by hinting that terrible supernatural revenge would follow if they were slighted or turned away empty-handed. Intimating at possession of powerful magical ability or secret knowledge through intensity of gaze or strange facial expressions, or by carrying mysterious-looking pouches and recounting their own feats of sorcery, gave the landless poor a certain leverage in soliciting charity from wealthier peasants. One informant recalled an elderly beggar who visited his childhood home at the end of the 1870s: 'she had been married to four men and then remained a widow and roamed about, begging and telling the most frightening tales of her magical abilities, so that farm mistresses, in their fear, put all kinds of things in her begging-sack'.[26] Another account reads as follows:

> I remember how dreadfully afraid we were of the sorceress named Pykly. I was a small girl on my home farm of Emoniemi. It was a completely different time than now, there were no railroads, nor anything else that was modern. The old beliefs were still alive. Every once in a while our home farm was visited by a tiny, old, extremely dark-complexioned woman with a bundle in her hand. She was the dreaded sorceress Pykly, with her magic objects in her bundle. 'Pykly is coming', it was said, 'now children, behave.' Cold shivers ran up and down my body. I would have wanted to run away, but there was nothing to do but remain in the farmhouse and be good, so that Pykly wouldn't work her magic. The adults tried to curry favour when dealing with Pykly. She was fed and given drink and gifts. Pykly was a malicious old woman, from whose brown face blazed a pair of keen black eyes. And she was capricious and quick to anger. Everyone heaved a sigh of relief when she left the farm. Many people used Pykly's 'services' during their lifetime. Pykly was in fact a capable sorceress, so it was said.[27]

Surprisingly large numbers of beggars and itinerant labourers appear to have been able to obtain food from farm households in the late nineteenth century. Given the fact that poor relief institutions were in their infancy, efforts by the political and cultural elite to stem the tide of beggary had little effect in the famine-ridden areas of northern and eastern Finland. While some farmers saw it as their Christian duty to assist the needy, many gave alms out of a deeply-rooted belief in the limited nature of good fortune which made them afraid of exposing their own hard-won resources to magical 'breaking' or 'ruining'. Narratives tell of households which refused charity to persons they mistakenly took for ordinary beggars and thereby suffered the consequences, whereas those who correctly identified which beggars were skilled in sorcery were able to appease them and thus escape magical harm. Correct identification, in turn, was aided by the circulation of folk narratives which told of well-known figures in the village or parish, as was the case with Poor-Lawrence (*Köyhä-Lauri*) from Uukuniemi in South Karelia, who was said to have bewitched livestock and magically prevented wedding guests from leaving weddings when refused food or alcohol. Poor-Lawrence was considered such a powerful sorcerer that 'if necessary he could have set all the denizens of the graveyard in motion'.[28] Narratives suggest that the most sensible precaution in dealing with beggars was a thorough knowledge of their reputations so that those who were versed in magic could be recognized and placated through gifts. This sort of almsgiving, while outwardly reminiscent of charity, was motivated by anxiety and self-interest rather than philanthropy.

Witches in the Finnish countryside were not simply *suspected* of harbouring resentment against those who withheld alms, they themselves made it clear, through boasting of their own skills in sorcery and actual performance of magic rites in full view of the farm household, that refusal of charity would not go unavenged:

> In order to demonstrate how much people feared 'breaking' and other sorts of ruinous magic practices, I tell the following story here: In a neighbouring parish, there lived in the days of my childhood a certain man who had made it his habit to travel from farm to farm every year in the late summer, not only in his own parish, but also in neighbouring parishes to claim his butter tax or tithe just like a clergyman, even though he hadn't any more right to it than a common beggar.[29]
>
> When this 'tax man' came to collect his due, as he put it, he asked for nothing, unlike others who would receive favours for free, instead, he wrinkled up his nose and twisted his jaw and said, 'now I came to collect my butter tax'. He needed say no more, and in some places didn't even need to say that much, before the butter pat was brought to him and he was humbly asked not to consider it too mean a gift by reason of its paucity or something else, but in no case was it said that the 'tax man' had no particular right to what he received.
>
> In addition to his pat of butter, the 'tax man' was given food and drink. You see, he was so feared for his sorcery that his hosts tried to be as humble and obedient as they possibly could. If, in his opinion, he was given too little, then he rarely complained about its paucity using words,

instead he wrinkled his nose and twisted his jaw even more, so that his face was puckered up. And then upon leaving he began his magical machinations, at the other end of the field if not before, thus frightening the people on the farm.

With these sorts of schemings he had made himself so frightening that farm mistresses, even farm masters, began to tremble with dread when this 'tax man' visited the farm. Once, however, it so happened that three men from one farm went after him and when they found him working his magic, they gave him quite a thrashing, and that's what he should have received from each place he visited instead of butter and refreshment, that dirty blackguard, but nobody dared to do it, they just waited on him hand and foot like a bishop in the parsonage.[30]

Not only begging but also petty theft might be tolerated if the perpetrator was known to be skilled in sorcery. One account from Eastern Finland describes a wealthy farm whose household members were well aware that a gravedigger was stealing grain from their granary to feed his family in the winter but dared say nothing about it because he was known to be a powerful sorcerer.[31] Such sorcerer-beggars may have been tolerated not only because members of the community believed in the efficacy of their magic, but also because they could be useful when one wished to perform sorcery against a third party. Itinerant beggars who visited farms or crofts where illness had suddenly or mysteriously arisen were in a position to benefit from their own claims of skill in counter-magic, and narratives suggest that their advice on magical matters was usually well received and rewarded.

Despite the frightening reputations of sorcerer-beggars, fear of the *tietäjä's* ability to work magic was even greater, and ensured that few dared to offend him deliberately. In one narrative, a farm master absentmindedly drove his wagon home past a known *tietäjä* walking some kilometres outside the village without inviting him in for a ride. The next morning the farm master's horse was seriously ill, having been 'eyed' by the *tietäjä*, but was cured when the farm master went to the *tietäjä* to kindly ask for help.[32]

It was especially dangerous to offend a *tietäjä* because the *tietäjä's* power or magical force was seen to come directly from his anger,[33] and could not always be countered through rituals or by injuring him. The famous *tietäjä* Pekka Tuovinen, for instance, told a folklore collector how a farmhand had vandalized a trap set for birds by an elderly *tietäjä*, despite warnings from others. 'At this the old man became furious. And later, when the farmhand went insane for the rest of his life, the old man said, "I became too angry, he cannot be saved", when he was asked to grant mercy.'[34] In another account, a man who had verbally offended the *tietäjä* known as 'Doctor Hirvonen' died of a haemorrhage the same night: 'Doctor Hirvonen said of himself that the person at whom he became angry would die right away.'[35]

Sorcery and the farm household

Throughout Finland and Karelia, farming households formed the basic unit of society, the fundamental community with which the individual most closely identified. For various reasons associated with land shortage and the low productivity of agriculture which resulted in the need for household members to engage in several different economic occupations simultaneously, actual farm households were quite flexible in terms of size and membership. Household members might not necessarily be related by blood or marriage, but might include unrelated 'partner families' and servants.[36] More important than blood ties was the fact that the Eastern Finnish and Karelian farming household ideally comprised a fundamental 'eating community', an aggregate which was seen to function as a single unit of social and economic production and consumption.

Descriptions of sorcery make it clear that in rural-traditional Finnish communities suspicions and accusations of sorcery tended above all to reinforce the boundary between separate farming households. From the perspective of landowning peasants or crofters, those who posed the greatest threat of magical harm were their neighbours. Narratives regarding sorcery reflect a cultural ideal in which the household was imagined to function as an integrated and harmonious whole. Tensions within households undoubtedly existed, but in numerous descriptions of sorcery, these tensions are silenced and glossed over, and it is the tensions *between* households which are emphasized. If, for example, household members or livestock fell ill or otherwise failed to thrive, the witch was never seen to be a member of the same farm household as the victim. In some cases the sorcerer and victim might even be related (as brothers, cousins, or in-laws), but lived in competing farm households, especially those which might have split off from a larger farm or were involved in disputes over inheritance or land use.[37] The only time that sorcery was seen to occur *within* a farm household was when an older woman performed sorcery on her son's new wife, if the incoming bride was seen to be a threat to the farm's continued prosperity.

For individuals and households who feared they were victims of magical harm, the primary recourse was counter-sorcery performed by a *tietäjä*. The identity of the sorcerer who had worked his or her magic against a farm was not always known at the moment in which counter-sorcery was undertaken. Yet it was believed that the agent of magical harm (referred to as a 'dog') would find its own way back to its sender or 'master', even if this sender had not yet been identified. If sent back to the witch, the 'dog' was thought to attack its master or mistress even more furiously than it had attacked its original victim, causing sudden pain, illness or even death, according to the *tietäjä's* instructions.[38] At this point the witch could be identified, once word circulated through the village that someone had suddenly suffered an inexplicable attack of pain or illness. The following narrative was sent to the Finnish Literature Society Folklore Archives in 1921 by a man born and raised in rural Eastern Finland, and depicts such an event which took place in his childhood:

> Once, the majority of the members of our household were feeling rather poorly. At that time, you see, nothing seemed to be going quite right in our life. Somebody had 'broken' the entire household. It was therefore necessary to fetch a sorcerer from somewhere who would correct the problem, release us from this 'breaking' [= magical harm], send the dog to its home, as was said concerning release from 'breaking'. That sort of sorcerer could be found some twenty or thirty kilometres from our farm, and so he was fetched.
>
> For smaller difficulties, 'releasers' could be found from closer at hand, from one's own village, in fact, but none of them could release a person from more serious 'breaking'. For that, he had to be an entirely 'toothy-mouthed man',[39] a man who knew all the magic tricks, who could put the Devil himself in pincers, who could drive a knife into his heart.
>
> And so! That sorcerer fetched from afar was, or at least pretended to be, the sort who was fully capable with his magic of making the Devil tremble in his trousers, of making the Evil One flee. And so the sauna was heated and the entire group of us, from the father of the family to the smallest child, went to the sauna with the sorcerer. There the demon-frightener first bathed us, slapping each of us separately with the sauna whisk made of birch leaves, and at the same time reciting an incantation so that he foamed at the mouth. Then he put each of us three times through a hoop fashioned from the blades of three scythes, first by lowering the hoop over each of us from head to foot two times, and then one time from bottom to top. While doing this trick, the sorcerer was in an extremely agitated state the entire time, but that was still nothing compared to what happened next. Now, you see, the sorcerer encircled each of our heads with a hunting knife, two times clockwise and one time counter clockwise, and then in a fit of frenzied rage, hurled the knife into the sauna whisk lying on the floor, and then, holding the knife, flung the whisk out of the sauna window and against the cooking hut so that the wall of the cooking hut reverberated. Apparently in this way he flung out our tormentor, supposedly pierced to the core by the knife, thus sending the dog to its own home to bite and gnaw the person who had 'broken' us.
>
> That sorcery seemed to have been very effective. A certain person living not far from us was heard to have become so violently ill in the same moment that he[40] nearly died. You see, a 'dog' sent home in the proper manner was exceedingly severe, it could kill the 'breaker' where he stood, depending entirely on what the person who sent it home wanted it to do. The sorcerer, in fact, usually asked the person he cured, from whom he sent the dog home ... how severe should be the bite of the dog sent home, should it kill right away, or merely torment?
>
> Usually people were sufficiently merciful toward the 'breaker', so that his life was spared, but otherwise to be dealt with as harshly as possible, since he had worked his magic in the first place without reason, in order to harm

another. Therefore that worthless lout should receive his just reward, and so be less willing to start bewitching a second time.

The release of our household from the 'breaking' occurred in the winter. In the spring, we boys found the sauna whisk which had been thrown from the sauna to the cooking hut, about a half kilometre from our farm, near the road that led to the cottagers who lived on our land. Apparently our sorcerer had taken it there, had given the 'dog' a ride that distance from our home. When we took the whisk apart, we found inside it a forked piece of alder wood about six inches long, and a bundle of alder twigs wrapped in the red string usually used for working magic.

That forked piece of alder wood in the whisk was naturally standing in for the person whom the 'dog' was sent back to bite. It was that piece of alder at which the sorcerer had aimed the thrust of his knife at the same time that he had chanted the incantation and glared and distorted his face in such a horrible manner.

I still remember the words of the incantation: 'Go, dog, to your home / to your master by supper / to your mistress by breakfast / to the rest of your family by mealtime / to bite, to gnaw / to cause extreme pain / Go far from the blameless / skirt round the innocent / go past the decent people.'[41]

Because the witch's fate hung in the balance between life or death, solely dependent upon the choice made by the victimized client, the *tietäjä's* counter-measures gave the client a sense of empowerment and functioned as an effective channel for clients' aggression and desire for revenge. Numerous accounts tell how *tietäjäs* gave their clients the choice of whether or not to 'send the dog back to its master', and if the answer was yes, how much damage the dog should do. While most clients asked that the witch's life be spared, others were reportedly not as merciful.

Despite the large number of narratives depicting acts of sorcery and the widespread fear in their efficacy, there is only one mention that sorcery-related cases were ever brought before the local courts by villagers, and there is no indication from the folklore materials that villagers were ever brought to trial for their over-zealous punishment of suspected sorcerers.[42] In general, retribution against witches tended to assume the form of counter-sorcery rather than physical violence. Only in cases where the witch was caught in the act was physical violence carried out:[43]

An old story of a witch from Vesanka village in Jyväskylä parish, which took place about one hundred years ago.

In the aforementioned village there was a certain farm mistress known for working witchcraft. And once she had been offended by something her neighbours did, and she began to summon a bear against the neighbour's cattle, so that it would attack the cows. She went to the forest near her neighbour's farm, where she knew her neighbours' cattle grazed during the day and began to climb up a tree upside-down so that her feet were in the air, and naturally in this way she was not able to climb very high.[44] But the master of the neighbouring farm happened to notice the mistress going secretly off into the woods, and he followed her in secret to observe what she did, and crept silently after her carrying a switch in his hand. When the mistress began to climb backwards up the tree, the master came up to her immediately and began to hit her on the backside with the switch while the mistress was still hanging onto the tree trunk with her feet in the air. The mistress yelled for help and did not manage to harm the neighbour's cattle, since her witchcraft had been interrupted in this way.[45]

While we may view the factuality of these narratives with a critical eye, keeping in mind their entertainment function, one thing is clear: these tales circulated by word of mouth for decades as part of a living oral tradition, which indicates that the world-view attributed to the characters in the narratives (in which climbing into a tree backwards or entering a neighbour's cowshed signified an intent to work witchcraft, constant watchfulness and suspicion of sorcery were commonplace, and mention of hostilities between farm households needed no further explanation) must have been to some extent familiar to both narrator and audience. Storytellers and listeners appreciated the tales because they understood the attitudes and background assumptions depicted in them, and any narrative gaps regarding context or motivation would have been filled in from knowledge of similar stories or even personal experience. The line between descriptions of actual magic practices and tales of magical fantasy is a hazy one, because as long as they were theoretically possible to carry out, the methods mentioned in even fanciful tales of sorcery could always serve as models for real attempts at magical harm. Oral tradition was therefore both the message *and* the medium of magical knowledge; it described sorcery practices while serving at the same time as the very means by which cultural knowledge of these practices was disseminated.

Legitimate versus illegitimate sorcery

Narrative accounts indicate that an important aim of sorcery was to prevent the dissolution of pre-existing social relationships. Numerous narratives allude to failed expectations regarding gifts not given (alms, hay from a neighbour's meadow, the milk or beestings from a neighbour's newly calved cow) yet the narratives do not go into the background of these expectations, to explain how the gift may have been awaited in return for a prior favour, for instance. What is depicted instead is a single act of charity refused at a particular moment in time – and this makes it difficult to reconstruct the social context behind the expectation or its refusal. In some cases, though, it seems clear that sorcery was used by dependent persons to prevent more powerful persons from breaking off relations of giving or exchange. In other words, the sorcerer was the weaker party, in danger of being excluded from a network of reciprocity from which he or she benefited. For instance, in speaking of the tensions in the tenant-landlord relationship, social historian Matti Peltonen points out that it was not the land tenure system and the dependence that it engendered *per se* which aroused bitterness in the crofter class, it was instead the *breakdown* in this system. During the period 1901–15, roughly 16,000 crofters were evicted from their homes by landlords who themselves were under new economic pressures.[46] This is reflected in the recollected narratives on sorcery as well, in which tenant farmers boasted of having caused magical harm to their landlords when their ties of interdependency had been, or were about to be, severed:

> I lived for eight years on the Kuusenjuuri croft in Mulikka village, Pylkön-mäki district. Since I didn't have a written contract, the master of Hokkala farm evicted me. Some time later I met an old Lapp man ... When he heard my story, he said: 'would you like for the entire family to become poor?' 'So be it,' I said. And thus it actually happened, the entire Hokkala family is now penniless.[47]

Another important context for sorcery was the power struggles that arose over disputes concerning theft, wages, or fair exchanges in barter. These were often disputes in which questions of legitimacy were unclear, often due to insufficient evidence to sway others to one's point of view. The motive behind the sorcery in all of these cases appears to have been the *overturning* of the sorcerer's position of dependency and powerlessness. When a neigh-bour's child fell ill, her cow was bewitched to stop giving milk, or a bear attacked her cattle, she was often forced to go to the sorcerer to ask for mercy, a request that was usually granted. Unlike the counter-sorcery in sixteenth- and seventeenth-century England described by Keith Thomas, in which the victim's aim was to compel the witch to ask for mercy, here it was often the victim who was forced to seek the mercy of the witch. In this way, the sorcerer strove to maintain the power equilibrium between self and victim which had been under threat:

> In former times when I was a child, my sister fell ill with epilepsy and people said that the girl is in the clutches of a sorcerer, of one old man, whose wife brought my mother berries [48] but in her opinion did not receive enough flour in return. Because my sister was the one to eat those berries first, it was said that the old man had bewitched the berries. Years later, my ailing sister went to this same man's house to ask if he would cure her of the illness, since he had been the one to bring it in the first place. The old man agreed and my sister told that he had proceeded in the following manner: 'we went into the forest and with the old man made a *naara* church from saplings (one naturally makes a cross with the trees so that it looks like the walls of a barn). Then a fire was lit in its corners and I had to walk through the hole of the window while they were burning. Then I had to take off my shirt and

burn it on a low, flat stone. During this whole procedure, the old man was mumbling something I could not make out.'[49]

Yet while the sorcerer may have hoped to force his/her victim to ask for mercy, in some cases persons went to apologize to and seek mercy from their tormenters only after months or even years, or after having sought the aid of other sorcerers (minor healers and *tietäjäs*). For the victims, humbling themselves and asking for mercy was a last resort. In many narratives, the story concludes instead with a third-party *tietäjä* healing the victim, and in some cases giving the victim the choice of whether or not to send the illness or harm back to its sender.

When was sorcery seen to be an act of illegitimate aggression, and when was it an act of self-defence or justifiable revenge? An analysis of folk narrative suggests that rural communities had their own value system and cultural categories for interpreting magical harm and human agents of sorcery. While some types of malevolent magic were clearly viewed as acts without social justification, other cases of harmful sorcery could be seen as defensible, as stabilizing social relations rather than escalating tensions.

On the basis of the folk narratives it appears that magical harm was divided on the one hand into categories of socially justifiable versus unjustifiable types of magical harm, and, on the other hand, pre-emptive sorcery, retributive sorcery and counter-violence. Combining these gives us, in theory, six different types of harmful magical acts. Socially justified, retributive sorcery included sorcery carried out against persons who insulted or refused to help the magic-user, or whose acts threatened the peace and order of the community, but above all the inviolability of the individual and his property. In practice this meant the identification and/or supernatural punishment of thieves, vandals and rapists.[50] It also included sorcery to punish men who had fathered children (especially by serving-maids) but refused to take financial responsibility for them.[51] Second, we have socially justified counter-sorcery which included sending back the 'dog' (e.g. illness-agent or bear summoned to attack an enemy's livestock) to its master. *Tietäjäs* might assist clients in both of these cases of socially justified magical harm:

> When about 60 years ago there was a bear in the midst of my cows and I found out that my enemy, the witch Nuija-Taipale from Ruovesi parish had bewitched it to attack my cattle, I went to the witch Kyyräläinen in Saarijärvi parish to ask for help. Kyyräläinen asked me: 'shall I send the dog home?' To which I answered, 'Do what you like, I'll not interfere.' The next day a bear attacked my enemy's cattle and killed his only cow, while the 'farmed-out cow' (which was rented to him for a year at a time in return for payment) was let alone.[52]

In traditional Finnish narrative, pre-emptive sorcery was never presented as justified. Persons who committed unjustified, pre-emptive sorcery generally operated alone, without the assistance of *tietäjäs*. Unlike the case made for early modern England by Thomas, most perpetrators of magical harm were not those most dependent upon neighbourly support; instead, they were persons who were only momentarily or *situationally* powerless, that is, they found themselves in situations in which sorcery was their only option. For example, with less freedom and mobility, but a considerable amount of power at stake, the goals of women of the landowning classes often ran counter to the goals of those who represented 'public good', namely farm masters. Because a rural Finnish woman's position in her marital household was often tied to the amount of milk produced by her own cattle (which she had brought with her as her dowry and therefore owned), examples of pre-emptive, illegitimate sorcery by women in rural Finland included the 'stealing' or 'breaking' of other households' cattle-luck.[53]

Another example of such illegitimate sorcery was *love magic*, an aggressive act of bewitching in which unmarried women placed their own bodily substances (menstrual blood, sweat, hair, etc.) in food or drink offered to the man whom they desired as a husband, but could not attract by other means, often a man of higher social standing. Numerous folk beliefs and personal reminiscences recorded throughout Finland and Karelia attest to the fact that both women and men believed in the effectiveness of this magic.[54] Women either practised love magic alone or were aided solely by their mothers, and generally only received assistance from outside sorcerers when the sorcerer wished to barter his/her knowledge for food or coffee.

Following the logic of the categories given above, one might also expect to find narratives regarding unjustified retributive sorcery and unjustified counter-sorcery, yet these do not seem to have existed in the Finnish folklore tradition. The reason for this is that retributive sorcery and counter-sorcery, as narrative devices, were *always viewed as justified* in order to signal the illegitimacy of the original, pre-emptive magic which preceded it and the guilt of the initial aggressor. Such counter-measures mentioned in the narratives also included physical violence, for example violence carried out against women by men who suspected themselves to be the victims of love magic.[55] In other words, when counter-sorcery was mentioned in the narratives, its function seems to have been to depict a situation in which social justice prevailed and equilibrium was restored. To have suggested that counter-sorcery was unwarranted would have violated these norms for storytelling. When, on the other hand, the narrator wished to signal that the first act of retributive magical harm was justified, then the story simply did not mention counter-measures at all.[56] The fact that punished sorcerers did not pursue their grudges in the stories' narratives does not necessarily reflect the ethnographic reality but rather the internal value system of the narratives, as well as the fact that the narratives tended to capture frozen moments of time rather than the diachronic processes of long-term hostilities.

Folk narratives also used other devices to signal whether the sorcery depicted in them was socially acceptable or unacceptable. Stories warned how the use of love magic by women in order to ensnare husbands, for instance, could end in the suicide or insanity of the husband, or the attempted murder of the wife:

> Just after the master of Pyykkö farm was fed the magic substance, they were married, but the couple became quarrelsome even though they had five children. The man was once again hostile: almost immediately after the marriage the feeling of closeness ended and in its place came the former feeling of disgust and revulsion. After having been married for about ten years the man went crazy and once he tried to kill his wife in the meadow with a scythe, but the wife got away.[57]

Sorcery that was seen to be justified, on the other hand, did not give rise to narratives that warned of the fateful consequences awaiting the magic-user.

Sorcery in the late nineteenth- and early twentieth-century Finnish country-side did not represent merely the vestiges of a once vital tradition, but comprised instead a system whose internal mechanisms were still functioning as late as the 1930s in some parts of the country. These mechanisms included belief in the efficacy of magic, circulation of narratives regarding sorcery, valuation of magic as cultural capital and the communal assessment of the legitimacy of different forms of magical harm. In the final analysis, sorcery in this cultural context appears to have been a strategy by individuals striving to maintain both their own social standing in society and their links to other persons. Exclusion from a relationship of aid or assistance was simultaneously a loss of one's place in the social matrix, and the insults that commonly sparked retributive sorcery likewise stripped persons of their social face. Persons undertook retributive sorcery in an attempt to maintain collapsing relations of dependency, whereas counter-sorcery was often a means by which households disengaged themselves from ties with non-beneficial groups or individuals while emphasizing their own internal cohesion.

Witchcraft accusations and the actual identification of witches seem to have played only a minor role in the sorcery dynamics of rural Finnish society when compared to the situation following the period of witchcraft trials in other parts of western Europe. Because the sorcerer did not lose face or social position by being suspected (sometimes quite the contrary), accusations were never an end in themselves, and *public* accusations are never mentioned in the narratives. To be known as a 'witch' (*noita*) was not necessarily a stigma to be avoided at all costs, since a reputation for magical harm elicited respect from others. The sorcerer or witch was never accused and then asked to remove a curse or pronounce a blessing.[58] The magical harm of sorcery could only be countered through supernatural strength or by crushing the sorcerer's will through frightening counter-measures, which included 'sending back the dog' and occasionally physical violence. One observation which emerges from my reading of the narratives is the importance of counter-sorcery and the role of the *tietäjä* in providing a legitimate outlet for airing grievances and tensions. From the Finnish material it appears that victims of supernatural misfortune placed their trust either in their own ability to counter sorcery, or in the *tietäjä's* capacity to find and punish the perpetrator, and therefore had no need to expend energy in ferreting out the evil-doer themselves, causing them bodily harm, or venting aggression against them in the form of long-term persecution.

In these folk narratives which highlight the tensions and tactics of everyday socio-economic struggles, sorcerer and victim appear as rational actors, even if they cannot always be pinned down with historical precision. Narratives were the *modus operandi* by which sorcery beliefs and practices were created, shaped and evaluated. When magical information was made more valuable through secrecy, this facilitated the circulation of narrative descriptions concerning it. Memorates and anecdotes simultaneously evaluated motives and situations, classifying them into socially acceptable and unacceptable forms of magical harm. By functioning as mechanisms of social ethos and control, narratives of magical harm were assured a place at the very heart of rural Finnish social dynamics into the twentieth century.

Notes

1 The author would like to thank the Academy of Finland for its funding of the research upon which this chapter is based.
2 The term sorcery here refers to magical harm caused by a human agent. Particularly in the eastern parts of nineteenth-century rural Finland, most sorcery beliefs had little diabolic content. Because a common term for sorcerer in Finnish, *noita*, has nonetheless been commonly translated into English as 'witch', I use the terms sorcerer and witch interchangeably in this paper to refer to both genders.
3 Many of these accounts deal with the physical traces left by witches of their activities: magic bundles (of dirt, hair, animal parts and the like) placed in cradles or under thresholds by malevolent visitors, or the bits of wool sheared from sheep in odd places discovered after a witch's night visit to the sheep pen.
4 Orivesi, 1953: Hugo Hörtsänä, 936.
5 Orivesi, 1953/1933: Hugo Hörtsänä, 925.
6 All translations from the original Finnish are mine.
7 The term Karelia refers to a region historically populated by a Balto-Finnic people related culturally and linguistically to the Finns. Karelia lies on both sides of the present-day border between Finland and Russia.
8 See Gwyn Prins, 'Oral History', in Peter Burke (ed.), *New Perspectives on Historical Writing* (Cambridge, 1991), pp. 119–20.
9 Michel de Certeau, *The Practice of Everyday Life*, trans. Steven Rendall (Berkeley, 1984).
10 Pierre Bourdieu, *Outline of a Theory of Practice* (Cambridge, 1977); Bourdieu, *The Logic of Practice* (Cambridge, 1990).
11 Keith Thomas, *Religion and the Decline of Magic* (London, 1971).

12 Max G. Marwick, 'Witchcraft as a Social Strain-Gauge', *Australian Journal of Science* 26 (1964) 263–8.

13 See Thomas, *Religion and the Decline of Magic.*

14 George M. Foster, 'Peasant Society and the Image of Limited Good', *American Anthropologist* 67 (1965) 293–315.

15 Toivo Vuorela, *Paha silmä suomalaisen perinteen valossa* (Helsinki, 1960).

16 Similar to leeching, 'cupping' was a practice of drawing blood for therapeutic purposes that involved suctioning blood from small cuts using hollow horns.

17 Laura Stark-Arola, *Magic, Body and Social Order: The Construction of Gender Through Women's Private Rituals in Traditional Finland* (Helsinki, 1998), pp. 108–11.

18 Ilomantsi, 1938: A. Turunen S. 1: 342: Heikki Hassinen, 51 years.

19 Asikkala, 1967: J. Maunula, *Kansantieto-lehti Kysely (Answers to the Questionnaire from the journal 'Folk Knowledge')*, 1936-present. Helsinki: Finnish Literature Society (hereafter *KT*), 394: 137.

20 Stark-Arola, *Magic, Body and Social Order*, pp. 105–6.

21 T. M. Luhrmann, 'The Magic of Secrecy', *Ethos* 17 (1989) 131–65.

22 Stark-Arola, *Magic, Body and Social Order*, pp. 39–43.

23 Leppävirta, 1935–36: Hannes Koskinen, *Kalevalan riemuvuoden kilpakeräys (Collection Contest in Honour of the 100th Anniversary of the Kalevala)*, 1935–6. Helsinki: Finnish Literature Society (hereafter *KRK*), 104: 17: Pekka Itkonen, 69 years; Nousiainen, 1930: F. Leivo, 25; Nilsiä, 1961: Aatto V. Korhonen, *Tarinakilpailu (Tale Competition)*, 1961. Helsinki: Finnish Literature Society (hereafter *TK*) 37: 51: Collector's father Adolf Korhonen (died 1935).

24 See Anna-Leena Siikala, Suomalainen šamanismi (Helsinki, 1992), pp. 108–11.

25 Satu Apo, 'Alkoholi ja kulttuuriset tunteet', in Sari Näre (ed.) Tunteiden Sosiologiaa II (Helsinki, 1999), pp. 101–44.

26 Sääminki, 1939: J. Vaahtoluoto, 419.

27 Valtimo Pyhäjärvi, 1955: Siiri Oulasmaa, 3116: Lempi Suurkoski.

28 Uukuniemi, 1935–36: Eino Kuutti, *KRK*, 143: 88: Toivo Mustajärvi, 50 years.

29 In the late nineteenth-century rural countryside, parishioners had to bring to the parsonage each year a certain amount of their produce, usually in the form of butter or cheese. In some cases parsons went from farm to farm every year to collect their butter, hence the comparison here between the itinerant sorcerer and a clergyman.

30 Kitee, 1921: Pekka Vauhkonen, *Vähäisiä keräelmiä (Minor Collections)*, 1900–1930s. Helsinki: Finnish Literature Society (hereafter *VK*), 107: 1.

31 Pälkjärvi, 1961: Olga Hirvonen, *TK*, 17: 155: Antti Eschner, b. 1875.

32 Koivisto, 1935–36: Väinö Santamo, *KRK*, 138: 23: Regina Rautanen, 76 years.

33 Anger can be thought of as the key component in Finnish-Karelian magical harm carried out by not only tietäjäs but ordinary persons as well. This was associated with the archaic belief that all persons possessed a supernatural force known as *luonto*, which 'rose' sometimes uncontrollably when one was angry. Because the *tietäjä's luonto*-force was seen to be harder (and sharper) than that of others, his *luonto* could penetrate the *luonto* of other persons, causing them physical or mental illness. See Stark-Arola, 'The Dynamistic Body in Traditional Finnish-Karelian Thought: *väki, vihat, nenä*, and *luonto*', in Anna-Leena Siikala (ed.), *Myth and Mentality: Studies in Folklore and Popular Thought*, Studia Fennica Folkloristica 8 (Helsinki, 2002).

34 Valtimo, 1939: Jorma Partanen, 1124: Pekka Tuovinen, 45 years.

35 Liperi, 1935–36: Tommi Korhola, *KRK*, 157: 143: Aapeli Ihalainen, 43 years.

36 Stark-Arola, *Magic, Body and Social Order*, pp. 78–81.

37 See Juha Pentikäinen, *Oral Repertoire and World View: An Anthropological Study of*

Marina Takalo's Life History, Folklore Fellows' Communications 219 (Helsinki, 1978), pp. 68–9, 220.

38 The 'dog' referred to any agent of harm sent by magical means, including an illness, curse, snake or bear sent to attack an enemy's cattle. In all of these cases, the dog was sent home by the *tietäjä* who spoke the words: '*Mene koira kottii*'.

39 Only *tietäjäs* who still had their teeth or carried iron objects in their mouths were considered to be supernaturally or magically powerful. See Stark-Arola, 'The Dynamistic Body in Traditional Finnish-Karelian Thought'.

40 The non-gendered Finnish pronoun *hän* here does not indicate whether the supposed perpetrator of the sorcery was male or female.

41 Kitee, 1921: Pekka Vauhkonen, *VK*: 107, 1.

42 On the other hand there are mentions that when a sorcerer was brought to court on charges unrelated to magic, such as refusal to repay a debt, he might perform (secret) magic aimed at bewitching the judge and jury and taking revenge on his accusers.

43 Also: Orivesi, 1941: Hugo Hörtsänä, 3548: Otto Sinkala, elderly farm master; Orivesi, 1932: Hugo Hörtsänä: Kustaava Välilä, eyewitness, born 1854.

44 Climbing backwards up a tree in the forest near the fields belonging to one's enemy was believed to be a common means of summoning a bear to attack that enemy's livestock, mentioned in numerous narratives.

45 Jyväskylä Korpilahti, 1945: J. Hyvärinen, 2665: Nikla Majander, born 1875.

46 Matti Peltonen, *Talolliset ja torpparit: vuosisadan vaihteen maatalouskysymys Suomessa* (*Landowners and Crofters: The Peasant Question in Finland at the Turn of the Century*) (Helsinki, 1992).

47 Pylkönmäki, 1935–36: Otto Harju, *KRK*, 70: 614: Otto Puttonen, 85 years.

48 Berries could be picked freely in the forest by everyone, and might be exchanged by poorer households for staple foodstuffs.

49 Tervo, 1935–36: Anna Heimonen, *KRK*, 92: 1069: Edla Heimonen, b. 1864. Parentheses are original.

50 Two narratives from South Karelia describe a magical punishment for the rape of a young woman. In them, a curse is uttered against the culprit which transforms his sexual organs ('May your organ always swell/ May it always stand like a pole/ And never be satisfied/ May it even be erect on your deathbed') so that he is doomed to 'chase wildly after women all his life, even though all the women were afraid of him and called him "Ville the Bull"'. Here we can speculate that in a community which believed in the effectiveness of the curse, it may have been enough for the rumours and narratives of both the rapist's act and the frightening new condition of his genitalia (which few would bother to confirm for themselves) to circulate throughout the community in order for him to be shunned (Koivisto, 1935–36: Ulla Mannonen, *KRK*, 129: 792: Ulla Kallonen, 79 years).

51 For example, Juva, 1914: Lauri Taskinen, *VK*, 98: b) 8: serving maid Hilma Väisänen, approximately 30 years of age.

52 Keuru, 1935–36: Alma Viitanen, *KRK*, 51: 108: Heikki Kurra, deceased, crofter.

53 Stark-Arola, *Magic, Body and Social Order*, pp. 169–72.

54 Stark-Arola, *Magic, Body and Social Order*, pp. 211–23.

55 Stark-Arola, *Magic, Body and Social Order*, pp. 222–3.

56 Stark-Arola, *Magic, Body and Social Order*, pp. 218–23.

57 Utajärvi, 1966: V. Lohi, 2484: Maija Ryynänen.

58 See Willem de Blécourt, 'On the Continuation of Witchcraft', in Jonathan Barry, Marianne Hester and Gareth Roberts (eds), *Witchcraft in Early Modern Europe: Studies in Culture and Belief* (Cambridge, 1996), pp. 335–52.

5

Boiling chickens and burning cats: witchcraft in the western Netherlands, 1850–1925

Willem de Blécourt

Towards the end of the nineteenth century The Hague newspapers reported that in a village between Gouda and Rotterdam a child was bewitched. The parents consulted an unwitcher who advised that they boil a live black chicken. This would draw the witch to the house of the bewitched. That evening, as the spell was enacted, it so happened that an old woman walked by. She was pulled inside and forced to unwitch the child, that is to say, to bless it. At the time this was certainly not an extraordinary account. Neither did it concern a 'single narrow-minded individual'. To the horror of the newspaper editors the whole village population participated in the 'witchcraft story' and this even 'in the centre of our fatherland'.[1] Yet today's historians pay attention to this and other cases of witchcraft in inverse proportion to the zeal with which such 'superstition' was combated at the time. In the historiography of the western Netherlands one searches in vain for discussion on witchcraft in this period.[2] The end of the nineteenth century is rather associated with a renewal of industrialization and improving communications than with witchcraft. This can at least partly be ascribed to the concept of culture that is current among historians who deal with this period. This concept is barely coloured by anthropology and therefore offers hardly any room for what has come to be called the history of everyday life.[3]

In this chapter I will apply an anthropological perspective. This way I will show what thinking and acting in terms of witchcraft, in short the witchcraft discourse, implied for the way people dealt with space and to a lesser extent with time, as well as for what they thought about the body. This analysis is embedded in an discussion about the bewitched, the people they suspected of bewitchments, and the people they called in to help them. The prevention of witchcraft will figure, too. It should also be clear from the outset that I do not consider manifestations of witchcraft as 'remains of magical thinking' mixed up with Christian elements, and which would be labelled as 'emotional' in contrast to 'rational' or 'sober-minded'.[4] Witchcraft, I will argue here, has its own logic that is neither more nor less rational than other ways of thinking.[5] This becomes especially evident when considering the underlying ideas about the 'second body'. In everyday life there is also no contradiction between witchcraft and religion since the former is strongly interwoven with religious opinions.

The geographical boundaries applied here have been derived from the work of Jozien Jobse-van Putten about self-support in the Netherlands. By the 'western' Netherlands she understands 'a continuous area … which included almost the whole of the provinces of North- and South-Holland and the western part of the province of Utrecht'. Compared to the other regions that can be discerned within the Netherlands, this area is characterized by a high degree of urbanization, a market economy and therefore a very low level of self-support. This kind of regional categorization is imbued with cultural relevance.[6] Since witchcraft serves to ascribe individual misfortune to others, it may also be considered as an expression of dependence within a community. It seems therefore reasonable to study it within a relatively homogeneous area where this dependence was less pronounced than elsewhere in the Netherlands.

Documentation and occurrence

Another reason for the neglect of witchcraft in the western Netherlands during the decades around 1900 can be found in Hans de Waardt's thesis on the subject. Although it is primarily concerned with the period up to 1800, the author thought research into manifestations beyond the eighteenth century was hardly fruitful. 'The witchcraft histories from this period can be characterized as isolated incidents,' he remarked. Furthermore, 'The belief in witchcraft was restricted to a fairly small group of people and it was no longer a social issue.' [7] These conclusions hardly invite further attention. They are not based on substantial research, however, and are part and parcel of the author's hypothesis about witchcraft's steady decline since the end of the sixteenth century.[8] In the supplements to his book, De Waardt refers to nine reports from the newspapers the *Nieuwe Gorinchemse Courant* and the *Schiedamsche Courant*, without informing his readers much about their content. Yet seven of the reports are dated between 1873 and 1882 and such a concentration of cases would, had it been found in the fifteenth or sixteenth centuries, easily have led us to call it an accusational peak. Moreover, newspapers actually reported many more cases. An indication of this can be found in the *Monthly* of the Society for the Repression of Quackery, which between 1893 and 1897 copied several reports from the *Nieuwe Rotterdamsche Courant*, one of the main Dutch newspapers. But since newspapers from the western Netherlands have not yet been systematically searched for information on the subject of witchcraft, I will mainly draw on newspapers from the province of Drenthe.[9] They reported about fifty cases from the western Netherlands, mainly in the second half of the nineteenth century. Editors from the eastern Netherlands liked to print reports on witchcraft from the west of the country, if only to relativize the image that 'superstition' was mainly rampant in the east. 'A striking example of superstition is reported, not from Drente or the Achterhoek [in the east of the province of Gelderland], but from Sliedrecht, one of the most prosperous villages in our country', the *Dordtsche Courant* wrote in 1894.[10] This prepared the reader to have his expectations dashed and at the same time it showed that these expectations were realistic. If witchcraft was of such little social importance at the time why was there so much journalistic attention?

To counter the notion of 'incidental' cases, it can be suggested that around 1900 witchcraft was still an integral part of people's experience, especially in the countryside. Intellectuals may have been sceptical, though some nevertheless eagerly participated in new 'superstitions' like spiritism and magnetism,[11] but this does not mean that today's historians have to emulate them. For it was a contemporary conclusion that witchcraft was still prevalent. For example the Dutch specialist Enklaar stated in his leaflet on 'superstition', after having discussed fortune-tellers: 'The medical practitioners in the countryside would be able to tell us a lot about a form of superstition which exceeds in importance all those mentioned earlier. I mean the belief in witches, which still reveals itself in many ways.' [12] This does not imply that the documentation of the witchcraft discourse becomes less fragmentary and anecdotal. This is especially the case with criminal justice material. Certainly, witchcraft may no longer have been persecuted, but the police could get involved when violence was employed to remove witchcraft or when an unwitchment specialist broke the law regarding the unlicensed practice of medicine. Only occasionally, however, did such events end up in court. Witchcraft was a subject 'which one often hears mentioned in the countryside, but which seldom leads to a criminal trial'.[13] When cases were tried, they are mainly to be found through newspaper reports.

Next to the newspaper reports, the responses to a survey carried out by the Bureau of Folklore in the 1930s offer the most complete overview of witchcraft's distribution, although this is not in totally reliable. Questions focused primarily on how to recognize witches. For the western Netherlands positive answers were returned from (small) places such as Bergen, Halfweg, Laren, Wilnis, Maassluis, Hoogvliet, Oud-Beierland and Schoonhoven.[14] Since the question presumed an active witchcraft discourse, this indicates that witchcraft was still reasonably widespread outside the big cities. Moreover, there are reasons to overvalue rather than to undervalue the responses. The Germanist Jan de Vries, who supervised the folklore research, found at the time that the folklorist was offered few chances to discover anything about witches: 'the minister and the teacher will tell him with indignation that these kinds of medieval practices have not occurred in his community within living

memory. If he asked a farmer about it, then he will think that the stranger
had come to make a fool of him.' [15] The number of positive responses could
thus have been larger. Comparison with the newspaper reports underlines
the diffidence that lies hidden in the negative responses. For the town of
Hoorn, for instance, the answer was simply: 'People don't believe in witches',
while reports from around 1860 nevertheless point to the contrary, and
complaints about 'superstitious' 'backwardness' were still expressed in the
early twentieth century.[16] Even affirmative answers may well have been
distorted, for example when witchcraft was placed too far back into the past.
The taboos surrounding witchcraft made it into a 'superstition' that, when
discussed at all, was ascribed to others. It concerned the inhabitants of
another village, or another province, or members of the 'lower classes of the
populace' or the 'rabble'.[17] It was therefore rarely possible to collect the
expressions of the very believers themselves. Cornelis Bakker, a general
practitioner in Broek in Waterland, just north of Amsterdam, and a student
of 'folk medicine' and related matters, began to collect stories and information
at the end of the nineteenth century. He made the following observation:
'People who know witchcraft stories, do not like to tell them to more educated
people, since they are often derided for their stupid superstition.'[18] Only
intensive research could yield results. 'Because we have been here very long,
we got to know the stories which were anxiously concealed,' a dialectologist
wrote about Volendam and Marken.[19]

Not only the accusers but also those who were considered to be witches
could have their reasons for reticence. Thus in 1886 a judge in the court of
Dordrecht asked a man from 's-Gravendeel, whose house had been invaded
and whose wife had been compelled to carry out an unwitchment, whether
he did not belittle the matter 'because he was afraid of new upsurges of
violence'? But the couple maintained that the accused who had forced his way
into their house 'was a good boy who did not want to harm them'. This led
to an acquittal for lack of evidence.[20] As late as the 1960s people on the island
of Goeree, south of Rotterdam, were afraid to tell 'witch stories'.[21] And when
people were willing to discuss witchcraft it still did not imply that they would
tell everything. The reports that survive are often superficial.

After Bakker, systematic oral research into all kinds of 'folk belief' was
only taken up again in the 1960s. The informants interrogated at this time
had come to consider witchcraft as a thing of the past – at least this is what
they conveyed to their interviewers. 'With us in Lopik there used to live
three witches,' said a factory worker from Haastrecht, south of Gouda; 'My
aunt also lived next to one.' Others expressed themselves likewise: 'Some
time ago people said, that there lived a witch in Ameide along the dyke.'
'There used to be old women in Sliedrecht who were able to bewitch.'
Occasionally it was explained that 'some time ago' meant 'a long time ago',
but mostly it probably concerned the period around 1900. 'We were only

school kids,' said a cattle farmer, born in Stolwijk in 1893, while talking about a local witch.[22] These expressions, collected by Henk Kooijman in the river area east of Rotterdam can be supplemented by the research of Engelbert Heupers which covered the region of Het Gooi, east of Amsterdam. A woman from Huizen, for instance, told the collector about her parents' experiences with the members of a witch family. A man from the same place, born in 1880, could remember stories from the time when his mother had still been a girl.[23] This may have been a strategy to avoid discussing later cases. It does show that the folklore texts refer to the same period as the newspaper reports, roughly between 1850 and 1925. Later cases have not been found.

The oral research conducted by folklorists only covered the edges of the provinces of North and South Holland. This had more to do with where fieldworkers enrolled by the Folklore Bureau lived than with a possible absence of the witchcraft discourse north of the Northsea Channel, which ran from Amsterdam westwards, or in the countryside between Leiden and Rotterdam. Scattered local publications fill the gaps in the other sources to some extent.[24] At Wieringen, in the Rijnland and in the Westland witchcraft was certainly known. The intensity of the phenomenon, however, is more difficult to ascertain. The reports vary from a few half-remembered stories, a remark about a local witch, to a case of bewitchment.[25] It could have concerned different phases in the decline of witchcraft, but for the time being it primarily shows that one place was more thoroughly researched than another. For the cities we have to rely again on newspaper reports; on the whole folklorists refrained from interviewing the urban population.

The bewitched and the witches

The newspaper reports show that the diagnosis of a bewitchment and an unwitchment ritual were not individual events; family members and neighbours were actively consulted. In 1851 in Hoorn it was recorded that the parents of a sick child, 'called the neighbours together and there was general agreement that the child was bewitched'. In Delft in 1866 'experienced female neighbours' were consulted for the same reason. In Dalem in 1896 it was said of an ill woman that, 'Neighbours and good friends convinced the patient that she had been bewitched. Immediately a witch doctor from Rotterdam was called in'.[26] In some cases we may even surmise that witchcraft was still a reality for most of the population. An old woman of Oud-Beierland referring to a time around 1890 observed, 'All ordinary people still believed in witchcraft then'.[27] In the same period it was reported from Utrecht: 'Who would ever have thought that in our enlightened century the belief in witches and the like was still rooted so strongly among a large part of the people?'[28] In Ameide it was usual to draw a little cross in the earth when people passed the house of the local witch. According to a building worker there, interviewed in 1962, 'Practically everyone in Ameide did this, certainly ninety percent'.[29]

The newspaper reports also allow a more precise description of the group of the bewitched, although mainly by age and gender. Occupations were only mentioned in exceptional cases: a 'simple labourer' in Gorinchem, a peat bargeman in Oude Wetering and a labourer in Charlois.[30] But bewitchment did not only concern the lower classes, since a farmer was also mentioned and 'well-to-do agriculturists'.[31] Small children made up the largest group of the bewitched (44 per cent), then adolescent girls (23 per cent). The same number of adult men and women thought themselves to have been the victim of a bewitchment (both 16 per cent). Since ill children were cared for by their mothers, this implies that the witchcraft discourse was for a large part situated within the female domain. The family members and neighbours who were consulted would also have primarily been women.[32] However, men were not missing from the discourse altogether. Apart from the fact that they occasionally felt themselves bewitched, like the man in Lopikerkapel whose, 'body was full of frogs' after he had drunk coffee with a certain woman,[33] they could also occupy several other positions. Once witchcraft had been diagnosed and the perpetrator had been identified, she had to be convinced to take away the bewitchment. Usually this called for forceful persuasion and most of the time men were the ones who carried out this action.[34] Men were also sent to witch doctors to obtain remedies and advice. Moreover, witchcraft was not restricted to the private sphere governed by women. A standard story, often related by men, was that a witch had stopped horses or had caused accidents when people passed her house.[35] In this case her influence transgressed the boundaries of her house and premises.

The witches themselves were predominantly women. In the newspaper reports only three men (6 per cent) were identified as witches. In the decades around 1900, as in the early modern period, every woman could be considered a potential witch.[36] This is sometimes apparent, for example, from the expressions about the number of witches in a certain region. 'Formerly Langerak was in such a bad way with witchcraft, that some people did not dare to admit that they came from Langerak when they were living else-where', the wife of a milk inspector related in 1963; 'that meant that you were involved in the free [magical] arts'.[37] In Sliedrecht it was discovered after a chicken test that '*all* women in the neighbourhood of the so-called Bosch as far as the Spuithuis (at least seventy) had taken part in the bewitchment'. In Lexmond there were eighty-seven witches 'according to popular rumour'; in Arkel there were sixty-three. Half of the inhabitants of Hornaar were capable of bewitching, it was thought, and it was said that Noordeloos swarmed with witches. In Schoonhoven there also used to be 'many witches' and in Utrecht at the road to Jutphaas between the railroad bridge and the Biesbosch lived seventeen witches.[38] This kind of information may often have originated with a witch doctor; the point is that it could be passed on and was believed by people.

There was an increased risk of being branded a witch if one's descendants had accrued a similar reputation. In the stories noted down by Bakker and by Heupers this is apparent from the motif of the girl who learns how to witch from her mother or her granny.[39] This was also one of the ways in which men came to be suspected of witchcraft. The man, who was said to have bewitched to death a fifteen-year-old girl in a little village near Dordrecht, had a great-grandmother, a grandmother and a mother, who were 'known as witches'.[40] The witchcraft that ran within the Keijer family in the fishing village of Huizen was also defined through the female line and among the most important were Aaltje (1843–1914) and Willem Keijer (1845–1929).[41] According to a local herring skewer, her granny Grietje Keijer had been a witch and Grietje was a sister of Willem and Aaltje. She also related: 'Father's sister and one of his nieces were capable of making mice. Just like that. It was told in our family. The whole of Huizen knew about it … It concerned Gerritje and Lammetje and those women were always sitting together. People were really scared of these two witches.'[42] A number of the stories about Willem concerned his teasing and his power over horses. The bewitchments he was accused of occurred within the male domain: he bewitched milk at a bakery and a cow belonging to a small farmer. His sisters Aaltje and Grietje could stop horses as well, but they also bewitched children.[43]

In patriarchal Holland province the boundaries between men and women were also well defined in the case of witchcraft. Men experienced bewitchments and dealt with local witches differently from women. When a boundary was occasionally crossed and a man was accused of having bewitched children, this was because witchcraft in his family was already defined in the female line. Male witchcraft was on the whole more about a display of power. Well-known male witches in Waterland, in the region of the river Zaan and in Hoorn (all in the province of North-Holland) were capable, so it was said, of immobilizing people and animals, and could perform tricks such as sending the jack of clubs to fetch a bottle of brandy.[44] In their turn women had to learn to deal with that. An example of this can be found in stories from Oud-Beierland, south of Rotterdam, which showed that women were not afraid of a male witch, that 'they kept their gaze fixed on him' and made him stop his whims.[45]

Unwitchment experts

Doctors could do little against bewitchments. 'We called the doctor, but he did not know what it was', a woman from Hilversum said. The remedies of the doctors did not help. And when the bewitched themselves had not already placed physicians outside the witchcraft discourse, then witch doctors would put them in an unfavourable light.[46] In Ransdorp a doctor was said to have been taken for a witch and beaten black and blue because he paid a visit in the middle of the night.[47] When the suspicion of a bewitchment had arisen, there were specialists who did react satisfactorily, be it a blesser (in the countryside), a fortune-teller (in the town), a priest or a member of the regular clergy, or a specialist unwitcher or witch doctor. We can see the actions of these specialists and especially the extent to which they were specialized as another sign of the scope of witchcraft. Intensive research reveals, for example, that the unwitchment specialists in the region Het Gooi had only a localized sphere of influence. Within this region a blesser could occasionally give advice in witchcraft cases in places such as Laren and Hilversum, though female witch doctors were also practising in Hilversum and Bussum.[48] At the most they were consulted from a neighbouring village. Female fortune-tellers were visited because of bewitchments from further away, but only sporadically. Newspapers report a fortune-teller in Amsterdam who was visited from Oude Wetering (near Leiden), and one in Maassluis (west of Rotterdam) who received visitors from Sliedrecht.[49]

Just as with female fortune-tellers, unwitching formed only a small part of the activities of Catholic clergy. Each instance is only mentioned once. People in Bovenkerk who felt bewitched went to the *Paterskerk* at the *Keizersgracht* in Amsterdam. Around 1900 there was an unwitching priest in Kortenhoef and a monk in Hilversum was also consulted.[50] Moreover, not every Catholic clergyman wanted to provide help. A certain Father van D. in Haarlem only reluctantly agreed to bless a house in which a six-year-old bewitched boy lived: 'he had, of course, not said that it was true, but did not deny anything either and the only advice he gave was to pray'. The boy's mother, however, had been convinced that the blessing would draw the witch to the house.[51] In 1879 a priest in Rotterdam was most unwilling to unwitch. One morning he had given a woman the last rites and in the evening of the same day he was called back. The brother of the woman had arrived in the meantime and was convinced that she 'had been touched by an evil hand' and that the priest could remove the spell. The latter refused because he found the idea superstitious, whereupon the brother started to threaten the priest: he became angry and took him hostage. But the priest said 'that he would rather die than to give in to this superstition'. This lasted for five hours until the priest devised a trick and escaped. In 1882, in the same town a cleric was asked to unwitch and when he declined and failed to change the mind of the parents and the bystanders regarding witchcraft, a horse doctor was consulted instead.[52]

In the region along the big rivers several unwitchers were active and they were also more specialized than their northern colleagues. Around 1860 a scrap-metal merchant in Delft, Jan Boogaarts, sold iron filings to bewitched people from Rhoon. To impress them with the power of his remedy he told his clients that the filings would become hot to touch and they should not show them to anyone else because otherwise the bewitched would die.[53] In

1896 'several witch doctors' were consulted from Zevenhuizen, among whom at least one was from Rotterdam.[54] In Streefkerk a well-known witch doctor from Beesd used to pay visits. This was Anthonie Mulheim, who was also consulted by people from Lexmond.[55] Informants of Kooijman mentioned witch doctors in Vianen and Giessen-Nieuwkerk. The last was once asked: 'I have heard that you can ride a broomstick through the air'. The witch doctor acknowledged this and added, 'but I am not doing it now. I find the weather too bad'.[56] This anecdote indicates the tall tales that circulated about witch doctors.

In Gorinchem the bewitched could obtain advice and remedies against bewitchments over the whole period under discussion here. Reports about this can be found in a range of sources. Only rarely, however, is the name of the specialist mentioned. One that is identifiable is Lelie the saddler.[57] He was from a long line of saddlers of whom particular members performed unwitching as a sideline. 'Gorinchem again possesses a famous witch doctor,' the *Schoonhovensche Courant* wrote in 1872. 'Many in the Alblasserwaard already have to thank their unwitchment to this noble man.'[58] Originally this family of saddlers was called Lille, but this soon turned into the more Dutch Lelie (Lilly). All three brothers Hermanus, Egidius and Anthonie were born around 1800 and were Catholics. So far we only know that the last two featured as unwitchment specialists. In 1857 Egidius (1804–59) had been indicted by the local court for practising medicine without a licence. He had provided bottles of 'medicine' to a woman in Meerkerk who had been affected by the 'evil hand'.[59] In 1876 Anthonie (1808–1885) was accused of a similar crime. He had supplied bottles with a certain liquid to men from Hellouw and Haasteren for their children. Both brothers were acquitted for lack of evidence, in Anthonie's case because the witnesses said that they did not know him and because he also said that he had never seen any of the witnesses either.[60] These incidents indicate little regarding judicial incompetence and say rather a lot about the considerable influence healers exercised over their clients.

It is plausible, although not certain, that one of the family specialized in unwitchments and that upon his death this task was taken over by a successor.[61] But although this allows us to identify a pause in the performances of the family, it does not explain individual approaches. Remedies and advice are likely to have been transmitted within the family. According to the writer of a letter in the *Nieuwe Gorinchemse Courant* the drink that was administered in the 1870s consisted of an extract of dried cherry stalks made into 'a kind of weak hot brandy toddy'. In 1882 white wine was prescribed, and a herbal extract in 1889. In 1926 Egidius's grandson provided blessed wine. This was not meant for the bewitched but for the witch herself. It 'tasted quite sour and I felt my lips withdrawing', she explained to a reporter. 'As soon as I finished it, they wanted me to bless the girl.' But the practices of the Lelies went beyond unwitching. They recommended a 'kind of poultice of fig leaves' for wounds and ruptures, for example. Furthermore, every remedy was accompanied by an instruction.[62] When it concerned bewitchments, it was strongly advised to prevent the witch seeing the jug to stop it from bursting, and to discuss witches after sunset was not permitted.[63]

The sphere of influence of the Lelies extended over a wide area around Gorinchem. In the course of time this area possibly diminished. At any rate, the oldest relevant sources, the newspaper accounts, indicate the furthest reach towards the west and the south. The replies to the 1934 survey show a somewhat smaller sphere of influence, especially to the north and east, and in the 1960s Kooijman's folklore notes suggest similar boundaries. Yet as late as 1926 a newspaper reported that, 'patients arrived almost daily who think that they are bewitched by someone or other'.[64]

Proxemics and kinesics

The witch doctor's advice contributed to the way in which the bewitched acted towards witches. In the first instance this was mainly a matter of keeping a distance, which could cause the suspected witch to become almost totally socially isolated. When the suspect was self-employed this could have severe financial ramifications. In a village in North-Holland a woman who sold haberdashery was boycotted after she had been identified as a witch. Similarly a saleswoman from The Betuwe was avoided by everyone. A wet nurse in Gorinchem had her income drastically reduced, and a seller of peat in Vlaardingen lost most of her clients.[65]

At a local level all kinds of warnings circulated to restrict a witch's influence. Thus one should not sit next to a witch in church, or accept food from her. It was also not very sensible to come close to a witch, or, according to a cattle farmer in Nieuwland, be near to a place where she had been. Bodily contact was to be avoided at all costs. It was said in Noordeloos: 'Don't touch or eat anything that belongs to her. Don't let your hair be stroked.' When she put her hand on your head, you had to hold your hand over hers, said a pig castrator at Haastrecht. This advice applied in Het Gooi as well.[66] For touching could result in a bewitchment. In Zuid-Beierland a girl had become unwell after a woman had shaken her hand. In Rijnsburg a woman had soothed a child, in Weesp and in Alkmaar she had even kissed it. In Utrecht a girl had become bewitched after she had been tapped on her shoulder by a woman and been asked for the way.[67] In Maartensdijk a woman had been punched in her back by a woman who was known as a witch. Since then she had become unwell, 'tired and always miserable'.[68] Being touched by some woman who was not supposed to do so, it appears from all these examples, affected people's bodily integrity and led to illness.

In the area of the great rivers people spoke about the 'evil hand'. Occasionally this could be prevented by a manual gesture. In the words of a farmer's wife of Haastrecht: 'When you wonder whether a woman had bewitched your child, then the best thing to do, is to quickly put your hand above the woman's head, then the evil returns to that woman.' Another counter-measure, used in Naarden, was to keep your thumb inside your hand. 'That little woman always stroke little children over their heads, along the face and then that child became bewitched, of course. They all said so here.'[69] It was rare, though, to become bewitched by means of looking, by the evil eye.[70]

In the various texts the precise picture of a bewitchment remains unclear. A young girl was suffering from 'heavy tightness of the chest and from an unknown illness'. Another girl was 'already suffering for some time, without anybody knowing the nature of her ailment'. Still another girl was also 'suffering'. A family was plagued by 'illnesses against which the doctors could not prevail'. A man was feeling 'unwell and depressed especially at night'.[71] Often less was known about her own condition than about the state of the mattress or the pillow on which the bewitched had been lying, in which all kinds of objects and feathers lumped into strange shapes were found. This combination of bodily vagueness and extra somatic certainty was typical of bewitchment. The experience of most of the men also differed in this respect from that of the women. Not only had they less to fear from being touched, when they did get bewitched because they had eaten something given by a witch, they felt beasts in their body. As one man told a doctor, 'My stomach is full of toads. I am bewitched'. His doctor ascribed this to bad teeth, however, which had prevented the man from chewing well.[72] These sorts of opinions were supported by the witch doctors in Gorinchem who told male clients that they had a stoat, a toad, or even a whole family of toads inside them.[73]

To repair the affected body the witch was required to pronounce a blessing over it. Occasionally she would come on her own accord 'to see the effect'. More often she had to be lured, with an excuse such as 'Come and have a look', or with violence.[74] In most cases the bewitched resorted to a ritual. It was possible to boil herbs which would burn the witch's face,[75] or to perform the chicken test. According to De Waardt the low frequency of this ritual in the seventeenth century was one of the examples of a declining 'witchcraft belief'.[76] This would have been correct if it rarely occurred later, but this is not the case. In the nineteenth century boiling a black chicken alive was, in fact, rather popular, especially in mid and western areas of the Netherlands. Not only can this be seen on the map which was drawn for the *Folklore-Atlas*, based on the 1934 witchcraft survey, but is also evident from newspaper reports from Delfshaven, Delft, Hoorn, Maartensdijk, Muiderberg, Oude Wetering, Rotterdam, Schiedam and Sliedrecht.[77] This ritual required a special screening-off of the boundaries of the house: the 'house was closed and the chimney filled up', 'all cracks and slits in the room and even the key hole' were filled. The meaning of this must surely be found within the ritual context, but there was also a practical aspect. In 1873 in Lexmond, for instance, the windows were covered with material to prevent people looking in.[78]

In some way the boiling chicken was connected to the witch and would draw her to the house. Numerous stories show a similar connection between witches and cats. When a cat was wounded, the same wound would also appear on a witch. In Rotterdam this was put into practice by rubbing a cat's head with oil and setting it alight. Consequently people would go to see whether the suspected woman had a 'burn sign' on her face.[79] This expected effect from a distance also appears in one of the Lelies' rituals: when a witch's face showed in the water they let a woman cut it with a coin. This would give the witch a cut on her face.[80] In all these cases the distance between bewitched and witch was bridged, but now the boundaries were maintained which had previously been broken.

This relation between the witch and animals can be understood from the concept of the witch's double that lies behind it, a second shape that could operate next to her actual body but that stayed connected to it. This was made explicit only in a few cases. A woman in Woerden, for instance, lured one of her neighbours to her house, saying: 'No ugly witch, you have bewitched my child, you crawl through the keyhole at night and you put the evil hand on my child.'[81] The witch doctor in Delft asked whether his patients would not have seen someone standing in front of them. The double could reach places that were normally inaccessible. Why cats and chickens were especially associated with witches is not totally clear. They are of course both domesticated animals. But while this may explain the cat, which was associated with witches all over Europe, the chicken remains specific to the central Netherlands in Western Europe. The concept of the double also explains why when a chicken was boiled every hole had to be closed. For only then the witch had to come herself. It was easier to manipulate the double than the witch's own body. The latter had to be kept at a distance as much as possible, and only with bodily violence could the witch be forced to express the words that would counter her evil influence: 'God bless you'.

Continuation or decline?

Although the material presented here covers a period of about seventy-five years, taken together it does not offer much more than a synchronic picture. Only with the necessary caution is it possible to draw conclusions about continuity or decline of the witchcraft discourse. This is especially the case in view of the insufficient research carried out in parts of the geographical area that has been described. The characterization of nineteenth- and twentieth-century witchcraft cases as 'isolated incidents' nevertheless appears to be false. Not only was the witchcraft discourse still firmly embedded in the local culture of a number of places, but so many cases can be pointed out that a wide distribution becomes visible. This certainly applied to the eastern part of the western Netherlands, roughly south-east of a line from Amsterdam to Delft.

As to the coastal area and North-Holland north of the North Sea Channel, at least in some places we have to acknowledge a lack of material rather than a total absence of witchcraft. This conclusion can be strengthened by considering the taboos that surrounded the discourse. Bakker's notes about Waterland certainly indicate a lively memory of witchcraft in the years around 1900, and there is no reason whatsoever not to suspect the possibility of bewitchment discourses in the Amsterdam quarter of the Jordaan at the time.[82]

In the coastal area witchcraft seems to have flourished in the Catholic context. The folklorist Tjaard de Haan did not find any traces of it in Zandvoort, but he did in the old Catholic Egmond aan Zee with its 'reminiscence of witch and witch expeller'. He also connected the continuation of witchcraft stories in Spaarndam with the local Catholic belief.[83] In the folklore survey of 1934 a respondent of Leiderdorp made a similar observation: the Roman Catholic part of the population still believed in the evil eye; the Protestant part did not.[84] In the area of the Kromme Rijn, where accusations certainly occurred till 1940, a relation between the local 'superstitions' and Catholic customs was likewise noticed.[85] Together with the Catholic unwitchment experts in Haarlem and Amsterdam, these accounts may indicate a certain predisposition for witchcraft among conservative Catholics.

This is not to say that Protestants had left the witchcraft discourse altogether. The eastern part of the western Netherlands, where both folklore investigations and my newspaper research found a fair amount of witchcraft cases, includes the orthodox Calvinist regions for which a preoccupation with witchcraft has already been determined before.[86] The strong indignation regarding members of the Keijer family in the orthodox Huizen was not without reasons: 'Such a dirty fellow'; 'a dangerous woman'; 'a very evil bitch'. Among these Calvinists witchcraft was defended on 'scriptural grounds'. A peat bargeman in Oude Wetering, whose children had been bewitched, was also 'of more than strict Christian persuasion'.[87] This image is even more strongly supported by remarks like those from Hilversum about the pharaoh's wizards in the Bible: 'who may not have been able to do everything, but who, when you read it, together did witch quite a cool bit'. This was a biblical justification for the existence of witchcraft, for the Bible 'does not lie'.[88] In 1887 a member of the Reformed Church in Giessendam asked for a day of prayer and fasting because his household had been hit by a bewitchment. More detailed investigation confirms the activities of a witch doctor from Oudewater, a Catholic and a 'seventh son' who had furnished the house with Catholic medals, statues of Maria and palms, and moreover had sprayed it with holy water.[89] Here the Calvinist susceptibility for witchcraft met with the unwitchment facilities from the Catholic repertoire. As a matter of fact, this was also the case with the Catholic Lelies and, in view of their region of origin, their mostly Protestant clients.

In general, however, Catholics and Protestants reacted differently to bewitchments. While Protestants often resorted to violence, both against the presumed witch and the animal that represented her, Catholics took a somewhat easier and conciliatory stand. After all, they had a clergy at their disposal who, whether willingly or not, supplied unwitchments and moreover possessed a collection of appropriate paraphernalia. This difference is well observed in Het Gooi. In Catholic Laren, a blesser named Calis could break a bewitchment by putting a scapulary in the pillow of the bewitched, or a simple blessing sufficed, or the power of the local priest could be employed.[90] Neighbouring Protestants boiled chickens and beat up witches.

The witchcraft discourse thus survived longer in conservative religious circles. Outside those it became presumably more and more marginalized and the expression 'witch' lost its substance. The man who had taken the priest hostage in Rotterdam was 'from elsewhere', and the family who in 1873 in Lexmond maltreated a woman had only lived there (according to the burgo-master) since 1862. These were partly the usual attempts to situate witchcraft outside one's own place of living. The particular descriptions of origin in these cases are thus not totally credible; both because in Rotterdam later cases were also recorded and because the family in Lexmond had only temporarily lived a few kilometres away. But it is nevertheless possible that witchcraft was sometimes more strange than normal. In a case in Alkmaar in 1910 a woman who suggested to a neighbour that her children had been bewitched, originated from Kampen, at the other side of the Zuiderzee.[91] Yet her ideas did not prove too exotic to be adopted.

The weakening of the content of the witchcraft discourse manifested itself through the disappearance of bewitchments and the distortion of stories about male and female witches. This may well have been the case in The Hague, where 'street urchins' took a woman for a witch and smashed her windows only because she had numerous and various pets. An actual bewitchment was never mentioned. Likewise a single woman at the border between The Hague and Wassenaar was branded as a witch, which some inhabitants found 'too ridiculous to consider, let alone to discuss it'.[92]

The cases in the western Netherlands that are available are for the most part situated at the eastern and southern edges of an area marked out by Jobse-Van Putten as only minimally self-supporting. Although there is too little material to conclude anything about the households of the bewitched, and thus about a possible direct link between witchcraft and a certain degree of self-support, such a link may nevertheless be plausible. The warning not to take any food from a witch at least indicates an exchange of primary provisions outside the market. It can also be of importance here that the part of the witchcraft discourse that concerned the household was mainly preserved by women. Whatever the case may have been, during the nine-teenth and early twentieth centuries witchcraft was certainly of social and moreover of cultural importance in large parts of the western Netherlands.

It may not be possible to indicate relations with economic or demographic developments, but enough people were thinking and acting in terms of witchcraft to call it a widely accepted phenomenon.

Notes

1 *Het toekomstig leven* 3 (1899) 217, taken from the *Haagsche Courant.*
2 Marijke Gijswijt-Hofstra, 'Witchcraft After the Witch-Trials', in Stuart Clark and Bengt Ankarloo (eds), *Witchcraft and Magic in Europe: The Eighteenth and Nineteenth Centuries* (London, 1999), pp. 95–189, especially p. 106.
3 See Alf Lüdtke, *The History of Everyday Life: Reconstructing Historical Experiences and Ways of Life* (Princeton, 1995); Richard van Dülmen, *Historische Anthropologie. Entwicklung. Probleme. Aufgaben* (Cologne, Weimar and Vienna, 2000).
4 C. de Gast, *Afscheiding en doleantie in het Land van Heusden en Altena* (Tilburg, 1989), p. 60; Jo Daan, *Wieringer land en leven in de taal* (Amsterdam, 1950), p. 106.
5 See Marijke Gijswijt-Hofstra, *Vragen bij een onttoverde wereld* (Amsterdam, 1997), p. 10, about the difference between science and magic.
6 Jozien Jobse-van Putten, 'De zelfvoorziening in ruimtelijk perspectief. Een cultuur-historische vergelijking van regionale indelingen van Nederland', *Volkskundig bulletin* 16 (1990) 21–48.
7 Hans de Waardt, *Toverij en samenleving* (The Hague, 1991), p. 291.
8 See Willem Frijhoff and Marijke Spies, *Bevochten eendracht. Nederlandse cultuur in Europese context, 1650* (The Hague, 1999), p. 426; J. C. Price, *Dutch Society, 1588–1713* (Harlow, 2000), p. 129.
9 See Willem de Blécourt, *Termen van toverij. De veranderende betekenis van toverij in Noordoost-Nederland tussen de 16de en 20ste eeuw* (Nijmegen, 1990), pp. 91–3.
10 *Maandblad tegen de Kwakzalverij* (hereafter *MtK*), 14 May 1894.
11 J. E. Enklaar, *Het bijgeloof in vroegeren en lateren tijd en de middelen om het te bestrijden* (Amsterdam, 1889), p. 30. See Roy Porter, 'Witchcraft and Magic in Enlightenment, Romantic and Liberal Thought', in Clark and Ankarloo, *Witchcraft and Magic in Europe*, pp. 189–282, especially p. 273.
12 Enklaar, *Het bijgeloof*, p. 12.
13 *Hoogeveensche Courant*, 12 May 1886.
14 A. J. Dekker and J. J. Schell, *De Volkskundevragenlijsten 1–58 (1934–1988) van het P. J. Meertens-Instituut* (Amsterdam, 1989), pp. 29–30; P. J. Meertens and Maurits de Meyer, *Volkskunde-Atlas voor Nederland en Vlaams-België. Commentaar*, vol. 1 (Antwerp, 1959).
15 Jan de Vries, *De wetenschap der volkskunde* (Amsterdam, 1941), p. 29.
16 J. M. M. Leenders, *Benauwde verdraagzaamheid, hachelijk fatsoen. Families, standen en kerken te Hoorn in het midden van de negentiende eeuw* (The Hague, 1991), p. 138; *Provinciale Drentsche & Asser Courant* (hereafter *PD&AC*), 27 Apr. 1861. See also K. Kooiman, 'Een praatje over kollen', *De Navorscher* 21 (1871) 524–9.
17 *PD&AC*, 4 July 1896, 4 July 1878.
18 C. Bakker, 'Iets over kollen en belezen', *Nederlandsch Tijdschrift voor Geneeskunde* 39 (1903) 680. His life and fieldwork are discussed and partly published in Theo Meder, *Vertelcultuur in Waterland. De volksverhalen uit de collectie Bakker in hun context (ca. 1900)* (Amsterdam, 2001).
19 Jac. van Ginniken, *Drie Waterlandse dialecten*, vol. 2 (Alphen a/d Rijn, 1954), p. 766.
20 RAZH, archief arrondissementsrechtbank Dordrecht, inv. no. 116, no. 132; *Hooge-veensche Courant*, 12 May 1886.

21 F. den Eerzamen, 'Het eiland Goeree: geschiedenis, volksleven, taal', *Neerlands volksleven* 16 (1966) 156.
22 Henk Kooijman, *Volksverhalen uit het grensgebied van Zuid-Holland, Utrecht, Gelderland en Noord-Brabant* (Amsterdam, 1988), nos 47, 109, 338, 591, 665.
23 Engelbert Heupers, *Volksverhalen uit Gooi- en Eemland en van de westelijke Veluwe* (Amsterdam, 1979, 1981 and 1984), nos 911–14, 1162.
24 For an overview of these kinds of publication up to 1989 see Fred Matter *et al.* (eds), *Toverij in Nederland. Bibliografie* (Amsterdam, 1990).
25 J. R. W. Sinninghe, *Hollandsch sagenboek. Legenden en sagen uit Noord- en Zuid-Holland* ('s-Gravenhage, 1943), pp. 67–100, 111–24; A. Bicker Caarten, 'Rijnlandse volksverhalen', *Jaarboekje voor de geschiedenis en oudheidkunde van Leiden en omstreken* 51 (1959) 135–7; 53 (1961) 139–44, especially 142–3; Arie Olsthoorn, 'De heks van Zouteveen', *Midden-Delfkrant* 6, 3/4 (1982) 38–9.
26 *PD&AC*, 22 Aug. 1851; 27 March 1866; *MtK*, 16 June 1896, from *NRC*.
27 L. Verhoeff, 'Volkskunde van Oud-Beierland (II)', *Neerlands volksleven* 16 (1966) 142.
28 *Nieuwe Provinciale Drentsche & Asser Courant* (hereafter *NPD&AC*), 9 Oct. 1889, from the *Werkmansbode*.
29 Kooijman, *Volksverhalen*, no. 109.
30 *Nieuwe Gorinchemsche Courant* (hereafter *NGC*), 15 Feb. 1873; *PD&AC*, 14 June 1877; *NPD&AC*, 1 Aug. 1890; *MtK*, 15 Feb. 1895, respectively.
31 In Muiderberg, Sliedrecht and Hornaar: *PD&AC*, 8 Oct. 1859, 27 Nov. 1860 and 4 July 1863.
32 See De Waardt, *Toverij en samenleving*, pp. 144, 208. From the end of the sixteenth century men's participation in the witchcraft discourse declined and the discourse subsequently became concentrated within the household.
33 *PD&AC*, 10 Feb. 1886.
34 *PD&AC*, 28 July 1860 (Sleeuwijk), 27 Apr. 1861 (Hoorn), 29 Sep. 1877 (Sliedrecht), 13 July 1893 (Hellouw) and 6 May 1897 (Oud-Beierland); *NPD&AC*, 25 Apr. 1890 (Zuid-Beierland); *Schiedamse Courant*, 21 Aug. 1875 (Ammerstol).
35 Daan, *Wieringerland*, p. 107; *PD&AC*, 14 Feb. 1884; Kooijman, *Volksverhalen*, nos 21, 289, 293, 427, 505, 532, 551, 591, 992, 1085, 1285; Heupers, *Volksverhalen*, no. 2826.
36 Willem de Blécourt, 'The Making of the Female Witch. Reflections on Witchcraft and Gender in the Early Modern Period', *Gender & History* 12 (2000) 287–309.
37 Kooijman, *Volksverhalen*, no. 875. According to a fruit grower it was told that all old women in Langerak were capable of bewitching: see nos 262 and 297.
38 *PD&AC*, 29 Sep. 1877; Volkskundevragenlijst 1934, K34; *NGC*, 23 Oct. 1873; Sinninghe, *Hollandsch sagenboek*, p. 97; *NPD&AC*, 9 Oct. 1889. See 'Eene reisontmoeting', *Geldersche volks-almanak* (1842) 164, about the infamous dyke between Tiel and Bommel, 'about which an old grandmother recently told her doctor that, when one included the part from Bommel to Gorinchem, there were 73 witches at it'.
39 *Bakker*, nos 387, 473; Heupers, *Volksverhalen*, no. 3580. See also *PD&AC*, 27 Sep. 1873.
40 *PD&AC*, 8 Sep. 1910. See also Willem Geldof, *Volksverhalen uit Zeeland en de Zuidhollandse eilanden* (Utrecht and Antwerp, 1979), p. 159, about a man in 's-Gravendeel whose mother and sister were taken for witches.
41 Heupers, *Volksverhalen*, nos 911–14, 1162, 1164, 1165, 1214, 1236, 2152; Everard Gewin, *Neerlands volksgeloof* (Arnhem, 1925), p. 87.
42 Heupers, *Volksverhalen*, nos 1560, 1563. The informant used 'father' to indicate her husband and 'granny' for the grandmother of her children. Her own father was unknown; she grew up with her mother and grandmother and she had a child in wedlock herself, too. See *Bevolkingsregister Huizen* (1888–1919), vol. 2, p. 361.
43 Heupers, *Volksverhalen*, nos 911, 1561, 1720, 1721, 2118.

44 *Bakker*, nos 173, 177–80, 201, 264–5, 276–7, 279, 281–2, 296, 396. See also Ton Dekker, 'Witches and Sorcerers in Twentieth-Century Legends', in Marijke Gijswijt-Hofstra and Willem Frijhoff (eds), *Witchcraft in the Netherlands from the Fourteenth to the Twentieth Century* (Rijswijk, 1991), pp. 181–95. These kinds of story seem to be primarily told by men.

45 Verhoef, 'Volkskunde', 143.

46 Heupers, *Volksverhalen*, no. 1775, see also nos 345, 2657; *PD&AC*, 29 July 1872; 26 Nov. 1887; 19 Apr. 1882.

47 *Bakker*, nos 11, 35.

48 *PD&AC*, 18 Feb. 1896; *MtK*, 16 March 1896; Heupers, *Volksverhalen*, nos 148, 352, 1702, 1751, 1815, 2203.

49 *PD&AC*, 14 June 1877; *MtK*, 14 Apr. 1894; *PD&AC*, 7 July 1910. I have discussed these women in Willem de Blécourt, *Het Amazonenleger. Irreguliere genezeressen in Nederland 1850–1930* (Amsterdam, 1999), especially pp. 68–9, 120–1.

50 R. J. C. Cornegoor, 'Heksenverhalen uit de buurt van Amsterdan', *Neerlands volksleven* 8 (1958) 165–7; Volkskundevragenlijst 1937, E124; Heupers, *Volksverhalen*, no. 3580.

51 *MtK*, 13 Nov. 1893. This article was found offensive by some Catholic readers.

52 *PD&AC*, 26 Apr. 1879, from *Maasbode*; *PD&AC*, 19 Apr. 1882. For the activities of Roman Catholic clergyman in Delft in 1851 see, L. E. Bosch, 'Tooverij', *Utrechtsche volks-almanak* 17 (1853) 163–4.

53 RAZH, archief arrondissementsrechtbank 's-Gravenhage, inv. no. 175, no. 216.

54 W. Paul, 'Toverij in Zevenhuizen', *Verleden tijdschrift* 5 (1986) 27–8. See also Kooijman, *Volksverhalen*, no. 1342.

55 Volkskundevragenlijst 1934, K56; K39; RAZH, archief arrondissementsrechtbank Gorinchem, inv. no. 55, no. 114 (1866). The influence of this man can also be recognized in an account about a bewitchment in Buren against which *Haarlemmer* oil was prescribed: *NGC*, 26 Apr. 1873.

56 Kooijman, *Volksverhalen*, nos 201, 315.

57 Vragenlijst 1954, K65. See also *Het Leven* 16 (1921) 1368–9.

58 *NGC*, 4 Sep. 1872.

59 RAZH, archief arrondissementsrechtbank Gorinchem, inv. no. 46, no. 114. The judicial considerations in the verdict cannot be consulted anymore. According to a note on the contemporary index he was acquitted.

60 RAZH, archief arrondissementsrechtbank Gorinchem, inv. no. 102, no. 86; *NGC*, 21 June 1876.

61 See De Blécourt, *Termen van toverij*, pp. 174–7, 218, about the witch doctors Brouwer and Rusken.

62 *NGC*, 19 March 1879; *PD&AC*, 3 Jan. 1882; 10 July 1889; *MtK*, 4 June 1924; *De Telegraaf*, 7 July 1926. See also *Het leven* 16 (1921) 1369, concerning medicines 'which tasted and looked like berry juice'. The 1924 case is more extensively described in Willem de Blécourt, 'The Witch, her Victim, the Unwitcher and the Researcher: The Continued Existence of Traditional Witchcraft', in Willem de Blécourt, Ronald Hutton and Jean La Fontaine, *Witchcraft and Magic in Europe: The Twentieth Century* (London, 1999), pp. 162–5.

63 Kooijman, *Volksverhalen*, no. 2102; *NGC*, 4 Sep. 1872.

64 *De Telegraaf*, 8 July 1926.

65 M. Kramer, 'Bijgeloof op het land', *Buiten* 4 (1910) 488–9; *PD&AC*, 29 July 1872; *NGC*, 15 Feb. 1873; *PD&AC*, 4 July 1878.

66 Verhoeff, 'Volkskunde', 142–3; Kooijman, *Volksverhalen*, nos 421, 361, 506; Heupers, *Volksverhalen*, nos 1578, 1751.

67 *NPD&AC*, 25 Apr. 1890; *PD&AC*, 28 Aug. 1890; 20 Aug. 1901; 7 Aug. 1910; 9 Sep. 1898.

68 Heupers, *Volksverhalen*, no. 3580.

69 Kooijman, *Volksverhalen*, no. 506. See also Sinninghe, *Hollandsch sagenboek*, p. 89; Heupers, *Volksverhalen*, no. 2576.

70 For instance Loosdrecht, where a woman had been looked at by a gypsy woman in a shop; Heupers, *Volksverhalen*, no. 2087.

71 *PD&AC*, 22 Aug. 1851 (Hoorn); 28 July 1860 (Sleeuwijk); 27 March 1866 (Delft); 6 Dec. 1876 (Delft); 29 Sep. 1877 (Sliedrecht); 3 Jan. 1882 (Meeuwen).

72 Kooijman, *Volksverhalen*, no. 1363.

73 Vragenlijst 1934, K35; *Het leven* 16 (1921) 1369; *PD&AC*, 3 Jan. 1882.

74 Heupers, *Volksverhalen*, no. 2079 (Loosdrecht); 1926 (Sliedrecht); 1873 (Lexmond).

75 Verhoeff, 'Volkskunde', 142.

76 De Waardt, *Toverij en samenleving*, p. 216.

77 *PD&AC*, 16 Nov. 1850; 22 Aug. 1851; 8 Oct. 1859; 27 March 1866; 11 Nov. 1874; 6 Dec. 1876; 14 July 1877; 29 Sept. 1877; 16 Sep. 1879. See also Willem de Blécourt, 'Heksengeloof: toverij en religie in Nederland tussen 1890 en 1940', *Sociologische gids* 26 (1989) 245–66, particularly 256–7; Heupers, *Volksverhalen*, nos 2078, 2084, 2211, 2830 (Loosdrecht, Naarden, Muiderberg); *Bakker*, nos 13, 44, 304, 350, 454.

78 *PD&AC*, 19 March and 28 Apr. 1873. On this case see also *Paleis van justitie* (1873) 21, 3–4; RAZH, archief arrondissementsrechtbank Gorinchem, inv. no. 62, no. 51.

79 See, for example, Sinninghe, *Hollandsch sagenboek*, pp. 92–6; *Bakker*, no. 22; *PD&AC*, 16 Sep. 1879.

80 Vragenlijst K148b.

81 *HC*, 25 Feb. 1891. For another 'keyhole' example see, Kooijman, *Volksverhalen*, no. 136. See also *Bakker*, nos 20, 442, 474.

82 For example, the bewitchment of an eel-seller's car in Amsterdam, which took place near the ferry behind the Central Station around 1952; Herman Pieter de Boer, *Waar gebeurd. Meer dan 60 verhalen die niemand geloven wil maar die waar gebeurd zijn* (Naarden, 1974), pp. 89–90.

83 Tjaard W. R. de Haan, 'Het vroegere volksleven', in Tjaard W. R. de Haan (ed.), *Gort met stroop. Over geschiedenis en volksleven van Zandvoort aan Zee* (The Hague, 1968), p. 122; de Haan, 'Volksleven van Spaarndam', in Tjaard W. R. de Haan (ed.), *Drie baarsjes en een ham. Over geschiedenis en volksleven van Spaarndam en zijn naaste omgeving* (The Hague, 1967), p. 68.

84 E171.

85 K. Vernooij, 'Bijgelovigheden en religieuze praktijken in het Kromme-Rijngebied', in H. Scholtmeijer, *Zuidutrechts woordenboek. Dialecten en volksleven in Kromme-Rijnstreek en Lopikerwaard* (Utrecht, 1993), pp. 160, 163.

86 de Blécourt, 'Heksengeloof', 258–60. See also de Blécourt, *Termen*, pp. 204–5, 251; de Blécourt, 'On the Continuation of Witchcraft', in Jonathan Barry, Marianne Hester and Gareth Roberts (eds), *Witchcraft in Early Modern Europe: Studies in Culture and Belief* (Cambridge, 1996), pp. 335–52; Gijswijt-Hofstra, 'Witchcraft after the Witch-Trials', p. 180.

87 *PD&AC*, 3 Jan. 1882; 14 June 1887.

88 G. van Bokhorst, *Het leven in Oud-Hilversum* (Zaltbommel, 1974), p. 91.

89 J. A. van Houwelingen, 'Kerkelijk leven in de jaren 1869–1910', in H. K. Bouwkamp, *'k Zal gedenken. Fragmenten uit de geschiedenis van de gereformeerde kerk te Giessendam en Neder-Hardinxveld* (Giessendam, 1985), pp. 98–9.

90 Heupers, *Volksverhalen*, nos 345, 352, 1485.

91 *PD&AC*, 7 July 1910.

92 *PD&AC*, 28 Aug. 1897; W. van Noord, 'Ons oude buurtje. Herinneringen aan de Witte Brug en omgeving', *Jaarboekje Vereniging die Haghe* (1967) 163.

6

Witchcraft accusations in France, 1850–1990

Owen Davies

The continued widespread belief in witchcraft and magic in nineteenth- and twentieth-century France has received considerable academic attention. Yet little of the relevant work has been published in English and, moreover, no thematic historical survey has yet been attempted to trace the continued social significance of witchcraft over the two centuries. As well as discussing the extent and nature of witchcraft accusations in the period, therefore, this chapter also provides a general survey of the published work on the subject for an English audience. As the reader will find, this requires considerable interdisciplinary awareness. Although historians, folklorists and anthropologists often find themselves in the same field of study, they rarely follow the same path across it. Despite a wealth of information, historians have ignored the history of French witchcraft accusations beyond the nineteenth century, while anthropologists, folklorists and psychologists, who have built up an impressive body of analysis from oral interviewing, have largely failed to trace the historical context of the contemporary beliefs they have studied. Reading through the publications of the various disciplines it soon becomes obvious that if we are to understand fully the recent history of witchcraft accusations, then a flexible interdisciplinary approach is essential. This is certainly being done in the broader context of the social history of the period, but has yet to be applied to more specific cultural themes such as witchcraft. Finally, my approach to the subject is much influenced by my own work on English witchcraft in the nineteenth and twentieth centuries. This introduces the puzzling question as to why two countries separated by a narrow stretch of water have such different recent histories regarding the continuation of traditional witchcraft accusations.

Most of the historical studies on the continuance of witchcraft and magic in French society during the modern period have focused on the late eighteenth and early nineteenth centuries. Matthew Ramsey's work on popular medicine between the years 1770–1830 has done much to highlight the profusion and diversity of magical practitioners and practices in that period.

Eloïse Mozzani's examination of the popularity of fortune-tellers, prophets, occultists and pseudo-scientists during the Revolutionary and Napoleonic years has provided further confirmation of the ubiquity of magical beliefs across French society at the time. Bernard Traimond's study of magic and religious politics in the *Landes de Gascognes* (1750–1826) gives us a detailed and vivid study of one serious witchcraft dispute that ended in court in 1826. The case illustrates the depth of popular feeling concerning the activities of witches in southern France. Judith Devlin's fascinating and impressive survey of witchcraft, magic and 'superstition' throughout the whole century has been widely cited by other historians, though it does present a rather static impression of popular belief over the century.[1] As well as these book-length studies, there are several articles by French historians that have made use of the criminal records of the period. Marie-Claude Denier has examined several late eighteenth- and early nineteenth-century trials concerning unbewitching in Mayenne, a *département* in north-western France. Jean-Claude Sebban has analysed twenty-three trials involving magical practitioners in nineteenth-century Berry, and Benoît Marin-Curtoud has considered, in more general fashion, the prosecution of magical practitioners under laws against illegal medicine between 1870 and 1940.[2]

There have also been numerous related studies on folk medicine and popular religion that help broaden our contextual understanding of the social relevance of witchcraft and magic in the period.[3] All these reveal the integral role of Catholicism in healing the bewitched and averting misfortune, either through the use of consecrated items such as herbs, holy water, rosaries and candles or through the action of prayer, mass, ritual and exorcism. Yet in nineteenth-century France there was considerable disquiet within the Church regarding clerical involvement in or tacit sanction of unofficial popular religious rites and rituals. There are numerous instances during the second half of the century of priests attempting to suppress customary activities, those centred on prehistoric sites and megaliths for example, and demolishing the shrines of local saints disapproved of by the Church.[4] Some priests also refused to exorcise or provide succour to the bewitched as they saw it as perpetuating 'foolish' beliefs detrimental to true piety. But it was an uphill struggle. As the retiring *curé* of Rezay wrote to his successor in 1901, 'to report a general failing: superstition'.[5] Furthermore, such policies only served to alienate the laity and encourage the resort to lay alternatives. During the trial of a *devin* or cunning-man named Shanly in 1845 it was heard how he had been consulted after the *curé* of Villegenon, Cher, had refused to bless the bewitched pigs of Jean-Baptiste Sénè.[6] Much of what people like Shanly practised was little different from the services offered by the clergy, and it is no wonder people sought out such healers who were willing to use religion for practical rather than purely spiritual purposes.

Not surprisingly, some members of the clergy saw the installation of a more sober, less participatory and inflexible relationship between priest and parishioners as being detrimental to the best interests of the Church. Evidence from surveys conducted by the Church during the second half of the nineteenth century indicated they were beginning to lose their grip on both the individual and the communal psyche, particularly in urban areas. Church attendance was declining, civil burial becoming more popular, and the Church's traditional ban on marriage during Lent and Advent was observed less and less, for example.[7] It was not so much a process of secularization but of decreasing reliance on the spiritual support of the Church. The only way of maintaining popular participation was to accommodate folk beliefs, involve people in the manifestation of the supernatural, and promote the practical application of religion. A classic example of such a clerical response was Abbé Olive's *Association de Notre-Dame des Sept-Douleurs de Boulleret*, which was created to bolster parochial faith. The *Association* promoted a series of visions experienced by a female parishioner between 1875 and 1904. According to Olive she was inspired and chosen by the Virgin to reform sinners in the parish of Boulleret. Strange occurrences also happened in the parish. People vomited blood and some claimed they had been wounded by the devil in the guise of a man dressed in black. Under Olive's astute guidance, the *Association* became a national movement with membership mushrooming from 10,000 in 1887 to 302,452 in 1903. It also drove a thriving trade in devotional objects such as medals, rosaries and images that had protective properties.[8]

This conservative reflex within the Catholic Church undoubtedly helped maintain a religious environment into the twentieth century that accommodated popular concerns regarding witchcraft. Yet we should not jump to the conclusion that the continued strength of belief, compared to England, was largely *because* of the influence of Catholicism. More detailed comparative research is required looking at supernatural beliefs in French Protestant areas. In the mid 1870s only around 600,000 people out of a population of thirty-six million were Protestant,[9] but did they think differently about witchcraft than the dominant Catholic population? Were they less concerned? Jacques Gutwirth's study of 'superstition' and religion in the predominantly Protestant Cévennes region during the mid twentieth century seems to indicate a comparative level of discourse regarding witchcraft and magic amongst more conservative Protestants.[10] We can also look to Willem de Blécourt's work on witchcraft in Dutch Protestant and Catholic areas in the late nineteenth and early twentieth centuries for comparison. He found that the belief and fear of witchcraft seemed to be weaker in Protestant areas generally but remained strong in conservative Calvinist communities. As he concludes, 'the decisive factor connecting witchcraft discourse to the creed is not adherence to the main Christian denominations but the degree of religiosity itself'.[11] Still, we need to be careful about over emphasizing the link between the prevalence of witchcraft beliefs and levels of religiosity generally. Both historical and ethnographic sources provide ample evidence that people can think in terms of witchcraft without being devoutly religious. The continued belief in witchcraft in modern French society, and elsewhere, needs, therefore, to be analysed within a framework of socio-cultural trends rather than religious persuasion, and consequently the role of conservative religious tendencies in maintaining witchcraft beliefs should be located in individual reflexes to social change.

Sources

During the late nineteenth and first half of the twentieth century many amateur folklorists and antiquarians collected and reflected upon the persistence of witchcraft beliefs in French society. Up until the 1930s the attitude of such authors was generally censorious, tempered with a confidence that the forces of modernity would eventually vanquish such 'old-fashioned' beliefs. The language was not quite as harsh as M. Hilarion Barthety's talk in 1874 of the 'imbeciles' who held such beliefs, but the word 'credulity' was used liberally.[12] One such author was Félix Chapisseau. Writing in 1902 of the area of La Beauce, in the plains south of Paris, he remarked that thanks to the eighteenth-century philosophers and the development of science in the following century, 'in our days there is hardly anybody other than very old folk who believe in witches'. But he tempered this confidence by admitting 'the terror has disappeared, but the influence remains. They speak about it rarely, but they think of it sometimes.' Nevertheless in those 'isolated hamlets' where there remained 'some vestiges of this credulity, it will be undermined by this disclosure: newspapers and time will do the rest'.[13] In 1911, Charles Lancelin, a prolific author on the subject of the occult, posed the question, 'At the present time, do country folk still believe in witchcraft?' The answer was, 'Yes – in various degrees'.[14] It was not so much the belief in witchcraft which annoyed Lancelin but the activities of those 'rogues' who cheated people out of money by pretending to be able to cure it. In the same year a country doctor from the Montagne Bourbonnaise in the Massif Central, was critical of his patients for believing in witchcraft. Although he believed such 'superstitions' had undoubtedly diminished in the region, they 'are unfortunately still too numerous'. The people remained 'credulous' because they lacked sufficient education, he thought. He noted some signs of progress though. The first response of farmers whose horses were sick was to disinfect their stables and call in a veterinary. However, under cover of darkness they still made their way to the local cunning-folk to lift the spells they believed were upon their horses.[15]

Such authors, like many folklorists at the time, were guided by their own sense of social evolution. Yes, witchcraft beliefs still existed fairly widely but they were anachronisms. Their pervasive influence was on the wane and once the programme of state education was firmly established their demise would surely follow. Similar views were still being expressed after the Second World War. One commentator wrote in 1946 that although he was 'delighted with the progress of popular education', ignorance was still 'in our rural areas, the great auxiliary of superstition'.[16] But the academic approach of the folklorist Arnold van Gennep in the 1930s, and his followers such as Claude and Jacques Seignolle and M. Leproux and other researchers like Marcelle Bouteiller did much to move the subject away from this patrician view of witch belief as a 'problem' and as a hindrance to social development in rural areas.[17] Although Van Gennep still referred to such beliefs as 'erroneous', he nevertheless distanced himself from the nineteenth-century folklorists' preoccupation with survivals, with the view that 'superstitious' beliefs should be seen and studied as remnant artefacts of past societies. For Van Gennep popular beliefs regarding the supernatural were living aspects of current culture, albeit a 'traditional' one at odds with modernity, and to record and measure them required a subtle and systematic method of oral interviewing.[18] As he found in the Dauphiné, for example, when people were first questioned about witchcraft they were 'unanimous in declaring that the belief in witches had disappeared nearly everywhere', but further patient probing usually revealed that the 'belief existed more than appeared at first'.[19] When, several years later in 1935–36, the Seignolle brothers conducted an oral folklore survey in Hurepoix, on the southern edge of Paris, they found that a 'reluctance to talk has been most strong regarding magic and popular medicine'.[20] Those who provided instances of witchcraft 'considered it good taste to display a certain scepticism and consigned them to the past'.[21] All the cases of witchcraft they collected were located in the second half of the nineteenth century, and were either childhood memories or stories received from older family members. They assumed that belief had declined significantly over the previous three decades: 'if this research had been done according to our extensive method at the beginning of the twentieth century the list [of witch legends] would, without doubt, have been longer still.'[22]

While recognizing the value of the work of this new breed of folklorist, the problem still remains as to how representative are the results of such oral surveys of the strength and relevance of witchcraft in France between the world wars. As folklorists and ethnographers both before and after have found, it is a common defensive reflex for people to situate their knowledge and experience of witchcraft a generation or so in the past. It was, as Willem de Blécourt has put it, 'using the past as a device to obscure the present'.[23] After all, those being interviewed knew full well that the people interviewing them almost certainly did not share their feelings on the subject, and they were sensitive about appearing 'credulous' or 'foolish' to others. Yet in their totality the various oral surveys conducted in the two decades either side of the Second World War certainly demonstrate that witchcraft continued as an integral aspect of rural popular discourse.

It was not only folklorists who were interested in the contemporary belief in witchcraft during the first half of the twentieth century. The role of witchcraft in popular aetiology and magical cures also caught the attention of the medical fraternity. This is not surprising considering that as a profession they, along with the clergy, were most exposed to popular concerns regarding witchcraft or satanically inspired illness. George Raviart, a clinical psychiatrist writing in 1936, recalled how one of his colleagues was consulted in the case of the exorcism of a man from a hamlet in northern France, who had once been convicted for practising illegal medicine.[24] In his memoirs, Cyrille Kaszuk, a doctor who set up practice just after the Second World War in the Sundgau, a rural area in the south of Alsace, recommended, 'witches should not be considered lightly, if one wants to practice medicine with impunity around here'.[25] He observed that in 1947 there were only three doctors in the region of haut-Sundgau but by 1990 there were twenty-eight. Nevertheless, Kaszuk's comments suggest the increasing access to orthodox medicine did not have a profound effect on the local population's resort to witchcraft diagnoses and counter-magic. Away from parochial general practice, the medical fraternity also maintained a strong academic interest in the subject. The continued belief in witchcraft and the practice of healing magic were the subject of a number of student theses during the early twentieth century, motivated in part by the need to 'know one's rivals' and better to counter the adherence to popular medicine.[26] The manifestation and cause of possession was another continued focus of attention, which represented the extension of a nineteenth-century tradition of medical investigation into the psychological aspects of possession influenced by the work of Jean Esquirol (1772–1849) and Jean Martin Charcot (1825–93).[27] Both attempted to explain away the sensational early modern outbreaks of mass possession as 'demonopathy' or 'hysteria'. Such phenomena were rooted not in the bowels of Hell but in mental illness. As cases of multiple possession effectively disappeared by the early twentieth century, however, the psychiatric emphasis shifted from the concept of contagious 'demonopathy' to the psychopathology of the bewitched individual.[28]

One of the most interesting of the post-war doctoral psychiatric studies was conducted by Jean Morel, who examined the medical records of the psychiatric hospital of Alençon, in the department of Orne. Taking a fifteen-year period between 1949 and 1963 he looked at the cases of forty-three men who were admitted as being delirious following witchcraft disputes. He produced a sociological breakdown of these men. He found that thirty-five were rural dwellers while the other eight came from local towns. Twenty of the people were over forty years old; thirteen were between thirty and forty, and the rest under thirty. Twelve were farmers, sixteen were agricultural workers, seven general labourers, four were skilled workers, and there was one craftsman and one tradesman. Eighteen were classified as mentally subnormal and a further twenty as possessing poor intelligence. In fourteen cases the 'delirium' of bewitchment was attributed to alcoholism, eight men were described as being schizophrenic and five suffered from clinical paranoia.[29] Although such analyses of psychiatric cases provide useful case studies concerning the dynamics of accusations, and a valuable window on to the way in which witchcraft was projected by the mentally ill, they also create the misleading impression that the continued profound belief in witchcraft amongst people in the twentieth century can be explained solely in terms of mental illness. In other words, it suggests that witchcraft belief is a pathological rather than a sociological expression. In this respect, the ethnologist Dominique Camus has been particularly outspoken in his criticism of the work of Morel and like-minded colleagues, describing their work as 'an approach so limited by value judgements that it can but only impede the understanding of the phenomenon of witchcraft'.[30]

During the second half of the century, while folklorists such as Claude Seignolle continued to provide the valuable service of recording oral beliefs and legends,[31] anthropologists of witchcraft, whose interests had long been dominated by a fascination with witch accusations in colonial Africa, realized that there were communities on their own doorsteps where the witchcraft discourse was as strong. The pioneer in this new wave of research was Jeanne Favret-Saada who, between 1969 and 1971, immersed herself in the world of parochial witchcraft suspicions and accusations in the *Bocage* (hedged countryside) of western France.[32] She was dismissive of the previous analytical efforts of the folklorists, stating that 'anthropology is a discipline infinitely more sophisticated than folklore', and her research and publications certainly moved the study of French witchcraft on to a whole new level.[33] Not surprisingly, her work was initially embraced within the established context of African research,[34] but soon the ethnography of contemporary French witchcraft became a subject area in its own right. Further regional studies appeared, though few researchers followed Favret-Saada's approach of immersing themselves fully in the popular discourse.[35] The area of western France where she conducted her research was later the subject of several revisionist doctoral studies,[36] and more recently the ethnologist and sociologist Dominique Camus has become something of a media presence appearing on television, radio and in newspapers discussing his own insightful research on witchcraft and magic in western France.[37] The importance of such anthropological work will become apparent later.

As well as folklorists another target of Favret-Saada's scorn was journalistic reporting on contemporary witchcraft. Journalism's contribution to the study of witchcraft in modern France is certainly rather mixed, but cannot easily be dismissed. Newspaper reports of relevant court cases are an invaluable source of information on witchcraft accusations for the nineteenth and twentieth centuries, yet at the same time newspaper reportage has often been shaped not by the sober objectivity of the academic but by sensationalism, mockery and gross value judgements. Numerous journalistic exposés have proclaimed they have 'discovered' or 'uncovered' a 'shocking' or 'surprising' continued belief in witchcraft, despite the fact that academics and folklorists have long written and published widely on the subject.[38] René Crozet, for example, in a book that received a good deal of media coverage in the early 1990s, wrote with implicit racism, 'like many, I imagined that witchcraft was the exclusive domain of the folklore of blacks or Haitians'.[39] But at the same time the immediacy of journalistic work has also helped highlight areas of recent developments in magical practice that the anthropologists and folklorists have yet to explore in detail, such as immigrant urban magic.

Manifestations of witchcraft

1850 has been chosen as the chronological starting point for this discussion not only for reasons of tidiness but also because in that year there occurred one of the most sensational cases of witchcraft in nineteenth-century France. The events in Cideville, a village of around 270 people in the Normandy *département* of Seine-Maritime, provide a detailed snapshot of the continued strength of the discourse concerning witchcraft across a wide cross-section of French society.

One day in March 1849 Father Tinel, *curé* of Cideville, paid a visit to an ailing parishioner. On learning that the parishioner was being treated by a local *sorcier*, or cunning-man, named Gosselin, Tinel condemned the cunning-man and urged that a proper physician be consulted. Not long after, Gosselin was arrested for practising medicine without a licence and sentenced to two years in prison. It was rumoured in the village that Tinel had orchestrated his arrest. It seems that a friend of the cunning-man, a shepherd named Thorel decided to exact revenge on the priest. During a local auction in the village Thorel espied the presence of two of Tinel's lodgers, Gustave Lemmonier and Clement Bunel, boys aged twelve and fourteen respectively. He approached them and touched them in the back, a strange action, which was subsequently interpreted as an act of witchcraft. In November 1850 the two boys began to complain of rapping noises in their study. Soon after, furniture and other objects were reportedly thrown around the parsonage. These disturbances went on for two months until the archbishop of Paris ordered that the two boys be removed from Tinel's care. The priest believed Thorel's witchery was the cause of the trouble and exacted his revenge. Tinel had a word with Thorel's master, and the shepherd lost his job. Not long after the priest and the shepherd got into a physical altercation that ended with Tinel beating him with a walking stick. On 7 January 1851 Thorel lodged a formal complaint of assault against the priest. When the case came to court Thorel demanded 1000 francs damages for the imputation of 'witchcraft' and a further 200 for the assault. He lost the case and ended up out of pocket. The Normandy press reported little on the extraordinary events, undoubtedly conscious of the mockery the Parisian press would heap upon the region's rural population. It was the accounts provided by the occult explorers Charles Jules, Marquis de Mirville, and Henri Gougenot des Mousseaux, which brought the Cideville affair to wider attention. The case coincided with the sensational development of spiritualism and table-rapping, and the noisy manifestations in the presbytery, whose origins lay in a classic witchcraft dispute, were assimilated into the educated empiric quest to prove the reality of the spirit world. The case later found its way into the work of the influential occultists Eliphas Levi (1810–75) and the founder of Theosophy Madame Blavatsky (1831–91).[40]

The Cideville affair was, however, by no means an isolated sensation. Only a few years later, in 1857, hundreds of miles away in the village of Morzine, near the Swiss border, a lengthy outbreak of mass possession attracted considerable attention.[41] Several adolescent girls and young women in the village claimed they were bewitched, several of them by male witches. One girl said she had been possessed after a witch made her eat some of his bread. Another's illness began after drinking some wine in the company of a witch. A local priest, Abbé Pinguet, performed several collective exorcisms but was forced to cease his active involvement in 1860 by the new French authorities (the region having been recently annexed), who were concerned by the destabilizing consequences of such 'superstitious' practices. A year later the number of females supposedly possessed in the village peaked at around 200. Events in Morzine were reported nationwide, and the case attracted the considerable attention of the medical and clerical professions, as well as the spiritualist movement in the shape of Allan Kardec. The case highlighted the divisions within the Church regarding participation in such popular manifestations of supernatural belief, with some clergy conducting exorcisms, including some Capuchin missionaries, while others like the government appointee Monsignor Magnin, refused to exorcise and was subsequently beaten up in the church by some villagers. For the medical establishment the mass possession was a classic demonstration of hystero-demonopathy. Roy Porter ironically observed that Morzine truly was the 'Devil's gift to psychiatry'.[42] As the affair slowly died down, further north a new possession sensation was developing. Between 1864 and 1869 two young boys, this time from Illfurt (Illfurth), a village in southern Alsace, began to exhibit the classic symptoms of the possessed. Thiébaut and Joseph were the sons of a pedlar named Joseph Burner and his wife Marie-Anne. As in so many such cases the origin of the affair lay in a classic witchcraft scenario.

One day the boys had eaten an apple given to them by a poor old woman with a bad reputation who had been chased out of her old village, presumably for being a witch although this was not made explicit in the detailed account provided by Paul Sutter the *curé* of Wickerschwihr, near Colmar.[43] The evil spirits, Orobas, Zolalethiel and Ypès, who possessed the boys, had many a lengthy conversation with the doctors, clergymen and local dignitaries who interviewed them in various languages including Latin and English, though German was the preferred medium. The devils naturally expressed their hatred of Catholicism and Napoleon III, but were enthusiastic about Protestantism and the masons.[44] Professor Hoppe of Bale University considered the case to be one of hysteria coupled with St Vitus's dance. The Bishop of Strasbourg was also sceptical about the boys' possession, but in April 1869 local pressure led him to set up an ecclesiastical investigation into the affair. Its report was inconclusive but the Bishop reluctantly sanctioned an official exorcism, which apparently succeeded. Thiébaut died two years after his exorcism on 3 April 1871 at the age of sixteen. His brother died in 1882 aged twenty-five.[45]

Moving into the twentieth century, exactly one hundred years after the events at Cideville began, a major witchcraft disturbance occurred across the other side of the country in Merlebach, a town on the German border. In November 1949 a district of the town was thrown into a state of great agitation by the claims of several people that they had been bewitched by the 49-year-old wife of a Polish immigrant coal miner. As recorded by the regional press, for several evenings in a row an effigy of the woman was paraded around the neighbourhood in an attempt to drive the couple out of town. Jean Schober, a 'Lumpendoktor' from the nearby German village of Lauterbach, and a self-styled 'Master of Witches', was consulted, and confirmed the suspicions of the townsfolk. The Polish couple made a formal complaint to the police who set about diffusing the tense situation. A local newspaper, the *Républicain Lorrain*, ran its account of the story under the headline, 'Malevolence or hallucination? Accused of witchcraft by her neighbours, a Merlebach family escape being lynched'.[46] Twenty-seven years later a trial took place at Argentan, which graphically exposed the continued strength of witch belief and the integral role of popular religion in the witchcraft discourse.

In 1977 Léontine Esnault, a 74-year-old fabric shopkeeper of Savigny-le-Vieux, a village in the west of Lower Normandy, was arrested for fraud and failing to assist someone in danger.[47] In the local dialect she was a *désencraudeuse*, an unbewitcher, a cunning-woman. The story recounted in court started back in the 1950s when Guy, one of the sons of Pierre and Léontine Esnault, was sent home ill from National Service in Morocco. It was suggested at first that he had reacted badly to vaccination jabs. They consulted numerous doctors and healers but none helped improve Guy's condition, so they approached l'abbé Noury, a renegade priest who had built his own chapel near Lisieux, from where he cured the sick and sold various religious protective charms. Noury divided illness into two sorts: those that could be cured by a doctor and those caused by witchcraft and evil spirits. He diagnosed that Guy was possessed by a demon and had been bewitched by one of Pierre's competitors, Pierre being a rather unsuccessful sheep-trader. At the beginning of 1955 Guy died and their other son Henri fell ill. The witchcraft was evidently directed at the whole family. Léontine wrote to the local bishop asking him to intervene and he sent her a copy of the popular exorcism against Satan and the rebel angels published by Leon XIII (1878–1903) for use by the laity as well as the priesthood. Next she wrote to a Parisian medium and *désenvoûteur* named Maurice Martini. For a fee of 500 francs he agreed to visit the Esnaults and put an end to the witchcraft. To their great shock he identified Pierre's mother as the witch and using various religious paraphernalia proceeded to cast a spell over her to force her to stop. Henri's condition improved, and impressed by Martini's powers he spent some time in Paris receiving instruction in the occult arts – for a fee of course. His mother too, was seduced by the lure of professional magic.

On the night of 3 January 1956, the first anniversary of Guy's death, Léontine claimed to have had a visitation from Christ, who announced that he had chosen her to be one of his servants and conferred upon her the gift of healing by prayer. Word soon spread around the locality and Léontine began to be consulted by the sick and bewitched in the sacred confines of Guy's bedroom. Unlike the various cunning-men and healers she had en-gaged, Léontine did not charge a direct fee but encouraged gifts in kind. Besides, she soon developed other moneymaking sidelines. One day a client fainted and Léontine gave her some tap water. The client subsequently believed that the water had healed her complaint, so Léontine began to market it as 'eau de Savigny', though she was careful not to claim that it was 'miraculous'. She also made money by arranging buyers for bewitched land, farms and livestock. Later, she teamed up with a notary clerk from Paris who dispensed financial advice to her bewitched clients. In 1968 and 1969 Léontine prophesied that Guy would shortly rise from the dead and two high-profile pilgrimages were organized to herald the event. On the first occasion 500–600 people filed slowly through Guy's bedroom and then made their way to his tomb in the local churchyard. The local press was highly critical of these events and of the activities of the Esnaults, but it was another seven years before the law intervened and suppressed her activities and the cult that surrounded her. It is worth noting that over the twenty years of Léontine's practice the local priest, l'abbé Mauduit, made no attempt to set his authority against her. Some of his neighbouring colleagues expressed their concern about her activities and tried to persuade their parishioners from consulting her, but Mauduit maintained a complicit silence, even regarding her very public pilgrimages.[48] Like some of his nineteenth-century colleagues, he presumably maintained a sceptical silence while welcoming the upsurge in religious devotion that Léontine's activities encouraged.

The above cases are snapshots of substantial communal expressions of witchcraft and the integral role of the Church in resolving related conflicts, but in the intervening years many other court cases and serious individual incidents occurred. Assaults on suspected witches were certainly not rare and tragic deaths periodically resulted from such encounters. On 24 January 1868, for example, M. Gouache, priest of la Loupe in the *département* of Eure-et-Loir, died after being stabbed in the leg by a man who had beseeched him to cure him of witchcraft. The man openly confessed to the arresting police that he had been bewitched for three years and he had gone to confession in a highly excited state to ask Gouache to take the spell off. When the priest turned away to deal with another matter the man stabbed him. 'I killed him to free myself,' he said, which suggests that Gouache was suspected of being involved in the bewitchment.[49] In 1880 the Vendée assizes heard how several neighbours had murdered a seventy-year-old *sorcier* named Joseph Cléon. Witnesses testified that Cléon boasted of his ability to transfer milk from his neighbours' cows to his own. Six years later the assizes at Blois dealt with a case where an old woman suspected of causing a series of agricultural misfortunes on a neighbouring farm was deliberately pushed into a fire to prevent further acts of witchcraft. The woman burned to death. The farmer was executed and his accomplices sentenced to life imprisonment with hard labour.[50] Such tragic witchcraft-inspired incidents continued well into the following century. In July 1902 a man named Lanzeral, of Beauvais (Tarn), shot a neighbour and his son one night believing they had cast a spell upon him. A cunning-man had confirmed as much.[51] Twenty years later the Parisian newspapers reported on a case from the Vendée where a young *paysan* shot a neighbour who he believed had bewitched him.[52] January 1926 witnessed the trial of two men, members of a small Catholic association called *Notre-Dame-des-Pleurs* founded by Marie Mesmin, a former Bordeaux concierge, who seriously flogged the priest of Bombon because they believed he cast spells upon them. One of the men, a 27-year-old street-sweeper accused the *abbé* of spreading diseases in Bordeaux by means of birds. The birds dropped their excrement in Mesmin's garden giving rise to fungi of obscene shapes, which omitted a foul odour and the said diseases.[53] In 1938, in the Vosges in eastern France, a farming couple accused a sexagenarian neighbour of having cast a spell on their farm animals. They beat the man so mercilessly that he died from the assault.[54] Morel's study on witchcraft and psychiatric illness in the *département* of Orne reported several similar serious incidents in the years following the end of the Second World War. In 1948, for instance, a farmer of Saint-Maurice-du-Désert, near Domfront, shot dead his neighbour and seriously injured another who he believed had cast a spell on his animals by making the sign of the cross the wrong way whenever he passed his property.[55]

In February 1954, near Lillebonne, Seine-Maritime, a car was found in the river Seine with the bodies of three people. Police investigations revealed that the driver was a local farmer who had suffered repeated livestock losses. He came to believe he was bewitched, sank into a terrible depression and resolved to kill himself. He took his wife and a farmhand with him to his death.[56] The following year a farming couple in Venzins, Manche, suspected their farm servant had '*jeté un sort*' (cast a spell) over their livestock. They locked him in his room and beat him with large crucifixes. He managed to escape and called the police. The farmer was taken to a psychiatric hospital.[57] In February 1961 a 63-year-old postman, of Guislain, Manche, lodged a complaint of defamation against his neighbour, a 42-year-old woman who had accused him of bewitching a number of animals in the vicinity.[58] In February 1976 Jean Camus, a fifty-year-old single man of Héloup, Orne, was found shot dead in his bed. The police investigation and subsequent trial revealed that his killers, Michel and Daniel Hérisson, aged twenty and twenty-eight respectively, believed Camus had bewitched their family. During the trial the men's mother defended them, telling the judge that Camus had cast a spell on them and that there was no other solution but to kill him.[59] In 1984 a trial took place in Haute-Savoie in which a small farmer was prosecuted for shooting his neighbour after a boundary dispute developed into accusations of witchcraft.[60]

In the last decade or so those accused of witchcraft have continued to lodge formal complaints with the police. I have been informally notified of at least two such instances in the environs of Le Havre and Rouen during the early 1990s. In May 1990 the newspaper *Paris-Normandie* interviewed the head of police in the small town of Valmont, Seine-Maritime, about witchcraft disputes in the area. The police officer said that in most cases the local priest or the local healer settled such disputes: 'We intervene at the moment when a complaint is lodged or simply when there is a disturbance of public order.' The procedure he and his men followed in such instances was first to confiscate any guns, then to listen to the complaints from both sides in the presence of the local mayor. They then tried to find a rational explanation for the supposed bewitchment to present to the supposed victims. In the case of animals they called in the local vet to provide a diagnosis. Finally, if the person accused of witchcraft wanted to take the complaint of intimidation further, they would send the case to the public prosecutor's department. By way of example, in November 1989 the Valmont police dealt with a witchcraft dispute in one of the villages in the surrounding district. Martin Sueur, who ran a small farm with his sister, fired some shots in the direction of his neighbour Régine Dubourg. She called the police who followed their usual procedure in such matters. The Sueurs accused Dubourg of having cast spells over their farm. Their guns were confiscated and no further disturbance occurred between the two neighbours. However, the Sueurs continued to experience misfortunes. Martin went blind and could no longer drive a tractor or maintain the farm, so two years later the sister wrote a letter to the local authorities beseeching them to stop four of their neighbours from destroying them by witchcraft. She told how she had consulted numerous priests and several *magnétiseurs* but to no avail. She also complained that the local mayor had refused to help restrain their neighbours. Following the receipt of this letter the local police were once again called in to try and pacify the Sueurs.[61]

As well as demonstrating the continued presence of violent witchcraft disputes in provincial France, these examples also highlight the ubiquity of gun ownership in rural French communities over the twentieth century, which contrasts significantly with the situation in England. They may also help explain the predominance of men in witchcraft-related violence in the period. Turning guns on suspected witches can be seen as an aspect of a continuing strand of French male culture where shooting is not only an important Sunday pastime but also held up as a customary right. It is defended as a key element of a traditional French way of life against the forces of modernity, as represented by environmentalists and the European Union. The wider significance of this observation will become apparent later on.

In France, as in England, cunning-folk drove a thriving trade during the second half of the nineteenth century. While the involvement of such practitioners sometimes averted the violent resolution of witchcraft disputes by providing magical-medical remedies, their service of identifying witches also instigated physical confrontations between witch and bewitched. Judith Devlin has provided numerous instances of the activities of cunning-folk culled from the work of folklorists and the *Gazette des Tribunaux*, but many other court cases were reported in the newspapers of the period, some of which also found their way into the national and regional English press, and even American newspapers. In September 1882, for example, the English *Daily News* recounted the details of the trial of Adèle Mathieu, who was sentenced to six months' imprisonment for false pretences by the tribunal of Lisieux. Mathieu claimed to be able to unbewitch and exorcise evil spirits. One of the cures she employed consisted of burning toads in a cauldron. To cure the seventeen ailing cattle of one farmer she burnt 570 toads in the presence of the locals. In her defence she told the judge that although she charged more than the doctor, she had done them more good.[62] Sebban's analysis of twenty-three such prosecutions in nineteenth-century Berry reveals that two-thirds of practitioners were male, the majority having an artisan or trade background. While they could be prosecuted under a variety of laws such as those concerning fraud and public decency, it was the statutes regarding the practice of illegal medicine that were most frequently invoked. One such victim was Henri Blancher who was arrested in 1875. He had no medical training, and claimed that he had received his magical healing gift from an apparition that had appeared to him one day at the age of twelve as he helped serve the Mass. The investigating police commissioner estimated that Blancher gave more than thirty consultations a week and earned the tidy sum of 1500 francs a year.[63] It is no surprise, considering the continued strength of feeling about witchcraft in the twentieth century, that unbewitching remained a service much in demand long after the trade had gone into terminal decline in England. Lancelin cited numerous prosecutions from the early decades of the century in which sums of as much as 14,000 and 30,000 francs (in old money)[64] were handed over to specialists to cure witchcraft.[65] The work of anthropologists and folklorists confirm the continued existence of cunning-folk and witch-doctors throughout the rest of the century.

The paysan and the culture of witchcraft accusations

Having given an impression of the depth of the continued belief in witchcraft, and described the limitations of the various disciplinary methodologies, it is time to get back to the central issue of *why* the belief in witchcraft remained so relevant and so vibrant in twentieth-century France? To tackle this question, however, it is first necessary to consider wider developments in French economy, society and culture over the period. In particular we need to consider the central role of the *paysan* or 'peasant'. Fortunately for the witchcraft historian there is a large body of academic work, particularly by American historians, on the changing nature of French society during the nineteenth and early twentieth centuries,[66] while anthropologists and sociologists have picked up the baton of studying post-Second World War change in the French countryside.[67] These studies focus on the modernization of rural France, and in particular the relationship between the *pays* and France and the *paysans* and the French: in other words, the conflict between regional and national identity, and traditional rural society and urban modernity. Before embarking on such a discussion it is necessary first of all to clarify the definition and usage of the French term *paysan* and its literal English translation as 'peasant'. The two words have quite different connotations. While in England 'peasant' has long been used as a derogatory term denoting a backward, lowly, subservient agricultural labourer, in France *paysan* has become a badge of honour. The *paysan* is a bastion of honourable, independent-minded communal rural life, the upholder of the traditional values of 'old' France. The significance of this distinction is central to the argument that follows, and so I shall stick to the French rather than the English usage.

The demise of the *paysan* has long been a subject of historical debate. Eugen Weber's impressive and influential book *Peasants into Frenchmen* placed it in the last decades of the nineteenth century. Under the onslaught of economic and social modernization a nationalized French culture was forged, usurping regional cultures and identities. But the evidence from the various twentieth-century sources outlined earlier suggests that Weber's thesis is premature in its chronology. The late nineteenth century certainly heralded the end of English rural cultures but not France's. It is quite obvious that France experienced industrialization and massive urbanization some fifty years later than England, and in terms of environment, economy, landscape and culture continued to be a rural-dominated society for much longer. In 1846, 75 per cent of the population was considered rural, and although France followed the general drift towards the cities from the mid nineteenth century onwards, by 1931 some 48 per cent of the population was still counted as rural. By way of contrast, in England by 1901 only 22 per cent of the country was counted as rural. In 1911 some 15.1 million French people were still listed as living from agricultural pursuits.[68] In 1931 only 7,500,000 French people lived in cities of more than 100,000 inhabitants. Of these, five million were concentrated in Paris and its suburbs.[69] Even allowing for different methods of statistical calculation there is no doubt that France remained a rural country of small communities decades longer than England. The pattern and character of agriculture did not follow the same developmental path either. The industrialization of agriculture, which involved the shift from polyculture to monoculture farming, the use of fertilisers and silage, the rationalization of landholding, and the marginalization of the subsistence farmer were all still ongoing processes in France during the mid twentieth century.

A comparison with England highlights further important cultural differences such as language. In England by 1850 the whole population by and large spoke recognizable English. The Celtic Cornish language had already died out, and although there were certainly strong regional dialects, in general everyone spoke a common tongue. In France in 1850 over a quarter of the population spoke no French. For many more it was only a second language.[70] A Parisian could travel through large parts of the country and fail to understand the local *paysans* and fail to be understood. In some areas it was a matter of dialects that were so strong they bore little relationship to standard Parisian French, such as some Occitan dialects in southern France. Elsewhere completely different languages were spoken: Catalan in Roussillon, Breton in Brittany, Flemish in Northern France and German in eastern areas such as Alsace. Of course the setting up of a state system of education, in particular the measures of compulsory and subsidized schooling introduced by Jules Ferry during the 1880s had the inevitable impact, albeit slow. The strong sense of regional and communal identity which language defined and reinforced began to break down. But to a certain extent being 'Frenchified' was a personal choice as much as a social determinant. As a Breton man explained to his grandson shortly after the First World War, who had complained of being taught in French at school, 'With French, you can go everywhere. With only Breton, you're tied to a short rope, like a cow to a post. You have to graze around your tether, and the meadow grass is never plentiful.' [71]

The spread of French has been viewed as part of a much larger process whereby local communities became part of a national community. The conscious decision-making about becoming part of a national French culture, about leaving or breaking the cultural ties with the *pays*, about shedding the *paysan* life, about dropping dialects, was and still is an aspect of an individual, regional and national discourse concerning identity. It is in the strains between these contrasting and conflicting identities, which continued to exist throughout the 1960s, 1970s and even 1980s, where we can situate explanations for the continued relevance of witchcraft for many people. A dissatisfaction and disillusionment with modern society led to the idealization and hankering after the *paysan* lifestyle, a 'traditional' existence that for many was in its death throes, threatened by the forces of modernity.

In France the *paysan* under any economic definition ceased to exist by the 1960s, but as a cultural construct it remains a strong, symbolic reality to this day. As the anthropologist Susan Carol Rogers, writing in 1987, put it, 'Peasants survive in contemporary France largely as a potent cultural category referring to various sets of ideas having little or no direct relationship with classic definitions of peasant tillers … but having a great deal to do with central tensions in French society.' [72] What this means on the ground is that some people brought up in rural communities before the large-scale modernization of agriculture from the 1960s onwards, continue to see themselves as *paysans* even though they no longer work the land or even live in the countryside. As Geneviève Delbos has suggested, the inability or unwillingness to participate in and adapt to the post-war agricultural 'revolution' has led to the paradoxical situation where some *paysans* 'actually left the land so as to remain "peasants", thereby constituting a distinct social group maintaining the old-established values of traditional society'.[73] She has identified this phenomenon by studying five villages in different parts of France between 1972 and 1977. These self-defined *paysans* see a stark difference between the 'old' agriculture they cherished and the 'new' agriculture they despise. Amongst these men and women Delbos found that 'the role and function of agriculture was defined in moral terms'; 'they remain rooted in the older social order which no longer exists and which confines them within the mystified view of a "more sociable" agriculture in comparison with another rebuilt so as to be "less sociable"'.[74] As part of that traditional lifestyle and values we can include a belief in witchcraft and magic.

As Yves Dupont observed in a little known collection of essays on witchcraft and magic in the *Bocage*, Favret-Saada was working in just such a 'traditional' community but she never properly attempted to assess the relationship between the witchcraft she studied with such insight and the wider impact of contemporary social and economic developments. For Dupont, Favret-Saada concentrated too narrowly on the psychoanalytic and symbolic dimensions of witchcraft, and he suggested that broader sociological research would further help us develop hypotheses to understand the continued relevance and function of witchcraft in modern French society.[75] The work on witchcraft which has paid attention to the social as well as the symbolic, suggests that the key reason for the continuance of bewitchment in post-war rural France lies in the socio-cultural friction created in rural communities by agricultural change, and the associated self-conscious defence of the *paysan* lifestyle and mentality against the forces of modernity, as described in a different context by Delbos.

The study of witchcraft in parts of Anjou and the Vendée during the early 1980s by the 'ethnopsychiatrist' Patrick Gaboriau is one such piece of research that places contemporary bewitchment in sociological context. Not surprisingly, of thirty cases he investigated, nearly all of those complaining of bewitchment were *paysans* or people 'close to the *paysans* by their way of life or their geographical situation'.[76] They expressed profound nostalgia for the past, and were devout in their religion. They all devalued reading as an activity. They associated it with sloth and illness, and described it as 'annoying' or as time wasted. Those concerned, whether in town or country, also shared a profound pessimism concerning the state of society in general, with some expressing apocalyptic views of the future. The background context to all this was the large-scale change in local society and economy that had occurred over the previous three decades. The majority of the population of the department of Maine-et-Loire, which contained a large portion of Gaboriau's survey area, had remained largely rural right up until the mid 1960s. From this point on, though, the fading rump of the *paysan* way of life was thoroughly undermined. The number of farmers in the department dropped from just over 102,000 in 1954 to just over 48,000 in 1975. In his smaller zone of study nearly 700 farms went out of business between 1972 and 1980. The result amongst certain sections of the local population was a feeling of insecurity, disillusionment and disorientation. During the same period the shop-keepers and small manufacturers, amongst whom Gaboriau found several cases of bewitchment, were experiencing a similar assault on their way of life and social values from the growth of supermarkets and corporate manufacturing industries in the region.

From his interviews with those who felt themselves to be bewitched, Gaboriau found that witchcraft was not necessarily an expression of intense conflict between individuals in isolated dramas, but signified, 'all the social apprehensions of the *paysans* towards the world today and of tomorrow'.[77] André Julliard's work amongst the small polyculture farmers of l'Ain revealed a similar outlook where witchcraft was more than an attack on the individual or his or her farm, but an attack on a way of life.[78] Becoming bewitched, then, was both a conscious and subconscious response to broad social developments, a withdrawal into the traditional past. However, the bewitchment-inducing conflict between tradition and modernity should not only be seen in a broad social context, in other words as a psychosomatic response to the helplessness felt in the face of socio-cultural change, but also in terms of more intimate clashes with the personification of those forces of modernity. In particular, the clash between the *paysan* and the new breed of entrepreneurial *novateur* farmer. Yves Dupont outlined how in the *Bocage* of western France from the 1960s onwards, the impact of *novateurs*, schooled by such bodies as the *Centre National de Jeunes Agriculteurs*, backed up by substantial bank loans, and driven by productivity – developments alien to *paysan* culture – was conducive to witchcraft conflicts at the time. Tensions were further created by several laws allowing the seizure of land in certain circumstances. The *paysans* considered this to be another attack on their way of life by the state and its agents.

Paradoxically, the accusations of witchcraft generated by such antagonisms were not only the response of the *paysans* – as Gaboriau's work might suggest. Dupont recounts the experience of a young *novateur* farmer from outside the *bocage* who bought a farm in the area, which had been managed along traditional lines. Characteristic tall hedges bound the farm's small fields, and there were a number of woods on the property that local hunters valued for their pigeons, boar and deer. The young farmer motivated by the desire to increase productivity ripped out the hedges and woods to create more land for cultivation. The locals saw this as a transgression of local norms and traditions, and he was ostracized. A series of misfortunes subsequently beset the farmer, and he gradually became convinced that he had been bewitched. Prior to his moving into the area, witchcraft was not something he had ever considered, but once enmeshed in a community where witchcraft was part of the popular discourse, he began to think in their terms even if he had not acted as they did. He associated witchcraft with the *paysan* culture, and saw his misfortune as being the result of communal ill will towards him and his farming methods rather than the work of any one individual.[79]

Despite her impressive perspicacity, in some respects Favret-Saada's micro-study of witchcraft engendered a narrowness of perspective, though, to be fair, this has become more obvious with the benefit of hindsight. She asserted, for example, that 'unbewitchers are today exclusively ruralites' and subsequent researchers have continued to concentrate on rural areas.[80] We should be very wary, however, about drawing such exclusive links between 'traditional' rurality and the continued belief in witchcraft and magic. Yes, such agricultural societies as have been discussed are conducive to certain types of witchcraft accusation and magic, but urban communities play their part as well. It is from urban areas that numerous unbewitchers and fortune-tellers operated and continue to operate. In 1938, for example, the *prefecture* of Paris calculated there were 5,200 such practitioners in the capital.

During the 1980s the influx of African immigrants to French urban centres generated a new and vibrant magical culture that has yet to be studied properly, but which seems to have fused to a certain extent with the 'indigenous' discourse on witchcraft and the practice of counter-magic. Central to this new magic service industry are the Islamic *marabouts* or cunning-folk from North and West Africa – Senegal in particular. As various prosecution cases have revealed, it would seem that most of them profess to have been *marabouts* back in their homeland to boost their prestige, but have in fact adopted the trade while in France. According to police figures by the end of the 1980s there were around 500 *marabouts* practising in Paris and many more in other French towns and cities.[81] Their core customer base would seem to be from African ethnic groups but they have also built up a white French urban and rural clientele as well. This is evident from a case heard by the Rennes tribunal in August 1986. A Bretonne woman from a small village in the region suspected her rabbits had been bewitched. She looked in a local free newspaper and found an advert for 'le grand marabout Touré'. She consulted him and he promised to remove the witchcraft for the sum of 7100 francs. The woman paid, and apparently happy with his magic she subsequently asked him to provide her with a spell to protect her from all misfortune. Touré informed her that such a great spell would cost the huge sum of 64,500 francs, partly because he said he would need the help of his father who lived in Senegal. The woman agreed to the price and the *marabout* escorted her to her bank to pick up the cash. The bank clerk, suspicious of the large sum involved, called the police and Touré was arrested and sentenced to two years in prison.[82] The case was by no means unique. Several years later a *marabout*, originally from Guinea, who had successfully established himself in the small Normandy fishing town of Fécamp, was arrested after defrauding a local woman who had consulted him about her ill daughter.[83] On a more elevated level a recent book has caused a media stir by claiming with some substance that Jacques Chirac's entourage hired some Senegalese *marabouts* to work against his former political rival Edouard Balladur when they were competing for the Gaullist party presidential candidacy.[84]

The journalists who have reported on the rise and activities of the *marabouts* echo the journalistic censorial tone of the nineteenth century regarding cunning-folk and their clients. They feel a certain sense of shock that people could still be 'duped' in such a way. The growth of the *marabouts* is accordingly 'most mysterious and also most worrying'.[85] Another sensationalist wrote more generally, 'the problem of witchcraft in France is serious. It is even more serious than that posed by drugs.'[86] Concern at this period can be seen as an aspect of the wider fears regarding immigration and crime that have dominated recent elections. Any crude linkage that the *marabouts* are somehow responsible for a recrudescence of belief cannot be substantiated. They have merely positioned themselves exceptionally well in an existing 'native' market for unbewitching and other magical services. *Marabouts* make up only a small percentage of the practitioners offering similar services throughout France, the majority of whom are white. For the 1980s various unsubstantiated figures have been bandied about. One author estimated there were 30,000 *désenvôuteurs* in practice, charging 250 francs on average.[87] Others have put the figure for the broader category of *voyants* at between 30,000–50,000.[88] Explanations for the popularity of *marabouts* and other occult practitioners are no longer linked directly to a lack of education – that connection has been patently undermined – but rather to a pervasive and irresponsible mass media. Journalists writing on the subject in the late 1980s like Edouard Brasey, were critical of the attention the press, radio and television gave to supernatural beliefs in general and the way they promoted astrologers, healers, mediums and occultists in particular.[89] There is always *something* to 'blame' for the continued belief in witchcraft and magic and the existence of those professionals who service that belief, rather than accepting that it as aspect of the human condition.

A sociological survey of the French population's belief in the 'paranormal' published in 1986 suggested that 18 per cent believed in witchcraft. Compare this with the 23 per cent who believed in horoscopes and the 33 per cent who believed in UFOs.[90] But that 18 per cent cannot be portrayed as a rump of traditional witchcraft. Witchcraft is not a timeless, unchanging cultural phenomenon. Accordingly, considerable differences can be detected in witch-craft beliefs and the social context of accusations between 1850 and 1990. There has been a general diminution in the scope of witchcraft. Contagious possession disappeared by the early twentieth century, although individual cases still occur. The number of priests willing to perform exorcisms and unbewitchments are few these days. One journalist researching the subject in the mid 1990s found only ten or so willing to talk, though the numbers who have performed exorcisms is undoubtedly greater.[91] Some of the misfor-tunes formerly attributed to witches were no longer being made by the mid twentieth century. Favret-Saada's comparison of her experience of witchcraft in the *Bocage* with the detailed depiction of witchcraft beliefs in Jules Lecœur's 'sketches' of *Bocage* life published in the 1880s, highlighted the demise of weather-related witchcraft accusations such as storm-raising.[92] Witchcraft directed at cottage industry activities such as baking, brewing, butter- and cheese-making rarely appears in sources concerning the second half of the twentieth century. Yet we should not assume that the activities of witches were restricted to objects and activities of 'traditional' ways of life. Witchcraft is an adaptable explanation for misfortune. While misfortunes long associated with witchcraft disappeared, new ones emerged. Léontine Esnault dealt with bewitched cars and fridges, for example, and a couple of decades later one clergyman exorcist had to deal with a possessed fax machine.

As with witchcraft *beliefs*, witchcraft *accusations* should not be viewed as static phenomena either; they too reflect social change. The classic scenarios of neighbourly witchcraft conflicts certainly still continue, as shown by the Valmont dispute outlined earlier. But in modern France the unstable subsistence existence in which many nineteenth- and early twentieth-century witchcraft accusations can be situated no longer exists. Yet new fears and insecurities have emerged during the second half of the twentieth century. The threat is less precise, more general, no longer parochial but global. The witch has become symbolic of unwanted social forces rather than the malice of the individual.

Notes

1 Matthew Ramsey, *Professional and Popular Medicine in France, 1770–1830: The Social World of Medical Practice* (Cambridge, 1988); idem, 'Magical Healing, Witchcraft and Elite Discourse in Eighteenth and Nineteenth Century France', in Marijke Gijswijt-Hofstra, Hilary Marland and Hans de Waardt (eds), *Illness and Healing Alternatives in Western Europe* (London and New York, 1997), pp. 14–37; Eloïse Mozzani, *Magie et superstitions de la fin de l'Ancien Régime à la Restauration* (Paris, 1988); Bernard Traimond, *Le pouvoir de la maladie: Magie et politique dans les Landes de Gascogne, 1750–1826* (Bordeaux, 1988); Judith Devlin, *The Superstitious Mind: French Peasants and the Supernatural in the Nineteenth Century* (New Haven, 1987).

2 Marie-Claude Denier, 'Sorciers, presages et croyance magiques en Mayenne aux XVIIIe et XIXe siècles', *Annales de Bretagne et des Pays de L'Ouest* 97 (1990) 115–32; Jean-Claude Sebban, 'La sorcellerie en Berry au XIXe siècle', *Cahiers de l'institut d'histoire de la presse et de l'opinion* 2 (n.d.) 137–61; Benoît Marin-Curtoud, 'Les process de sorcellerie pendant la IIIe République', in Jean-Baptiste Martin (ed.), *Le défi magique: satanisme, sorcellerie*, vol. 2 (Lyon, 1994), pp. 161–73. See also Tessie P. Liu's discussion on bewitchments and household gender politics, 'Le Patrimoine Magique: Reassessing the Power of Women in Peasant Households in Nineteenth-Century France', *Gender and History* 6 (1994) 13–36.

3 For example, Nicole Edelman, *Voyantes, guérisseuses et visionnaires en France 1785–1914* (Paris, 1995); Thomas Kselman, *Miracles and Prophecies in Nineteenth-Century France* (New Brunswick, 1983); idem, *Death and the Afterlife in Modern France* (Princeton, 1993); B. Plongeron (ed.), *La religion populaire: Approches historiques* (Paris, 1976); M. Bouteiller, *Médicine populaire d'hier et d'aujourd'hui* (Paris, 1966); Jacques Léonard, 'Les guérisseurs en France au XIXe siècle', *Revue d'histoire moderne et contemporaine* 27 (1980) 501–16; René Luneau, 'Monde rural et christianisation: Prêtres et paysans français du siècle dernier', *Archives de sciences sociales des religions* 43 (1977) 39–52; Marie-Véronique Le Meur, 'Le culte des saints dans le diocese de Blois aux environs de 1840', *Cahiers de l'institut d'histoire de la presse et de l'opinion* 2 (n.d.) 9–25; Eugen Weber, 'Religion and superstition in nineteenth-century France', *Historical Journal* 31 (1988) 399–423.

4 See Eugen Weber, *Peasants into Frenchmen: The Modernisation of Rural France 1870–1914* (Stanford, 1976), ch. 20.

5 Sebban, 'La sorcellerie en Berry', 158.

6 Sebban, 'La sorcellerie en Berry', 158.

7 See, for example, James R. Lehning, *Peasant and French: Cultural Contact in Rural France during the Nineteenth Century* (Cambridge, 1995), ch. 7; Kselman, *Death and the Afterlife*, ch. 3.

8 Sebban, 'La sorcellerie en Berry', 157–8.

9 Weber, *Peasants*, p. 339.

10 Jacques Gutwirth, 'Superstition, ancêtres et piétisme en Cévennes', in Françoise Loux (ed.), *Panseurs de douleurs: Les médicines populaires* (Paris, [1978] 1992), pp. 199–214. See also Philippe Joutard, 'Protestantisme populaire et univers magique: Le cas cévenol', *Le Monde alpin et rhodanien* 1–4 (1977) 145–71.

11 Willem de Blécourt, 'The Witch, her Victim, the Unwitcher and the Researcher: The Continued Existence of Traditional Witchcraft', in Willem de Blécourt, Ronald Hutton and Jean La Fontaine, *Witchcraft and Magic in Europe: The Twentieth Century* (London, 1999), p. 206. See also his contribution in this volume.

12 M. Hilarion Barthety, *Pratiques de sorcellerie, ou superstitions populaires du Béarn* (Pau, 1874), p. 7.

13 Reprinted in [unauthored], *Contes populaires et legendes du Val de Loire* (Paris, 1976), pp. 224–6.

14 Charles Lancelin, *La sorcellerie des campagnes* (Paris, [1911] 2nd edn, no date, c. 1920s), p. 189.

15 Docteur Brisson, *En Montagne Bourbonnaise* (Roanne, 1911), pp. 156, 157, 227.

16 Ernest Sevrin, 'Croyances populaires et médicine supranaturelle en Eure-et-Loire au XIXe siècle', *Revue d'histoire de l'Église de France* 32 (1946) 304, 303.

17 See, for example, Arnold Van Gennep, *Le folklore de la Flandre et du Hainaut français*, 2 vols (Paris, 1935–36); M. Leproux, *Contributions au folklore charentais* (Paris, 1954); Claude Seignolle, *En Sologne, enquête folklorique* (Paris, 1946); Marcelle Bouteiller, *Sorciers et jeteurs de sort* (Paris, 1958).

18 On the development of French folklore studies see Charles Rearick, *Beyond the Enlightenment: Historians and Folklore in Nineteenth-Century France* (Bloomington and London, 1974). For an appraisal of Van Gennep's approach see Nicole Belmont, *Arnold Van Gennep: The Creator of French Ethnography* (Chicago, [1974] 1979); idem, 'Ethnologie et histoire dans l'œuvre d'Arnold Van Gennep', *Ethnologie française* 5 (1975) 184–9.

19 Arnold Van Gennep, *Le folklore du Dauphiné*, 2 vols (Paris, 1932–33), vol. 2, p. 467.

20 Claude and Jacques Seignolle, *Le folklore du Hurepoix: mœurs et coutumes d'Ile de France* (Paris, [1937] 1978), p. 13.

21 C. and J. Seignolle, *Le folklore du Hurepoix*, p. 204.

22 C. and J. Seignolle, *Le folklore du Hurepoix*, p. 206.

23 De Blécourt, 'The Witch, her Victim', p. 161.

24 George Raviart, *Sorcières and possédées: La démonomanie dans le nord de la France* (Lille, 1936), pp. 57–8.

25 Cyrille Kaszuk, *Les sorciers du Sundgau et autres souvenirs* (2nd edn, Mulhouse, 1993), p. 28.

26 For example, R. Kaufmann, 'Pratiques superstitieuses et médicales en Poitou', Thèse de médicine, Paris, 1906; J. P. Odendhal, 'Etudes sur la sorcellerie médicale en Dordogne', Thèse de médicine, Bordeaux, 1923; M. Igert, 'Les Guérisseurs mystique. Etude psychopathologique', Thèse de médicine, Toulouse, 1928.

27 See, for example, Sarah Ferber, 'Charcot's Demons: Retrospective Medicine and Historical Diagnosis in the Writings of the Salpêtrière School', in Marijke Giswijt-Hofstra, Hilary Marland and Hans de Waardt (eds), *Illness and Healing Alternatives*

in Western Europe (London, 1997), pp. 120–40; H. C. Erik Midelfort, 'Charcot, Freud, and the Demons', in Kathryn Edwards (ed.), *Werewolves, Witches, and Wandering Spirits: Traditional Belief and Folklore in Early Modern Europe* (Kirksville, 2002), pp. 199–215; Devlin, *Superstitious Mind*, conclusion.

28 For example, R. Cassins, 'Délire et sorcellerie. Contributions à l'étude de la psycho-pathologie de la sorcellerie à propos d'observations recueillies en Ille-et-Vilaine', Thése de médicine, Rennes, 1975. For examples of other theses on the subject see, André Julliard and René Luneau, 'La medicine populaire dans les campagnes française aujourd'hui: Bibliographie thématique', *Archives de sciences sociales des religions* 43 (1977) 81–2.

29 Gilberte Jacquel and Jean Morel, 'Sorcellerie et troubles mentaux: étude faite dans le département de l'Orne', *L'Encéphale* 1 (1965) 15–16. This article is based on Morel's thesis, 'La sorcellerie et ses incidences psychiatriques dans le départment de l'Orne', Thése de médicine, Paris, 1964.

30 Dominique Camus, *Pouvoirs sorciers: Enquête sur les pratiques actuelles de sorcellerie* (Paris, 1988), p. 69.

31 For example, Claude Seignolle, *Le Berry traditionnel* (Paris, 1969); Jacques de Wailly and Maurice Crampon, *Le folklore de Picardie* (Amiens, 1968).

32 Jeanne Favret-Saada, 'La malheur biologique et sa répétition', *Annales: E. S. C*%20.26 (1971) 873–88; idem, *Les mots, la mort, les sorts* (Paris, 1977) (English edition *Deadly Words: Witchcraft in the Bocage* [Cambridge, 1980]); Favret-Saada and J. Contreras, *Corps pour corps; Enquête sur la sorcellerie dans le Bocage* (Paris, 1981).

33 Favret-Saada, *Les mots*, p. 19, n. 3.

34 See Marc Augé, 'Ici et ailleurs: sorciers du Bocage et sorciers d'Afrique', *Annales: E. S. C.* 34 (1979) 74–83.

35 See, for example, André Julliard, 'Dans l'Ain, des leveurs de sorts', in Loux, *Panseurs*, pp. 99–106; Julliard, 'Le malheur des sorts: Sorcellerie d'aujourd'hui en France', in Robert Muchembled (ed.), *Magie et sorcellerie en Europe du Moyen Age à nos jours* (Paris, 1994), pp. 267–315; Patrick Gaboriau, *La pensée ensorcelée: La sorcellerie actuelle en Anjou et en Vendée* (Paris, 1987); Robert Jalby, *Sorcellerie et médecine populaire en Languedoc* (Nyon, 1974); Jean-Pierre Pinies, *Figures de la sorcellerie Languedocienne* (Paris, 1983).

36 See the various papers by research students in *Cahiers du LASA* (Laboratoire de sociologie-anthropologie de l'Université de Caen, 1985).

37 Dominique Camus, *Pouvoirs sorciers: enquête sur les pratiques actuelles de sorcellerie* (Paris, 1988); idem, *Paroles magiques, secrets de guérison: les leveurs de maux aujourd'hui* (Paris, 1990); idem, *Jeteurs de sorts et désenvoûteurs*, 3 vols (Paris, 1997–2000).

38 For example, Philippe Alfonsi and Patrick Pesnot, *L'œil du sorcier: une histoire d'en-voûtement aujourd'hui en France* (Paris, 1973); René Crozet, *La France ensorcelée* (2nd edn, Paris, 1993); François de Muizon, *Les derniers exorcistes de l'épiscopat révélent!* (Paris, 1996).

39 Crozet, *La France*, p. 45.

40 Eudes de Mirville, *Des esprits et de leurs manifestations fluidiques* (Paris, 1851); idem, *Pneumatologie: Des esprits et de leurs manifestations fluidiques* (Paris, 1853); Henri Roger Gougenot des Mousseaux, *Mouers et pratiques des démons* (Paris, 1854); Madame Blavatsky, *Isis Unveiled* (New York, 1877), vol. 1, p. 106; Eliphas Levi, *La clef des grands mystères* (Paris, 1861). See also I. Bertrand, *La sorcellerie* (Paris, 1899), pp. 19–27. More recent research on the case can be found in Jean-Claude Marquis, *Loups, sorciers, criminals: Une histoire du fait divers au XIXe siècle en Seine-Inférieure* (Luneray, 1993), pp. 126–33.

41 Ruth Harris, 'Possession on the Borders: The "Mal de Morzine" in Nineteenth-Century France', *Journal of Modern History* 69 (1997) 451–78; Jacqueline Carroy, *Le*

mal de Morzine: De la possession à l'hystérie (Paris, 1981); Laurence Maire, *Les possédées de Morzine, 1857–1873* (Lyon, 1981).

42 Roy Porter, 'Witchcraft and Magic in Enlightenment, Romantic and Liberal Thought', in Marijke Gijswijt-Hofstra, Brian P. Levack and Roy Porter, *Witchcraft and Magic in Europe: The Eighteenth and Nineteenth Centuries* (London, 1999), p. 271.

43 Paul Sutter, *Le Diable, ses paroles, son action dans le possédés d'Illfurt* (Arras, [1921] 1926).

44 Sutter, *Le Diable*, p. 119.

45 Sutter, *Le Diable*, p. 148.

46 See also *Le Lorrain*, 19 Nov. 1949; cited in Jean Vartier, *Sabbat, juges et sorciers: quatre siècle de superstitions dans la France de l'Est* (Paris, 1968), pp. 251–60.

47 As well as widespread newspaper reportage, the story of Léontine Esnault has been told in detail by Danièle Carrer and Geneviève Yver, *La désencraudeuse: une sorcière d'aujourd'hui* (Paris, 1978).

48 Carrer and Yver, *La désencraudeuse*, pp. 140–3, 73.

49 Ernest Sevrin, 'Croyances populaires et médicine supranaturelle en Eure-et-Loire au XIXe siècle', *Revue d'histoire de l'Église de France* 32 (1946) 303.

50 Marin-Curtoud, 'Les procès de sorcellerie', p. 164; Bouteiller, *Sorciers*, pp. 65–6.

51 C. Rabaud, *Phénomènes psychiques et superstitions populaires* (Paris, 1908); cited in Devlin, *Superstitious Mind*, p. 113.

52 Lancelin, *Sorcellerie*, p. 200.

53 *The Times*, 6, 7 and 25 Jan. 1926.

54 Vartier, *Sabbat, juges et sorciers*, p. 250.

55 Jacquel and Morel, 'Sorcellerie et troubles mentaux', 17–18.

56 Roger Vaisan, *Les secrets des sorciers modernes* (Lyon, 1956), p. 86.

57 *La Presse de la Manche*, 23 Apr. 1955; le Tenneur, *Magie, sorcellerie*, p. 401.

58 *Ouest-France*, 13 Feb. 1961; le Tenneur, *Magie, sorcellerie*, p. 405.

59 *Le Journal du Dimanche*, 7 March 1976; *Le Monde*, 14 May 1977; le Tenneur, *Magie, sorcellerie*, pp. 410–12.

60 Julliard, 'Le malheur des sorts', p. 268.

61 Jean-Paul Lefebvre-Filleau, *Mystères en Normandie* (Luneray, 1994), pp. 161–6.

62 *Daily News*, 13 Sep. 1882; *Folklore Journal* 1 (1883) 331.

63 Sebban, 'La sorcellerie en Berry', 150, 153, 158.

64 To gain an approximate conversion to new francs simply subtract a zero from the figure.

65 Lancelin, *Sorcellerie*, pp. 191–209.

66 For example, Weber, *Peasants into Frenchmen*; Robert Forster and Orest Ranum (eds), *Rural Society in France*, trans. Elborg Forster and Patricia Ranum (Baltimore and London, 1977); Lehning, *Peasant and French*; Caroline Ford, *Creating the Nation in Provincial France* (Princeton, 1993); Roger Price, *A Social History of Nineteenth-Century France* (New York, 1987); Alan R. H. Baker, *Fraternity among the French Peasantry: Sociability and Voluntary Associations in the Loire Valley, 1815–1914* (Cambridge, 1999); Ted W. Margadant, 'Tradition and Modernity in Rural France in the Nineteenth Century', *Journal of Modern History* 56 (1984) 668–97.

67 For example, Henri Mendras, *The Vanishing Peasant*, trans. Jean Lerner (Cambridge, Mass., 1970); Gordon Wright, *Rural Revolution in France: The Peasantry in the Twentieth Century* (Stanford, 1964); M. Débatisse, *La revolution silencieuse: le combat des paysans* (Paris, 1963); Susan Carol Rogers, 'Good to Think: The "Peasant" in Contemporary France', *Anthropological Quarterly* 60 (1987) 56–63; Geneviève Delbos, 'Leaving Agriculture, Remaining a Peasant', *Man*, new series 17, 4 (1982) 747–65;

B. J. Lammers, 'National Identity on the French Periphery: The End of Peasants into Frenchmen?', *National Identities* 1 (1999) 81–8.

68 Paul Hohenberg, 'Change in Rural France in the Period of Industrialisation, 1830–1914', *Journal of Economic History* 32 (1972) 223.

69 Georges Gurvitch, 'Social Structure of Pre-War France', *American Journal of Sociology* 48 (1943) 538.

70 See Weber, *Peasants*, ch. 6.

71 Pierre-Jakez Hélias, *The Horse of Pride* (New Haven, 1978), p. 135; cited in Susan Cotts Watkins, 'From Local to National Communities: The Transformation of Demographic Regimes in Western Europe, 1870–1960', *Population and Development Review* 16 (1990) 253.

72 Rogers, 'The "Peasant"', 61.

73 Delbos, 'Leaving Agriculture', 748.

74 Delbos, 'Leaving Agriculture', 762, 754.

75 Yves Dupont, 'Sorcellerie et modernisation de l'agriculture en pays de bocage', in *Sorcellerie, bocage et modernité, Cahiers du LASA* (Caen, 1985).

76 Gaboriau, *La pensée ensorcelée*, p. 154.

77 Gaboriau, *La pensée ensorcelée*, p. 139.

78 Julliard, 'Le Malheur des sorts', p. 303.

79 Dupont, 'Sorcellerie et modernisation', pp. 21–7.

80 Jeanne Favret-Saada, 'L'invention d'une thérapie: la sorcellerie bocaine 1887–1970', *Le Débat. Histoire, politique, société* 40 (1986) 41.

81 Edouard Brasey, *Sorciers: Voyage chez les astrologues, envoûteurs, guérisseurs, mages et voyants* (Paris, 1989), p. 189.

82 Frederic Meridien, *Ma sorcière bien payée* (Paris, 1992), pp. 30–1.

83 Lefebvre-Filleau, *Mystère en Normandie*, pp. 149–54.

84 Sylvie Jumel, *La sorcellerie cœur de la République* (Paris, 2002).

85 Brasey, *Sorciers*, p. 188.

86 Crozet, *La France ensorcelée*, p. 46.

87 Crozet, *La France ensorcelée*, p. 83.

88 Devlin, *Superstitious Mind*, p. 262, n. 2.

89 Brasey, *Sorciers*, pp. 12–13.

90 Daniel Boy and Guy Michelat, 'Croyances aux parasciences: dimensions sociales et culturelles', *Revue française de sociologie* 27 (1986) 175–204, 177.

91 François de Muizon, *Les derniers exorcistes de l'épiscopat révèlent! Possessions et envoûtements analysés par des religieux et des psychiatres* (Paris, 1996), p. 9. See also Claude Béziau, *Les exorcistes parlent face à la sorcellerie* (Sable-d'Olonne, 1978).

92 Favret-Saada, 'L'invention d'une thérapie', 29–46; Jules Lecœur, *Esquisses du Bocage normand*, 2 vols (Brionne, 1883 and 1887).

7

Magical healing in Spain (1875–1936): medical pluralism and the search for hegemony[1]

Enrique Perdiguero

Was magic an essential part of the Spanish population's cultural repertoires for understanding and dealing with illness during the late nineteenth and early twentieth centuries? By 'cultural repertoires' is meant 'the ways in which people have conceived and explained illness and reaction against illness'.[2] For various reasons that will be discussed, the question is difficult to answer categorically, but in attempting to do so it is necessary to move beyond the typical generalizations found in the history of medicine. Like the other contributors in this volume, this chapter aims to explore the presence of magical elements in everyday life during the modern period, and thereby broaden the usual location of magical practice in the medieval and early modern periods.[3] The chronological focus of the following discussion is defined by two major political events: the restoration of the monarchy and the outbreak of the Civil War.[4] These years can be described as a period of far-reaching transformation in Spanish society. From a demographic point of view the most significant development was what can be described as the 'sanitary transition'. From a social, economic and political perspective the perception of the so-called 'social issue', which showed the weaknesses and contradictions in the socio-economic system, became sharper. The loss of Spain's last colonies in 1898 shook the national conscience. The country saw itself as being backward, and calls for national renewal became commonplace. In this situation social medicine claimed an important role for itself in the regeneration of the country.[5]

To assess the relevance of magic in the popular discourse and interpretation of illness it is important to consider the structure of health care more generally. This is a topic that still needs more in-depth research.[6] Nevertheless, during the period concerned we can identify two main forms of collective medical care: charity provided by authorities and individuals, and so-called 'friendly societies'. Charitable health care funded by public authorities (municipalities, provinces and the central government) covered home and institutional help for those defined as poor and who clearly had no means to take care of themselves. But the authorities' provision for the

majority of the rural population was described as clearly inadequate by
general practitioners, who kept demanding its nationalization. 'Friendly
societies' were more or less widespread depending on regions. They were
very important in Catalonia as a result of its large industrial workforce.[7]
Another arrangement particularly adopted by middle-class families was to
pay a pre-determined fee for general medical cover. The popularity of such
self-help strategies underlines the fact that despite efforts made in some
quarters, a national medical welfare system failed to emerge before the Civil
War.[8] Only maternity was covered by national social protection after 1931
and only after hard negotiation.[9] Although it would be too simplistic to say
that the lack of a collective welfare system explains the continuation of
magical means of dealing with illness, I do think there is a link, especially
considering how this reality was used by general practitioners to justify both
their attacks on popular medicine and their calls for the nationalization of
medical provision. This situation has been described by one historian as the
'health care conflict'.[10]

The problem of sources

As the editors of this volume have already highlighted in some of their work,
two key sources for understanding the role of magical healing during the
period are folklore surveys and newspapers, though their use is fraught with
problems.[11] The following discussion is based largely on the first of these
two sources, with care being taken to ensure that the folkloric material used
was collected in the period concerned.[12] Only occasionally are journalistic
sources employed, and mostly in the restricted context of my own research
on the local press of the town of Alicante.[13] The study of the subject will
undoubtedly benefit greatly from a greater awareness of the newspaper
archive. Folklore sources for the period are abundant.[14] The rise of the
folklore movement, which spread through various areas of Spain, was complex
and had different roots.[15] The most significant attempts to involve Spanish
intellectuals in the study of folklore were made by the group formed around
Antonio Machado y Álvarez (1846–93) in the city of Seville. Their initiative
only had an ephemeral success, although it acquired some relevance in
Andalusia, Extremadura, Galicia and Madrid.[16] Both the Machado y Álvarez
group, and those whose approach was usually associated with nationalistic
political beliefs, tried to find 'survivals' in popular culture.[17] It is difficult,
therefore, to assess whether their numerous collections of 'superstitions'
accurately reflect widespread popular responses to illness, or whether
they consist of 'rarities', which were recorded precisely because they were
considered archaic remnants of belief.

This problem of interpretation has been faced by several researchers
such as Ingrid Kuschick.[18] Although her work, first published in 1989, was

meant to focus on 'the practices and conceptions of popular medicine in contemporary Spain' much of her discussion is based on folkloric, anthropo- logical and medical writings from the early part of the century. But with the support of her own and others' field work she was able to contextualize and qualify the early ethnographic material. The result, though, is that her work tells us more about the situation of popular medicine at the beginning rather than at the end of the twentieth century. Another author who has analysed the problem of using folk sources to study cultural repertoires of illness is J. M. Comelles.[19] One of his findings worth emphasizing here is the relevance he attributes to doctors as the main characters as far as ethnographic tasks are concerned. He sees them not only as folklore collectors but also as health professionals interested in fixing the cultural limits to their own health care activities. In practice this led to a whole range of medical discourses giving detailed descriptions of popular medical beliefs and action considered to be inferior or wrong. This kind of literature focused especially on mother-and- child health,[20] which makes sense considering the high infant mortality rates during that period.[21] For the historian the problem posed by these sources lies in the preoccupation of medical authors to locate the world of 'popular beliefs' in the context of the 'irrational' supernatural, thereby ignoring other aspects of popular medicine considered less 'superstitious' that were also part of the cultural repertoires about illness.[22]

An examination of the sources discussed above certainly proves the significant presence in Spanish society of diverse types of healers who applied magical procedures, although the data is rarely sufficient to conduct an in-depth analysis of the totality of their business. The existence of what we would nowadays call, using a rather unfortunate expression, 'culture-bound syndromes' is also evident.[23] Most of the diagnostic and therapeutic methods that will be discussed below also reveal the presence of medico-religious elements related to miraculous saints, pilgrimages and sanctuaries. However, I have not treated this matter in a systematic way, because this would lead us to another field of study that, albeit concomitant with our research, requires more dedicated attention. Obviously, it is often difficult to establish boundaries between more clearly religious elements and magical ones, simply because the population did not necessarily establish them.

Folk healers [24]

It is difficult to use a single label to define the people who, despite not being health professionals, were seen by the population as a therapeutic alternative, and whose expertise included, in some way or other, the use of magic. The historiography has paid attention to this problem in recent years,[25] but it is far from easy to transfer words and concepts from one cultural context to another. In Spain, the most commonly used word for folk healers was and is *curandero*. However, under the heading of *curandero*, folklorists and medical authors referred to various types of practices: healers who treated a wide range of illnesses; people specialized in curing specific culture-bound syndromes; healers of sprains, herbalists and bone-setters. The latter three groups mostly used empirical procedures, though magical elements were commonly present. The label of *curandero* was also given to other individuals who not only diagnosed and cured, but also practised fortune-telling, spiritualism and *sonámbulo* – which in Spanish not only equates with the English term for sleep-walking, but also concerned the possession of mesmeric powers.

In the context of health professionals' efforts to achieve hegemony in health and illness management, the label of *curandero* was the most often used to refer to an unspecified reality considered as a 'moral illness that swarms everywhere like a confederate indestructible germ which poisons all it touches'.[26] *Curanderos* were regarded as people who had curative skills derived from their 'special gift', that is, as people whose activity was based not on their knowledge but on their 'power'. This feature additionally made it possible to distinguish them from other rivals of doctors who were labelled as 'intruders' or 'charlatans', although the limits separating them from *curanderos* with a 'gift' are blurred at times.[27]

Reports of the population's frequent resort to folk healers are commonplace in medical literature, but it is difficult to find examples with enough data to draw a detailed profile of their characteristics. One exception is the case of José Cerdá Baeza, the 'Baldaet',[28] who practised his profession in Alicante.[29] He claimed to have a 'gift' and cured using 'magnetized' water. The reason for our detailed knowledge of him is because we have the reports of his prosecution. Although initially found guilty he was finally acquitted. Another example is that of the so-called 'apostles', three healers who became very famous in Madrid in the year 1884, to such an extent that the large number of people who wanted to be treated by them generated law-and-order problems.[30] As they stated at their subsequent trial, they cured by praying over the sick and prescribing water over which they had also said some prayers. In mitigation they asserted: 'They do not think water acquires any medical virtues or any new properties that distinguish it from ordinary water as a result of this process, pointing out that they only give it to comfort the ill, or as a souvenir for the spirit, having sometimes resorted to this method after having unsuccessfully applied other techniques'. They were less fortunate than El Baldaet, as the Supreme Court of Justice sentenced them to thirty days' imprisonment.[31] However, their activities can still be traced after this sentence, since they went on to treat ill people using the same curative method and even, after offering their services in several cities, moved to El Baldaet's territory, the city of Alicante, which gave rise to conflict between them due to the similar healing methods they used.[32] They also performed their activity in other localities in the province of Alicante, in some of which similar *curanderos* practised their profession.[33]

This type of urban *curanderos/as* was the one that received the most attention in medical journals. This was because they were seen as a major threat.[34] Nevertheless, references are not too illustrative about their practice, though it seems they treated all kinds of ailments, like the healer who settled in the city of Burgos, who said he could diagnose because 'he saw inside the human body, the same as one can see the water in a crystalline glass', or the *saludadora* who was recorded as practising in Madrid in 1887.[35] The word *saludadores* or *saludadora* did in fact refer to a more specific type of folk healer whose 'gift' usually concerned the cure of rabies, mainly using the saliva or the breath. In the eighteenth century such healers formed part of the municipal health staff.[36] In the period under study there is abundant evidence of their continued popularity as folk healers, as is proved by the performance in Orihuela (Alicante) in 1887 of the *saludador* called 'tío Matamadres', which ended in the death of a person suffering from hydrophobia.[37]

Tantalizing but frustrating scraps of information regarding healers can be found in a series of articles written in the 1880s for the professional journal *La Fraternidad Médico-Farmacéutica* by a doctor working for the Alicante Town Council, Esteban Sánchez Santana.[38] Santana mentions, for example, an episode of mental derangement suffered by a woman in Alcoy (Alicante) after another woman with 'very bad antecedents' had given her 'a potion to cure the spell under which the ill woman was supposed to be'.[39] There are a few lines about a homicide caused by an accusation of bewitchment made by an old lady in the locality of Teya (Barcelona).[40] Folk healers mentioned include 'la Pelá', a specialist in cartomancy, and various *curanderos*, among who were specialists in all kinds of spells, including love charms.[41] However, a clear and complete overview of healers will not be available until further newspaper and periodical research is conduct for other areas of Spain. All the same, it is worth observing that the information available suggests that urban *curanderos* were not part-timers but made their living from healing, even though they sometimes had no fixed fees and only received what was known as the *voluntad*, voluntary payment in cash or kind.[42] The situation is less clear regarding rural *curanderos*.

Health professionals also reported on the existence of a specifically female category of folk healer who dealt with mother-and-child health. Although it is indeed mentioned, the use of magical procedures does not seem so important in references to this type of folk healers.[43] The main concern about these healers was their interference, based on the ignorance doctors attributed to women, during the birth[44] and, in particular, what was considered to be a very bad influence in the diet of children still on milk.[45]

In Catalonia, the huge folklore compilation made by Joan Amades provides a detailed and thorough study of a wide range of healers. He makes a distinction among those who really believed in their power and charged nothing for their performance and those who earned their living from healing. In Amades's opinion, both types were widespread, although he pays attention to those who considered their healing capacity as a 'gift' they obtained through different procedures. Amades classifies them in several groups depending on the activities they performed, though no precise information is provided about their relative importance and we cannot deduce how often the population resorted to them.[46] The fact that males prevailed among these folk healers is striking. As well as *saludadors*, who often did far more than cure rabies, there were *setens* (seventh sons); *xucladors* who were born on Saint Judas's Day and had the power to heal wounds by sucking on them; *endevinetes* born with the power to see inside the body to cure it; *caterins*, born on St Catherine's Day, who healed burns; *oracioners*, whose healing power was in proportion to the number of prayers they knew; *senyadors* who as well as citing incantations made the sign of the cross and marked the patient's ill area; *Samaires* who specialized in saying prayers that either gave luck or warned of the arrival of illness, and which could also be used negatively to make people emaciated.

The work by Amades is complemented by another Catalan folklorist, Cels Gomis.[47] He insists on the fact that the population trusted folk healers much more than doctors and cites numerous examples of these predominantly male healers' activities.[48] However, Gomis's work places more emphasis on the Catalan population's belief in the figure of the *bruixa* (female witch)[49] in the final years of the nineteenth century and the early years of the twentieth century. The witch was, according to the material collected by Gomis, a figure who could cure as well as cause illness. In fact, the main activities attributed to witches during the period under study in this chapter were those attributed to cunning-folk. He also underlines that all social classes asked for their help, including the aristocracy.[50]

The presence of these women who could ambivalently cause and fight illness is common in the writings of other authors. Witches – *sorguin/sorgui-ñak* in the Basque language – received special attention in the works of Barandiarán, the renowned Basque ethnologist.[51] Caro Baroja also dedicates a chapter of his well-known work to the role of Basque witches during the second third of the twentieth century.[52] As well as 'witches', *astue*, or cunning-folk, also practised as *curanderas*.[53] *Saludadores* are also mentioned in the Basque region.[54] Barriola points out that the presence of *curanderos* who used spells and other magical procedures were more visible in the rural milieu of the region and says that the area where they performed their activity was very restricted, while empirical *curanderos* with the ability to massage, make poultices and prescribe potions were the best known and usually lived on their curative activities.[55]

Turning to Alto Aragón, the area of the region nearest to the French border, we find scattered data about *curanderos* whose 'gift' was transmitted as an inheritance, and was usually complemented by manual procedures or those based on the preparation of poultices or herbal remedies.[56] One of these families of healers was 'los Castros', who specialized in sprains, fractures and dislocations, and who transmitted their power from parents to children, but only through the male line.[57] Although this type of healer is said to have been the most widespread in this northern part of the country, additional cases are mentioned of healers whose diagnostic and therapeutic methods were hardly empirical and were based above all on the 'gift'. One of them was Baltasar Ena Mosené, from Ayerbe, who practised during the first half of the twentieth century and who diagnosed by touching. He attributed his 'gift' to an apparition he saw when he was a child. His therapeutic methods did not rely much on magic and he preferred using massage. Others, like Maria de Gregorier de Curtillas, who practised in the early years of the century, claimed their saliva had magical properties.[58]

For Galicia, one can find numerous references to similar folk healers in various writings.[59] However, as in previous cases, these references are usually brief comments that only enable us to state that the role of these healers was very important in dealing with illness. However, in addition to the wealth of information provided in Victor Lis Quibén's work about healers who cured specific ailments, Lisón Tolosana's anthropological work contains a vast amount of information on the wider activities of folk healers in Galicia during the second half of the twentieth century, thus giving us a counterpoint which is revealing about the situation in previous decades.[60] In particular Lisón Tolosana provides a very detailed portrait of *bruxas* (witches) and *sabias* (cunning-women), which highlights the ambiguities reflected in their capacity to cause harm and illness as well as cure it – especially the *sabias*. These are mostly women, though some men perform these activities too. The ethnography-based description of the late 1960s and early 1970s characterizes them as women of a certain age who dealt with 'culture-bound syndromes'. Their therapeutic methods combined empirical and magical elements and, although the transmission of knowledge and therapies usually took place within the same family via women, what really matters once again is the fact of having a 'gift'. In the Galician material there is an emphasis placed on the ambiguity involved in the categories of *bruxas* and *sabia*. The latter tried to show that they were not harmful witches, but did not succeed completely. According to Lisón Tolosana, not every *sabia* was considered a witch, but every witch was considered a cunning-woman. Regarding the 119 examples of witches (twenty-seven males and ninety-two females) analysed by Lisón Tolosana, it is important to highlight that many of them started their activities while they were emigrants in South and Central America and they continued to practise their specialities when they came back to their home country.

Information is not so abundant for other areas of Spain, although data on female specialists known as *santiguadoras* in the Canary Islands is very detailed.[61] Otherwise there is some relevant source material regarding Asturias, Extremadura, Madrid and Andalucía.[62] Broader folkloric compilations about the whole of Spain, which cover the first four decades of the twentieth century, also inform us of the presence of fortune-tellers and bewitchers.[63] As explained above, it is difficult to give an accurate assessment of the degree to which people resorted to these types of healer, but judging by the importance the sources place on illnesses that could be caused by other people and which, therefore, required the services of this type of specialists for their treatment, the role of these healers must have been a significant one. The next section is dedicated to those ailments.

The illnesses

The evil eye and similar ailments

In all the sources that have been consulted a lot of attention is paid to ailments with a 'personalistic' etiology, in the sense used by the anthropologist George Foster.[64] The main examples are the evil eye and demonic possession (*meigallo, endemoniados* or *endemoniats*). Once again, it is difficult to assess whether this great attention is in direct proportion to the relevance these ailments had in the popular cultural repertoires concerning disease, or whether they were deliberately collected and highlighted because they were good examples of the presence of irrational elements in the popular world. This is particularly evident in material collected by doctors and folklorist doctors. Enrique Salcedo, writing in the 1890s, dedicated a long chapter to the evil eye in which detailed explanations were given for the impossibility of its reality from the point of view of medical science.[65] The popular resort to *curanderos* for a cure was also associated with high child mortality rates – a problem health professionals were preoccupied with at the time.[66] However, the fact that a number of later anthropological studies have highlighted the importance of the evil eye and possession in understanding illness among the Spanish population of the second half of the twentieth century seems to suggest they were also relevant in the period concerned.[67]

   Willem de Blécourt has underlined the inconsistency of studies in which the evil eye is isolated from research on witchcraft as well as the fact that explanations about this ailment are insufficient, even in the largest and most thorough works dedicated to it.[68] In the abundant Spanish sources there is a clear tendency to link evil eye and witchcraft. They also reveal numerous regional terms and variations with imprecise limits, which often make it difficult to distinguish culture-bound syndromes. *Mal de ojo* or *aojo* were generally used in those areas where Spanish was the only language spoken by the population, as in Extremadura and the Canary Islands, for example.[69] In Catalonia, however, they spoke about the *ullpress* within the somewhat larger concept of the *mal donat*, while *begizkoa* was used in the Basque Country and *mal de ollo* in Galicia, where considerable polysemy (multiple meanings) exists.[70]

The social relevance of the evil eye in the period is well attested to in a survey conducted on birth, pregnancy and death by the section of Moral and Political Sciences of Madrid's *Ateneo* in 1901–2.[71] Using the materials collected, not all of which were published at the time, Rafael Salillas produced a monograph that was entirely dedicated to the evil eye, in which he provided abundant information.[72] However, his comments on the prevalence of the belief are not in keeping with other folkloric compilations. This was because Salillas based his study exclusively on the answers received by the *Ateneo*, which led him to say incorrectly, for example, that the evil eye was very unusual in the Basque Country, Navarre, Aragón and Valencia.[73] Once again the problem of sources is revealed.

Although the evil eye could affect people of all ages, as well as animals and crops, most reports say that children were the most likely to suffer and die from it. Frequent discussions have taken place about whether the *aojo* was voluntary or involuntary, but what is most important to highlight is that, when trying to find possible causes of the illness, the population often believed that some people deliberately caused it using the power of the sight. It is the bewitchment component that is most important. Envy as an expression of personal conflicts in predominantly rural areas – which does not mean the belief was excluded from the urban milieu – and its materialization in the *aojo* or the *mal donat* are often present in many of the descriptions. The *aojo* was most frequently caused by women, who were commonly described in terms of the classic witch-stereotype – old, marginal, ugly and poor. Gypsy women were frequently cited as a habitual source of evil eye.

Given that the cause was considered supernatural, the elements used to cure and prevent it also incorporated the supernatural. Thus a wide range of amulets and charms were used, most notably the *higa* – where the thumb rises up between the ring and middle fingers, and the *evangelios*, a little cloth bag containing some verses from the gospels written on a piece of paper. The rituals used for the diagnosis of the ailment are also varied, but the most frequently cited is that in which oil drops are poured in a container with water, the subsequent behaviour of the drops telling whether the evil eye was present or not. The number of drops and what the oil is supposed to do are changing elements. What is perhaps most relevant in this context is that, despite the 'personalistic' etiology, it is apparently not always important to identify the person who had caused the evil eye. On many occasions it sufficed to have evidence of the fact that the illness was due to evil eye. On some occasions, though, it was indeed important to know who was responsible, as in some cases reported in Catalonia or Galicia.[74]

What leads to suspicions of evil eye is the exhibition of a series of very varied and even non-specific symptoms. The reports by medically educated people tend to associate the symptoms with a recognizable medical condition. Lis, for example, associated evil eye with deficiency diseases like rickets.[75] However, it is precisely the lack of specific symptoms that makes it difficult to distinguish evil eye from other culture-bound syndromes that sometimes present peculiar features but which, according to other accounts, represent a continuum in which it is difficult to differentiate one ailment from the rest. On the basis of his clinical and ethnographic experience, Lis himself often insists on this overlapping problem. He refers, for instance, to the *mal do aire* as a belief that is 'most widespread and vulgar, the one that is due to the most causes and the one with the widest range of symptoms'.[76] This polysemy often appears when it comes to giving names to this and various similar ailments. Take the *enganido*, for example.[77] This refers to an illness that is caused by the air emanating from objects, animals or people, which always has a supernatural origin based on the deliberate desire to cause harm. It is true that such etiologies are very wide; anything from pregnant women to the moon can trigger physical decay in others.[78] The moon is actually held to be responsible for a variety of this type of ailment, such as the *alunamiento* ('mooning') in Extremadura, which has been the subject of recent anthropological research.[79] Salillas also reflects on the problems of overlap between evil eye and similar 'entities' which had assumed a relevant role in various Spanish regions. This happened, for example, with the *mal de filu* in Asturias, in which the etiological process is similar to that of evil eye, but whose symptoms were apparently considered more serious.[80] The label used to name it refers to the thread with which the potentially ill person was measured in order to diagnose the presence of the ailment.[81]

Prevention, diagnosis and cure of these ailments, in which other people's will to cause harm may be present, involved the use of numerous amulets as well as rituals and avoidance behaviour. It is important to underline here the meticulousness with which some doctors illustrated, as richly as possible, every single aspect of popular actions linked with these illnesses. The aim of accumulating bizarre descriptions of the way the population responded to these ailments considered as 'imaginary', was to focus on the antagonistic relationship between the scientific progress doctors wanted to demonstrate and the perceived backwardness and gullibility that characterized popular beliefs and behaviour.

The endemoniados

Apart from the illnesses caused by the look or the influence of others, in which the bewitcher-victim-unwitcher triangle was more or less visibly present, there are others that could also be attributed to possession by demons or the spirits of the dead. This phenomenon, which is largely documented from the anthropological point of view in the Galicia of the late 1960s and the early 1970s also appears in various sources from the late nineteenth and early twentieth centuries.[82] It is also recorded in other regions like Aragón.[83] An outstanding example is that concerning the chapel of Zorita del Maestrazgo (Castellón), located in the intersection of the Valencia, Aragón and Catalonia.[84] Lisón mentions other sanctuaries and chapels that attracted those who considered themselves possessed: Santa María de Cervera (Lerida, Catalonia), Santa Orosia de Jaca, Torreciudad and the Monastery of Cillas (Huesca, Aragón), and finally the Santo Cristo of Calatorao and the Corporales of Daroca, both in the province of Saragossa.

Although Lis also highlights the overlapping between the *meigallo* or *ramo cativo* (the variant of the *endemoniados* in Galicia), and similar ailments we have already referred to above while dealing with evil eye, the truth is that what characterized the *endemoniados* was the fact that victims suffered the intrusion of demons or spirits, although that intrusion could be induced by another person, as with the evil eye. This is clearly explained in the sources, as, for instance, in some of the accounts from the late 1920s about the *endemoniats* of the sanctuary la Balma, whose journalistic structure confers upon them great value in accordance with recent re-evaluations.[85] The cause is not always directly related to individuals. Thus certain places (crossroads, paths, forests), certain times (around midnight), or simply on occasions when fear was felt, were circumstances believed to facilitate the invasion of demons or spirits. The solution to possession was often sought in visiting certain sacred sites, such as sanctuaries, chapels and monasteries, or *corpiños* as they are known in Galicia.[86] The name of *pastequeiros* was given to the experts in exorcising in Galicia (the exorcism they used being called *Pax tecun*). A thorough study was published by Lis about those who performed their activities in Santa Comba and San Cibrán.[87] They were all males. This was not always so, however, as shown in the case of the *caspolinas*, the female 'witches' who were in charge of exorcism ceremonies in la Balma (Zorita del Maestrazgo). These women took their name from Caspe (Saragossa), the locality they were supposed to come from, though they were actually native of other areas in Aragon.[88] The sources often refer to the stronger incidence of possession in women. Symptoms included restlessness, the tearing of their clothes, and the use of strange signs, such as the tying of bows.

The resort to sanctuaries and sacred sites in order to 'take out' the demons from the bodies of the 'possessed' easily fits in with wider popular religious behaviour, namely commending oneself to certain holy images or visiting sacred sites in search of a cure. The purely religious component is obviously more evident than the magical one here. In many of these cases, the cause of the illness was not necessarily considered 'supernatural', though God's power to send illness was widely acknowledged. This is the reason why I have not treated this topic, which, as has already been explained, shows very peculiar features and thus deserves a separate analysis.[89]

Other diseases cured by supernatural means
The medical and folkloric sources also describe many other magic-based
therapeutic procedures dedicated to treating diseases whose etiology was not
usually popularly associated with the supernatural. The ones that were by
far the most frequently cited concern children's hernias, erysipelas and warts,
though many other illnesses could be mentioned. The procedures used to
cure skin conditions such as warts and erysipelas were highly varied.[90] We
find more consistency, however, in the numerous references to the healing
methods for hernias.[91] The ritual, which consisted of passing the ill child
through a crack in a tree, the child being given and collected by people with
names such as Juan (John), María (Mary) or Pedro (Peter), always had to be
performed during the night of St John. After it had been performed, reciting
the corresponding prayer, of which numerous variations existed, the tree's
later 'behaviour' was the element that usually showed whether the healing
had taken place or not. This is yet another example of the abundant presence
of sympathetic magical elements in popular therapeutic procedures.

All the available evidence undoubtedly confirms the presence of considerable
belief in supernaturally-inspired illnesses and the resort to magical diagnostic
and therapeutic means of cure during the late nineteenth and early twentieth
centuries in Spain. Their significance in relation to other medical alternatives
is more difficult to assess. However, it can be deduced from doctors' efforts
to fight both folk healers and folk beliefs that they represented an important
hindrance to the hegemony doctors wanted to achieve in the management of
health and illness. Unfortunately, at present the sources we have used are
insufficient to gain better knowledge of the reasons for the presence of
magical elements in the management of health and disease, and of the
characteristics both of healers and of the population who visited them. Many
questions and issues remain unresolved. A sharper profile, for example, needs
to be drawn between the practices of urban and rural *curanderos.* More
attention must be dedicated to figures like the various kinds of cunning-
women and somnambulists, who appear only tangentially in the documents
we have consulted, and whose relevance elsewhere has been highlighted in
other studies like those by the editors of this volume. More generally, much
more research is required regarding questions of gender, which will shed
light on women's fundamental role in health and disease management. Moreover, in a country like Spain, regional diversity must definitely be taken into
account. Reaching general conclusions like those provided by Owen Davies
for England is simply impossible considering the basic research material that
has been considered so far for Spain.[92] It remains for the future to try and
learn why the magical element had acquired more or less relevance within
the cultural repertoires applied by the Spanish population in dealing with
illness. This will only be achieved when more thorough case studies provide

us with the context required to understand what really happened. The general survey offered in this chapter can only provide an initial guide to this complex matter.

Notes

1 I wish to thank Victor Pina for his translation into English and Josep M. Comelles for his help with the sources.
2 Marijke Gijswijt-Hofstra, Hilary Marland and Hans de Waardt, 'Introduction: Demons, Diagnosis and Disenchantment', in Marijke Gijswijt-Hofstra, Hilary Marland and Hans de Waardt (eds), *Illness and Healing Alternatives in Western Europe* (London, 1997), p. 1.
3 We must make clear at this stage that, the same as in other countries, this task is still far from complete in Spain. Research on magic and witchcraft in the early modern period has been abundant in recent years after the influence exerted one decade before by a work like that written by Julio Caro Baroja, *Las brujas y su mundo* (Madrid, 1961), as is attested by Ricardo García Cárcel in the prologue to one of the works belonging to this tradition: María Tausiet, *Ponzoña en los ojos. Brujería y Superstición en Aragón en el siglo XVI* (Zaragoza, 2000), pp. 7–17. In the specific case of the consideration of the supernatural when studying the conceptions of illness and the ways to face it, an additional element that makes the task more difficult in Spain is the excessive compartmentalization among disciplines such as History, History of Medicine and Social and Cultural Anthropology, which surely hinders fluent communication.
4 A standard account of this period can be found in Miguel Martínez Cuadrado, *Restauración y crisis de la monarquía (1874–1931)* (Madrid, 1991).
5 Juan Luis Carrillo edited a monographic study about the relationship between the 1898 crisis and medicine which was published in *Dynamis* 18 (1998) 21–314. See also the seminal work by Esteban Rodríguez Ocaña, *La constitución de la medicina social como disciplina en España (1882–1923)* (Madrid, 1987), pp. 9–51.
6 For overviews of rural health care from the point of view of health professionals, see Agustín Albarracín Teulón, 'La asistencia médica en la España rural durante el siglo XIX', *Cuadernos de Historia de la Medicina Española* 13 (1974) 123–204; Francisco Villacorta Baños. 'La opinión médica rural en 1924: resultados de una encuesta', *Estudios de Historia Social* 24–25 (1983) 165–85. See also Esteban Rodríguez Ocaña, 'Medicina y acción social en la España del primer tercio del siglo XX', in Carmen López Alonso (ed.), *4 siglos de acción social. De la beneficencia al bienestar social* (Madrid, 1985), pp. 246–62 and idem, 'La asistencia médica colectiva en España, hasta 1936', in José Álvarez Junco (ed.), *Historia de la acción social pública en España. Beneficencia y Previsión* (Madrid, 1990), pp. 321–59.
7 Rodríguez Ocaña, 'La asistencia médica', p. 331.
8 Rodríguez Ocaña, 'La asistencia médica', pp. 350–5.
9 Rodríguez Ocaña, 'La asistencia médica', pp. 336–50.
10 The expression is used in Llorenç Prats, *La Catalunya rància. Les condicions de vida materials de les classes populars a la Catalunya de la Restauració segons les topografies mediques* (Barcelona, 1996), pp. 210–36.
11 Willem de Blécourt, 'The Witch, her Victim, the Unwitcher and the Researcher: The Continued Existence of Traditional Witchcraft', in Bengt Akarloo and Stuart Clark (eds), *Witchcraft and Magic in Europe: The Twentieth Century* (Philadelphia, 1999), pp. 158–62; Owen Davies, 'Newspapers and the Popular Belief in Witchcraft and

Magic in the Modern Period', *Journal of British Studies* 37 (1998) 139–65; idem, *Witchcraft, Magic and Culture 1736–1951* (Manchester, 1999), pp. 168–74.

12 The dates of publication are, however, wider. Especially the Civil War (1936–39) acted as a distorting element and materials collected in the late 1920s or 1930s did not see the light until the 1940s or even much later.

13 Enrique Perdiguero, 'La "Fraternidad Médico-Farmacéutica. Revista Quincenal de Medicina, Cirugía y Farmacia" (Alacant, 1886–1888): la lluita per l'hegemonia en la gestió de la salut y la malaltia', in *Llibre d'Actes. Catorzè Congrés de Metges i Biòlegs de Llengua Catalana* (Palma, 1995), vol. 2, pp. 630–6. See also Agustín Albarracín Teulón, 'Intrusos, charlatanes, secretistas y curanderos. Aproximación sociológica al estudio de la asistencia médica extracientífica en la España del siglo XIX', *Asclepio* 24 (1972) 323–66.

14 An extensive but incomplete relation can be seen in Joan J. Pujadas, Josep Maria Comelles and Joan Prat, 'Una bibliografía comentada sobre Antropología Médica', in Michael Kenny and Jesús M. De Miguel (eds), *La Antropología Médica en España* (Barcelona, 1980), pp. 323–53.

15 See, for example, Angel Aguirre Baztán (ed.), *La Antropología cultural en España. Un siglo de Antropología* (Barcelona, 1986); idem, *Historia de la antropología española* (Barcelona, 1992); and Carmen Ortiz García and Luis Ángel Sánchez Gómez (eds), *Diccionario histórico de la antropología española* (Madrid, 1994).

16 Encarnación Aguilar Criado, *Cultura Popular y Folklore en Andalucía (Los orígenes de la Antropología)* (Seville, 1990).

17 See the characterization of the 'ideal types' of the different scholars of folklore in the diverse Spanish nationalities in Joan Prat i Carós, 'El discurso antropológico y el discurso folklórico en el Estado Español: un ensayo de caracterización', in *IV Congreso de Antropología* (Alicante, 1987, unpublished).

18 Ingrid Kuschick, *Volksmedizin in Spanien* (Münster, 1989). I have used the Spanish translation *Medicina popular en España* (Madrid, 1995). See pp. xv–xvi and 1.

19 The author of numerous publications of which the following are of most interest: Josep Maria Comelles, 'Medical Practice and Local Knowledge: The Role of Ethnography in the Medical Hegemony', in Yasuo Otsuka, Shizu Sakai and Shigehisa Kuriyama (eds), *Medicine and the History of the Body* (Tokyo, 1999), pp. 261–83; Josep Maria Comelles, 'De las supersticiones a la medicina popular. La transición de un concepto religioso a un concepto médico', in Xosé Manuel González Reboredo (ed.), *Medicina popular e Antropoloxía da Saúde* (Santiago de Compostela, 1997), pp. 247–80; and Angel Martínez Hernáez and Josep Maria Comelles, 'La medicina popular. ¿Los límites culturales del modelo médico?', *Revista de Dialectología y Tradiciones Populares* 64 (1994) 109–33.

20 Esteban Rodríguez Ocaña and Enrique Perdiguero, 'Ciencia y persuasión social en la medicalización de la infancia en España, Siglos XIX–XX', Practices of Healing in Modern Latin America and Spain Conference (New York, 2001, unpublished).

21 Elena Robles and Lucia Pozzi, 'La mortalidad infantil en los años de la transición: una reflexión desde las experiencias italiana y española', *Boletín de la ADEH* 15 (1997) 165–99.

22 Comelles draws his attention to the lack of information about behaviours which were not considered erroneous: Comelles, 'De las supersticiones a la medicina popular', pp. 275–6.

23 As has been highlighted from Medical Anthropology this label fell into the trap of considering Biomedicine as the 'golden standard'.

24 Relevant for this whole chapter is the discussion carried out by Kuschick, *Medicina popular*, pp. 130–7. Although the study refers to the present, because of

the materials used, some of its conclusions can more easily be applied to the early twentieth century.

25 See Gerda Bonderup, 'Danish Society and Folk Healers', in Robert Jütte, Motzi Eklöf and Marie C. Nelson (eds), *Historical Aspects of Unconventional Medicine* (Sheffield, 2001), pp. 76–7. As examples of papers about specific types of folk healers we can cite some works of the editors of this volume: Willem de Blécourt, 'Cunning Women, from Healers to Fortune Tellers', in Hans Binneveld and Rudolf Dekker (eds), *Curing and Insuring. Essays on Illness in Past Times: The Netherlands, Belgium, England and Italy, 16th–20th Centuries* (Hilversum, 1993), pp. 53–5; Willem de Blécourt, 'Witch Doctors, Soothsayers and Priests. On Cunning Folk in European Historiography and Tradition', *Social History* 19 (1994) 285–303; Owen Davies, *Cunning-Folk: Popular Magic in English History* (London, 2003); idem, 'Cunning-Folk in the Medical Market-Place During the Nineteenth Century', *Medical History* 43 (1999) 55–73; idem, *Witchcraft*, pp. 214–70.

26 Enrique Salcedo y Ginestal, *Madre e Hijo. Doctrina científica y errores vulgares en Obstetricia y Ginecología* (Madrid, 1898), p. 23.

27 'Intruders' were, in this context, people who were not, but passed themselves off as, health professionals; while *charlatanes* (quacks) are people who, with or without a title, devoted themselves to boasting about their healing skills. There was still another last group whom doctors were concerned about: the people who sold secret remedies, known as '*secretistas*'. See, about these different figures, Albarracín, 'Intrusos'. For example of studies in other countries see, among others, Roy Porter, *Health for Sale: Quackery in England, 1650–1850* (Manchester, 1989); Matthew Ramsey, *Professional and Popular Medicine in France, 1730–1830* (Cambridge, 1988).

28 Catalan diminutive used to indicate a physical disability.

29 Enrique Perdiguero, 'Healing Alternatives in Alicante, Spain, in the Late Nineteenth and Late Twentieth Centuries', in Gijswijt-Hofstra *et al.*, *Illness and Healing*, pp. 206–13.

30 *El Siglo Médico* XXXI (1884) 446. Cited by Albarracín, 'Intrusos', pp. 363–4.

31 *El Siglo Médico* XXXII (1885) 839. Cited by Albarracín, 'Intrusos', p. 364.

32 *Buenas Noches* (Alicante), 13 Dec. 1886. Dr Zechnas (Esteban Sánchez Santana), 'Siempre lo mismo', *La Fraternidad Médico-Farmacéutica* 16 (1887) 241–2; *Buenas Noches* (Alicante), 6 May 1887; *La Fraternidad Médico-Farmacéutica* 24 (1887) 369–72.

33 *El Constitucional* (Alicante), 7 Nov. 1885; *La Fraternidad Médico-Farmacéutica* 12 (1887), 177–8; Dr Zechnas, 'Siempre lo mismo', *El Semanario Católico* (Alicante), 26 May 1883, 307–8.

34 The concern about the abundance of folk healers in Madrid is reflected by folklorists themselves using the medical press as their source. See Luis de Hoyos Sainz and Nieves de Hoyos Sancho, *Manual de Folklore. La vida popular tradicional en España* (Madrid, 1947), p. 228.

35 Ramiro Ávila, *Medicina Rural*, 25 March 1882. Cited by Salcedo, '*Madre e Hijo*', p. 39; *El Siglo Médico* XXXIV (1887) 464. Cited by Albarracín, 'Intrusos', p. 365.

36 See José Miguel Sáez and Pedro Marset, 'Profesionales sanitarios en la Murcia del siglo XVIII. Número, evolución y distribución', *Asclepio* 45 (1993) 73; Enrique Perdiguero and Josep Bernabeu, 'La asistencia médica pública en el Alicante del siglo XVIII: los médicos de la ciudad', *Canelobre* 29–30 (1995) 166.

37 *La Fraternidad Médico-Farmacéutica* 16 (1887) 255–6.

38 Perdiguero, 'La "Fraternidad Médico-Farmacéutica"'.

39 *La Fraternidad Médico-Farmacéutica* 1 (1886) 16.

40 *La Fraternidad Médico-Farmacéutica* 11 (1887) 176.

41 *La Fraternidad Médico-Farmacéutica* 14 (1887) 209–12.

42 However, there are reports of clearly swollen fees like the 20 pesetas charged by the female healer from Alcoy for breaking a spell: *La Fraternidad Médico-Farmacéutica* 1 (1886) 16; *La Fraternidad Médico-Farmacéutica* 11 (1887) 176.
43 See for example, Salcedo, *Madre e hijo*, pp. 384–437.
44 See as an example Dr Zechnas (Esteban Sánchez Santana), 'Cuestión vital', *La Fraternidad Médico-Farmacéutica* 10 (1887) 145–7.
45 A classic formulation in this respect is that by Juan Aguirre Barrio, *Mortalidad en la primera infancia. Sus causas y medios de atenuarla* (Madrid, 1885), pp. 168–70. The work about Catalonia carried out through medical topographies also gives us abundant information about this phenomenon: Prats, *La Catalunya rància*, pp. 225–36.
46 Joan Amades, *Folklore de Catalunya* (Barcelona, 1969), vol. III, pp. 944–52.
47 Cels Gomis i Mestre, *La bruixa catalana. Aplec de casos de bruixeria, creences i supersticions recollits a Catalunya a l'entorn dels anys 1864 a 1915* (Barcelona, 1987).
48 Gomis, *La bruixa catalana*, p. 137.
49 I use 'witch' in English every time the word 'bruja' appears in the sources, which always conveys the connotation of causing harm and illness. The word for male witches is *bruixots*.
50 Gomis, *La bruixa catalana*, pp. 43, 87–9.
51 A compilation of his writings on this topic can be found in José Miguel Barandiarán, *Brujería y brujas en los relatos populares vascos* (San Sebastián, 1998). They are materials collected since 1921 in the Basque region.
52 Caro, *Las brujas y su mundo*, pp. 280–97. This work, originally published in 1961, has been translated into the main European languages.
53 José Miguel de Barandiarán, 'Paleoetnografía vasca', in *Obras Completas* (Bilbao, 1975), vol. V, pp. 256 and 278.
54 Ignacio María Barriola, *La Medicina Popular en el País Vasco* (San Sebastián, 1952), pp. 125–33.
55 Barriola, *La Medicina Popular*, pp. 17, 135–51. See also the same author's book dedicated to one of these healers who performed his activities in the early nineteenth century and whose descendants continued to practise until the twentieth century: Ignacio María Barriola, *El curandero Petrequillo* (Salamanca, 1983).
56 Rafael Andolz, *De pilmadores, curanderos y sanadores en el Alto Aragón* (Zaragoza, 1987), pp. 39–43, 53–5.
57 Andolz, *De pilmadores*, pp. 11–15.
58 Andolz, *De pilmadores*, pp. 81–8.
59 Among others: Bernardo Barreiro, *Brujos y astrólogos de la Inquisición de Galicia y el famoso Libro de San Cipriano* (Madrid, [1885] 1973), pp. 52, 88, 94–5, 108, 126; Víctor Lis Quibén, *La Medicina Popular en Galicia* (Pontevedra, 1949), pp. 15, 18; Jesús Rodríguez López, *Supersticiones de Galicia y preocupaciones vulgares*, (8th edn, Lugo, [1895] 1979), p. 158.
60 Carmelo Lisón Tolosana, *Brujería, estructura social y simbolismo en Galicia* (Madrid, 1983). More data can be found in Carmelo Lisón Tolosana, *Las brujas en la Historia de España* (Madrid, 1992), pp. 299–350.
61 José Pérez Vidal, 'Contribución al estudio de la medicina popular canaria', *Tagoro* 1 (1949) 31, 35, 72; Domingo García Barbuzano, *Prácticas y creencias de una santiguadora canaria* (10th edn, Gran Canaria, 1998); idem, *La brujería en Canarias* (6th edn, Tenerife, Gran Canaria, 1997), pp. 75–105.
62 Eugenio Olavarría y Huarte, 'El Folk-lore de Proaza', in Antonio Machado y Álvarez (ed.), *Biblioteca de las tradiciones populares españolas* (Madrid, 1885), vol. 8, pp. 231, 273; Isabel Gallardo de Álvarez, 'Medicina popular y supersticiosa. Mal de ojo', *Revista de Estudios Extremeños* 1–2 (1947) 182–3; Eugenio Olavarría y Huarte, 'El Folk-lore de

Madrid', in Antonio Machado y Álvarez (ed.), *Biblioteca de las tradiciones populares españolas*, (Madrid, 1884) vol. 2, pp. 86–7; Luis Montoto, 'Costumbres populares andaluzas', in Antonio Machado y Álvarez (ed.), *Biblioteca de las tradiciones populares españolas* (Seville, 1883), vol. 1, pp. 90–1. Alejandro Guichot y Sierra, 'Supersticiones populares andaluzas', in *El Folk-lore andaluz* (1881–82), pp. 271–2, 418 (facsimile edn, Seville and Madrid, 1981).

63 Hoyos and Hoyos, *Manual de Folklore*, pp. 207–10, 228.

64 George M. Foster, 'Disease Etiologies in Non-Western Medical Systems', *American Anthropologist* 78 (1976) 773–82.

65 Salcedo, *Madre e Hijo*, pp. 759–821.

66 Salcedo, *Madre e Hijo*, p. 819.

67 In addition to the rich material provided by Lisón in *Brujería*, numerous studies have been carried out that are collected in the bibliographical references of the work by Antón Erkoreka, *Begizkoa. Mal de ojo* (Bilbao, 1995), pp. 38, 153–67. We ourselves have been able to check the importance of evil eye when it came to facing children's diseases in the south of the current province of Alicante: Enrique Perdiguero, 'El mal de ojo: de la literatura antisupersticiosa a la Antropología Médica', *Asclepio* 28 (1986) 47–71.

68 De Blécourt, 'The Witch' , pp. 192–7; Alan Dundes (ed.), *The Evil Eye: A Casebook* (Madison, 1992); Amica Lykiropoulos, 'The Evil Eye: Towards an Exhaustive Study', *Folklore* 92 (1981) 221–30; Clarence Maloney (ed.), *The Evil Eye* (New York, 1976).

69 Gallardo, 'Medicina popular'; Pérez, 'Contribución', p. 78. See also the information collected by Kuschick, *Medicina Popular*, pp. 21–3, 34–7, 44–7, 58–9, 112–29.

70 Amades, *Folklore*, vol. 3, pp. 933–44; Gomis, *La bruixa catalana*, pp. 141–2, 149; Resurrección María de Azkue, *Euskaleriaren Yakintza. Literatura popular del País Vasco*, (2nd edn, Madrid, 1959), pp. 121–7; Barandiarán, 'Paleoetnografia Vasca', pp. 288–96; Lis, *La Medicina Popular*, pp. 89–110; Vicente Risco, 'Apuntes sobre el mal de ojo en Galicia', *Revista de Dialectología y Tradiciones populares* 17 (1961) 66–92.

71 See the annotations in Antonio Limón Delgado and Eulalia Castellote, *Costumbres populares en los tres hechos más característicos de la vida, nacimiento, matrimonio y muerte (1901–1902). Edición crítica de la información promovida por la Sección de Ciencias Morales y Políticas del Ateneo de Madrid* (Madrid, 1990), 2 vols; and numerous editions have been published of the materials corresponding to specific regions among which it is worth highlighting, for the quality of the report, the annotated edition of Antonio Bethencourt Alfonso, *Costumbres populares canarias de nacimiento, matrimonio y muerte* (Santa Cruz de Tenerife, 1985). For a contextualization of this survey, see Carmelo Lisón Tolosana, 'Una gran encuesta de 1901–1902. Notas para una historia de la Antropología en España', in idem (ed.), *Antropología social en España* (Madrid, 1971), pp. 91–171; and also Ángel Aguirre Batzan, 'La antropología cultural en España. Un siglo de antropología', in Aguirre Baztán, *La Antropología cultural en España*, pp. 36–8.

72 Rafael Salillas y Panzano, *La Fascinación en España. Estudio hecho con la información promovida por la Sección de Ciencias Morales y Políticas del Ateneo de Madrid* (Madrid, 1905).

73 Salillas, *La Fascinación*, p. 21.

74 Gomis, *La bruixa catalana*, pp. 142–4; Risco, 'Apuntes', pp. 89–90; Lis, *La Medicina Popular*, pp. 97–8.

75 Lis, *La Medicina Popular*, p. 95.

76 Lis, *La Medicina Popular*, p. 31. Throughout his monograph on witchcraft in Galicia, Lisón also repeatedly insists on the topic of overlapping.

77 Barreiro, *Brujos y astrólogos*, pp. 64–5; Marcial Valladares, 'Medicina popular', in

Antonio Machado y Álvarez (ed.), *Biblioteca de las tradiciones populares españolas* (Madrid, 1884), vol. IV, p. 129; Kuschick, *Medicina popular*, pp. 17–21.

78 Lis, *La Medicina Popular*, pp. 33–4.

79 See Yolanda Guío Cerezo, 'El influjo de la luna: acerca de la salud y la enfermedad en dos pueblos extremeños', *Asclepio* 40 (1988) 317–41; Salillas, *La Fascinación*, pp. 46–7; Gallardo, 'Medicina popular', p. 186.

80 Salillas, *La Fascinación*, pp. 45–7.

81 Another example of this ailment can be found in Salcedo, *Madre e Hijo*, pp. 682–3.

82 Carmelo Lisón Tolosana, *Demonios y exorcismos en los siglos de oro* (Madrid, 1990), pp. 8–9; Lis, *La Medicina Popular*; Rodríguez, *Supersticiones de Galicia*, pp. 204, 215, 233–6, 251–2.

83 Andolz, *De pilmadores*, pp. 92–3; Antonio Castillo de Lucas, 'Los endemoniados', *Clínica y laboratorio* 42 (1946) 447.

84 Alardo Prats y Beltrán, *Tres días con los endemoniados. La España desconocida y tenebrosa* (Barcelona, 1999). The original edition was published in Madrid in 1929.

85 Álvar Monferrer, *Els endimoniats de la Balma* (Valencia, 1997).

86 Carmelo Lisón Tolosana, *Endemoniados en Galicia hoy* (Madrid, 1990), pp. 5–65. In general, all sanctuaries in Galicia that specialized in the *endemoniados* (possessed) were and are known as *corpiños*, and the ailment itself is called 'mal de corpiño'.

87 Lis, *La Medicina Popular*, pp. 239–57.

88 Prats, *Tres días*, p. 100.

89 See, on this subject, the classic study by William A. Christian Jr, *Religiosidad popular: estudio antropológico en un valle español* (Madrid, 1978). In this context are also of interest works on ex-votos, numerous at present; see, as an example, Salvador Rodríguez Becerra and José María Vazquez Soto, *Exvotos de Andalucía: milagros y promesas en la religiosidad popular* (Seville, 1980).

90 Information about them can be found, among other works, in: Amades, *Folklore de Catalunya*, pp. 997–8, 1005–6; Barandiarán, 'Paleoetnografía vasca', p. 269; Gomis, *La bruixa catalana*, pp. 135, 152–3; Guichot, 'Supersticiones populares andaluzas', pp. 296–7, 412, 417; Pérez, 'Contribución al estudio de la medicina popular canaria', pp. 47–8, 72; Salcedo, *Madre e hijo*, pp. 744–6 . See also Kuschick, *Medicina popular*, pp. 62–3.

91 See, for example, Barandiarán, 'Paleoetnografía vasca', p. 283; Barreiro, *Brujos y astrólogos*, pp. 227–8; Gomis, *La bruixa catalana*, p. 186; Sergio Hernández, 'Supersticiones populares', in idem, *El Folk-lore fexenense y bético-exteremeño 1883–1884* (facsimile edn, Seville, 1988), pp. 136–7; Pérez, 'Contribución', 73–6; Rodríguez, *Supersticiones de Galicia*, p. 137; Salcedo, *Madre e hijo*, pp. 699–703. See also Kuschick, *Medicina popular*, pp. 26–7.

92 Davies, *Witchcraft, Magic and Culture*, pp. 271–93.

8

Witchcraft, healing and vernacular magic in Italy

Sabina Magliocco

Field notes, 29 October 2001: Bessude, Sardinia. I am walking in the country-side outside this highland pastoral town of 500 inhabitants with Mario, a shepherd in his mid-forties, and his cousin Pina, whom I have known for approximately fifteen years. Mario is telling us how his grandfather taught him and his cousins, Tonino and Basiliu, to charm warts when they were working for him as *terrakos* (tenant-shepherds) in the 1970s. 'I didn't know you could cure warts too; I thought it was just *giaio* (grandpa) and Uncle Basiliu,' exclaims Pina. 'He taught all of us this *meikina* (medicine) before he died. He couldn't die until he had passed it on,' Mario explains. 'Does the cure consist of *berbos* ('words', a spell) or are there also actions and herbs that you use?' I want to know. 'Only words,' says Mario. 'But does it work?' asks Pina. 'It depends; sometimes,' he replies. He tells us how he recently cured a friend who called him on the phone from Rome to ask for a healing; but he also showed us warts on his own hands that he has not been able to charm away. When I ask him what the words are, he says he believes the cure must remain secret, because passing it on means passing on the power to heal. 'There were lots of people in the village who knew *berbos* for things: to make birds leave a newly-sown field, or to make dogs go away,' he explains. 'How about keeping eagles away from the lambs?' I ask, thinking of spells I have read in folklorists' collections. 'For that you need a gun,' he says, deadpan.

While the last formal accusations of witchcraft in Italy took place around 1750, and by the early nineteenth century Enlightenment discourses had relegated supernatural beliefs to 'superstition' among the educated elite and the clergy, vernacular religion and folk belief were far from dead in Italy. Legend complexes about witches and related beings flourished well into the twentieth century, and folk healers continue to practise their craft in both urban and rural areas. In this chapter, I will give a general overview of vernacular magical beliefs and practices in Italy from the time of unification to the present, with particular attention to how these traditions have been studied. It is my contention that while many ethnologists have made these practices the focal point of their studies, certain crucial aspects have been ignored or silenced due to the biases of the researchers. I would like to argue for a more experience-centred approach to the study of Italian vernacular religion and belief – one rooted in careful attention to practice, embodied experience and the role of these aspects in daily life, in addition to factors of historicity and power. Only by examining the role of these practices in their entire context can we come to a fuller understanding of what they mean to their practitioners.

Witch beliefs, folk healing and the legend complexes related to them have generally been studied as aspects of 'folk', 'unofficial' or 'popular' belief or religion. But as Leonard Primiano notes, these terminologies presuppose the existence of a hierarchical, dualistic system in which 'official' religion or belief, sanctioned and adopted by the hegemony, has primacy over 'folk', 'popular' and 'unofficial' systems, which are then viewed as inferior or illegitimate.[1] According to Primiano, the assumption that such practices exist separate from hegemonic practices is inaccurate, since the continuum between official and unofficial religion and belief is fluid and varies according to context. Further, he asserts that this terminology has led to a devaluation of 'folk' belief and a denigration of popular practices.[2] He proposes instead the use of the term 'vernacular' to describe the dynamic process of lived religion and belief.[3] In this chapter, I am adopting Primiano's use of the term 'vernacular' and broadening its application beyond the study of religion to include magic. By 'vernacular religion', therefore, I mean the entire range of lived religion, with its complement of material, verbal and behavioural manifestations. By coining the term 'vernacular magic' after Primiano's 'vernacular religion', I am rejecting the dualistic system of 'high magic' versus 'low magic', on the grounds that these, too, constitute an artificial separation of complex, dynamic practices that cut across lines of class and power within a single society.[4] Of course, power relationships do profoundly influence belief and practice; my adoption of the term 'vernacular' is not meant to deny this, but rather to call attention to how particular individuals shape their own beliefs and practices in response to their social position, as well as to the many ways that vernacular religion and magic can both contest and reinforce power relations in a society.

It is problematic to speak about an 'Italian' vernacular religion or magic before 1861. Italy achieved statehood in 1861 after a thirteen-year struggle known as the *Risorgimento*. Previously, it was made up of a patchwork of Papal States, principalities and kingdoms without a common language or government. The area we now recognize as Italy spanned areas vastly different in culture, dialect and belief. Nevertheless, there was a certain commonality in vernacular magic and religion that also extended to other areas in Europe. It is perhaps more useful to look at the development of broad culture areas within which one can find a certain range of traits: northern Italy, comprising the regions along the Alps and the coastal Venezia-Giulia; central Italy, consisting of areas in Emilia-Romagna, Tuscany, and the northern sections of Umbria and Lazio; and southern Italy, from Civitavecchia (just north of Rome) down to the tip of the boot, including the islands of Sicily and Sardinia. Of course, within these divisions, there exist even finer boundaries, so that each individual region, city, town and small village has its own unique dialect and culture. Italy is part of a broader geographic and cultural region encompassing the western Mediterranean; within this area, regional cultures form distinct clusters. Thus Italy is by no means homogenous, and any generalizations about an 'Italian' vernacular culture need to be treated with great caution.

After Italian unification in 1861, the cultures and traditions of rural peasants in the twenty regions of the new nation-state became the focus of an emergent field of study, variously called *storia delle tradizioni popolari* (the history of popular traditions), *etnologia* (ethnology), *demologia* (the study of the common people), or *antropologia culturale* (cultural anthropology). Over the course of the late nineteenth and twentieth centuries, these studies drew predominantly from two interpretive strains: survivalist theories and Gramscian materialism. I will argue that while there is much to be said for the deep historicity of many Italian folk practices, and their rootedness in systems of social and economic oppression, these scholarly approaches, embedded as they are in Enlightenment discourses of progressivism, ultimately failed to address the spiritual meaning of the practices. I will argue instead for an experience-centred approach to folk practice that allows us to view it as an integral part of the individual experience of the numinous. Of course, any attempt to convey an overview of not only vernacular practices, but also the ways in which they have been studied, is bound to be limited in scope, especially in a brief article. Italian folklore scholarship spans over one hundred years and twenty separate regions; this overview cannot pretend to be comprehensive. However, for English readers interested in Italian folk magic and popular religion, I hope I can provide a point of departure from which to evaluate existing sources and discover new ones.

The study of Italian vernacular religion and magic

Most of the data on which my chapter is based were collected by Italian ethnologists and folklorists between 1880 and 1980, with interruptions during the First and Second World Wars. The study of folklore is never a politically neutral act, however. The kinds of materials collected, and the ways they were presented, were conditioned by the preconceived notions of the scholars collecting them. Italian unification in 1861 was followed by a great wave of urbanization, especially among the elite and middle classes,

who sought in the life of the cities and the new capital a level of cosmopoli-
tanism and sophistication unavailable in rural areas. This movement led to a
surge of Italian nationalism, and a new focus, partly born of nostalgia, on
what came to be called *tradizioni popolari*, popular or folk traditions. Italians
located the source of their national identity and cultural authenticity in the
Classical period, the last time the peninsula had existed as a unified entity
under the aegis of the Roman Empire. Early Italian scholars sought in folklore
some kind of link to that Classical past, as well as to that other touchstone
of Italian national identity, the Renaissance, in order to show that contemporary Italian culture carried on an ancient, uninterrupted tradition that
legitimized the existence of the state.

The early collectors worked from an evolutionary premise. They assumed
that the practices of the Italian peasant class were remnants of an ancient,
'primitive' belief system dating back to pre-Classical times, which was des-
tined to disappear as its bearers became 'civilized'. Their attitudes ranged
from the affectionate respect that Sicilian collector Giuseppe Pitrè brought
to his informants, most of whom were also his medical patients, to the disdain
of Giuseppe Bellucci, the title of whose 1919 work *Il feticismo primitivo in
Italia e le sue forme di adattamento (Primitive Fetishism and its Adaptations in
Italy)* speaks for itself.[5] While the work of early collectors has left us a wealth
of material, including proverbs, charms, spells, cures and narratives, these
scholars made few attempts to understand the role of magical belief systems
and practices in the context of the lives of rural agricultural workers. Instead,
they often preferred to compare them with the customs of ancient civiliza-
tions, so they could 'prove' an uninterrupted oral transmission of culture from
Classical times to the founding of the Italian state. Beliefs and practices were
presented as fragmentary and incomplete, not as parts of the integrated belief
systems of individuals and small communities. They were also stigmatized
as the ignorant productions of a peasant underclass. Because most early
collectors were men, their concerns reflect those of their male informants.
So, for example, we have a great many reports from men about women's
power to bind with potent love spells, but we do not know whether this
reflects women's actual behaviour, or men's fears and anxieties. More significant still is the absence of ethnographic attention to women's ecstatic
traditions connected to saints' cults. It was not until the 1970s that women
began to enter the ethnological professions in greater numbers, and conduct
fieldwork centred around women's issues, that more information on women's
actual practices became available.

Survivalist perspectives flourished well into the Fascist period in Italy
(1922–44), supported by a government whose political interests were served
by the projection of contemporary cultural praxes into a gloriously imagined
past. But, ultimately, survivalist perspectives were themselves rejected as
outdated after the Second World War, as scholarship began to reflect a

greater interest in contemporary social conditions and issues of power im-
balances between the industrialized north and the underdeveloped *Meridione*
(south) in the developing nation-state. It was the Socialist writer Antonio
Gramsci, who was imprisoned by Mussolini, who most strongly influenced
the post-Second World War generation of Italian ethnologists. Gramsci's
writings on folklore were brief, but significant, for they moved Italian
ethnology away from survivalism at last. For him, folklore was not a 'survival'
that was quickly disappearing, but an integral part of the cultures of rural
Italian peasants, and a product of particular historical and cultural circumstances, and worthy of study in its own right alongside literature and history.
In genres such as festivals and celebrations, he saw emergent forms of peasant
resistance – clever, creative ways the rural underclass subtly undermined the
power that the hegemony exercised over their daily lives. Following Karl
Marx, Gramsci saw folklore as part of the 'superstructure' of society – those
forms and accretions that grow out of particular economic configurations. He
also believed that folklore, especially certain forms of folk belief and magical
practice, were a kind of 'false consciousness' that ultimately blinded peasants
to the forces that oppressed them by hiding the real sources of domination
under a veil of mysticism. So while Gramsci idealized folklore as peasant
resistance, and sought to legitimize its study as a form of culture in its own
right, he also saw popular religiosity and magical practice as ultimately
crippling, a relic of the past that needed to be discarded to bring about a
more equal distribution of power in society.

This philosophy was very much at the heart of the work of two great
Italian folklore scholars of the mid-twentieth century: Alberto Maria Cirese
and Ernesto De Martino. Cirese expanded upon Gramsci's theories of folklore,
urging its study as part of subaltern culture that existed in contraposition to
the hegemony of church and state. De Martino was interested in documenting
and analysing Italian magical practice to understand thoroughly how magic
worked within the economic, cultural and historical context in which it
existed. Thus his groundbreaking studies of the evil eye belief complex and
tarantismo emphasize peasants' captivity in a system of social relations rooted
in economic, social and gender oppression. Still, despite De Martino's own
origins in Naples, centre extraordinaire of the occult in southern Italy, and
his deep knowledge of ethnology, he and his followers, like Cirese, saw magic
as primarily a tool of the poor and weak, a form of resistance against
systematic forms of domination that was ultimately unsuccessful. They
assumed that as economic opportunities became available to the subaltern
class, folk magical practices would cease to exist.

Both the survivalist perspective and the Marxian attention to materialist
context made important contributions to the understanding of folk magical
practices by emphasizing their historical continuity with earlier systems of
thought, and their relationship to systems of power and domination. However,

both approaches ultimately failed to address the deeply spiritual nature these practices had for their practitioners. This spiritual significance is, I suspect, the reason why despite the disappearance of Italy's grinding poverty and backwardness by the mid-twentieth century, vernacular magical practice has persisted, albeit in mutated forms. Nor are its manifestations limited to underdeveloped rural areas. As ethnologist Cecilia Gatto Trocchi has shown, urban centres are now the sites of a variety of occult and esoteric practices, from traditional fortune-telling to New Age religious movements, which are rooted in earlier systems of magic and healing.[6] Today, a new generation of seekers is reviving old practices such as *tarantismo* as a way of affirming local and regional identities in an increasingly globalized Europe.[7]

The context of Italian vernacular magic

Italian vernacular magic is rooted in a world-view that developed in small-scale communities where life was difficult and precarious. Until after the Second World War, the majority of the Italian population were *contadini* (peasants) who resided mostly in small, agricultural towns and villages. Rural conditions varied widely depending on the region, but for most *contadini*, living conditions were harsh. Many lived under feudal conditions as virtual serfs to powerful landowners. Life in small-scale communities involved intense social relations which often became strained, leading to quarrels, feuds and mutual suspicions between neighbours. Witch belief and accusations of witchcraft must be understood as part of this political and social climate. As Davies and Favret-Saada have demonstrated, such accusations flourish in communities where inhabitants live in close proximity with one another and have histories of conflicts and disagreements.[8]

Another factor contributing to witch beliefs and accusations was lack of access to basic health care and sanitation. Malaria, tuberculosis and typhoid fever were endemic in much of rural Italy before the First World War; in addition, many suffered from congenital blood disorders such as thalassemia and favism. Medical doctors were rare and expensive until 1866, when government-funded physicians were stationed in every small town and hamlet. Still, ordinary people relied on folk healers to cure their ailments and on local midwives to deliver their babies. These women often had extensive knowledge of herbs and their uses, and were able to alleviate a number of minor illnesses, although they could do nothing against life-threatening diseases. There was a sense that life was a precarious enterprise, full of dangers at every turn; magic was one of many protective strategies people employed to ensure their survival and that of their family members. Against this background, most people maintained a magical view of the world.

Vernacular religion played an important part in people's attempts to ameliorate their situations. Before Italian unification, the Catholic Church was the most important institution common to all Italians. Catholicism penetrated deeply into the fabric of everyday life, dividing both the year cycle and the life cycle into a series of rites and celebrations that accompanied the individual from cradle to grave. Invocations to the saints, prayers and the use of holy water and sacred objects were an important part of magical practice. Popular saints' cults and celebrations often had at their core both a *promessa*, or promise of devotion in exchange for good health, and an ecstatic component that could involve dancing, drumming, and extraordinary efforts on behalf of the saint that resulted in participants achieving alternate states of consciousness. These states played an important role in individual spirituality – one that has sometimes been overlooked by researchers. In my fieldwork, I observed that some individuals were deeply and spiritually attracted to religiosity. These people often became involved in religious fraternities and sororities which maintained various calendar customs and saints' shrines, while at the same time running a lively practice in folk healing on the side. Both aspects of their practice could involve ecstatic states. They did not see their practices as incompatible, since they were part of a logical continuum of vernacular religiosity. Priests, as representatives of the power hierarchy within the Catholic Church, often frowned upon (and continue to disparage) such activities; but this never seemed to trouble the spiritual individuals I interviewed. Italians have always harboured a rather healthy anti-clericalism and distrust of institutions and their representatives, and they were able to insert the priest's disapproval into this larger framework of understanding and view it with irony and scepticism.

The folkloric witch

Belief in witchcraft – that is, that certain individuals, both male and female, had supernatural powers to heal or harm – was once widespread in all regions of Italy. The witch has always been an ambiguous figure in the popular imagination. On one hand, the witch was essential as a healer and unbewitcher in a society that had little access to, and much distrust of, formal medicine. Yet witches were also feared for their supernatural powers and their reputed ability to do harm. Witches were therefore both real individuals living in communities and frightening supernatural figures, and these categories overlapped considerably in people's minds, sometimes giving rise to specific accusations of witchcraft. It is clear that many activities attributed to witches were folkloric in nature – that is, no living member of any community, even traditional magic-workers, practised them. Following Davies's recent work on witch belief in Britain I call these the province of the 'folkloric witch' – the supernatural figure of legends and folktales.[9] The word *strega* (plural *streghe*), from the Latin *strix*, 'screech-owl', is often used in Italian to refer to the folkloric witch, and the word has ancient negative connotations. Pliny the Elder wrote about *striges* (plural of *strix*), women who could transform into birds of prey by means of magic, and who would fly at night looking for infants in their cradles to slaughter.[10]

The folkloric witch appears predominantly in legends (accounts about supernatural events that were told as true) and folk tales (purely fictional accounts set in a magical world). In Italian folklore she is usually female. Folkloric witches perform feats that are obviously supernatural: they transform into animals; fly through the night sky on the backs of goats; tangle people's hair in their sleep; steal milk from nursing mothers and livestock; suck blood from living beings; and torment their enemies by paralysing them in their beds at night.[11] By the nineteenth century, the legend of the walnut tree of Benevento (near Naples) as a gathering place for witches was well known throughout much of the peninsula. Folkloric witches' activities sometimes overlap with those of fairies and the dead: in Italian folklore, noisy night raids and circle-dancing in the cemetery or church square are attributed to all three. There are important distinctions, too, between witches and fairies. Giuseppe Pitrè reported that Sicilian peasants distinguished between the vampiric, maleficent witch (*stria, nserra*) and the *donna di fuori*. Sicilian *donne di fuori* ('women from the outside') or *belle signore* ('beautiful ladies') documented by Pitrè are creatures somewhere between fairies and witches.[12] They appear as beautiful women who can enter homes at night through the keyhole. If all is in order, they reward the householders, but they punish dirt and disorder; however, too much attention from the *donne di fuori* can cause illness, especially in infants.[13] A similar distinction is made in Sardinia between *cogas* (lit. 'cooks'), maleficent witches who are said to spiritually cook and eat the bodies of their victims, who slowly decline in health and die; and *janas* (from Latin *Dianas*, 'followers of Diana', cf. Neapolitan *janare*), beautiful women who live in Neolithic shaft tombs, are expert spinners and weavers, and can on occasion intermarry with humans.[14]

Clearly, the folkloric witch is fictional; she represents an embodiment of rural people's worst fears, and her actions do not correspond to any real folk practices documented by ethnographers. Nevertheless, the presence of this character in Italian folklore from all regions indicates the ambivalent feelings villagers had towards those who practised traditional magic and who just *might* be dangerous *streghe*.

Il Malocchio, or the evil eye, and its relations

Much of Italian vernacular magic and healing centres around the evil eye belief complex, a set of interrelated beliefs and practices focused around the idea that an individual can psychically harm another person through the gaze.[15] Anthropologists have commonly treated the evil eye belief complex as a problem separate from witchcraft; but the two belief complexes are clearly interrelated.[16] The evil eye belief complex encompassed a range of phenomena, from the often inadvertent *jettatura* or *malocchio* (evil eye) to more intentional magical attacks, known as *attaccatura* ('attachment'), *fascino* or *legatura* ('binding'), and *fattura* ('fixing').[17] Afflicting someone with the evil eye could happen accidentally, and did not always signify that the guilty party was a witch; but trafficking in the more complex forms of ritual magic necessary to bind or fix involved greater magical knowledge and intent, and was often attributed to witches and folk healers.

The evil eye belief complex is one of the most widespread in the world, spanning the area from the western Mediterranean to North Africa, the Middle East and Central Asia. According to most scholarship the evil eye is the envious eye.[18] The harsh economic conditions under which most peasants struggled gave rise to a world-view of 'limited good' in which the good in the world (fertility, prosperity, etc.) was thought to exist only in limited quantity.[19] Therefore, whatever good one had was at the expense of one's neighbour, and vice versa. In the dry Mediterranean climate, good was often associated with moisture and fecundity, while dryness signified barrenness.[20] This symbolic system extended to the human body: youth was relatively 'wet', while old age was 'dry', and bodily fluids such as semen, milk and blood were symbols of the capacity to reproduce and nurture. Those in a condition of 'wetness', or fecundity, were particularly vulnerable to the envious looks of strangers because they had what others did not; newborn babies, young livestock, new brides, pregnant women and nursing mothers were thought to be especially susceptible. Conversely, those who had cause to feel envy were thought to be able to give the evil eye. In Naples, priests – men who had renounced sexuality and fatherhood – and hunchbacked women, who suffered from a disability that perhaps had made them less than desirable marriage partners, were avoided because they were believed to be intrinsic casters of the evil eye, or *jettatori* in Neapolitan.

The evil eye can also be given accidentally just by admiring something. When I was in Sardinia, I was cautioned never to express admiration for any living thing without taking pains to remove any evil eye I might have inadvertently placed upon it by touching it and saying '*che Dio lo/la benedica*', 'may God bless him/her/it'. The evil eye can also be avoided by ritually spitting (no saliva is ejected, but a 'p' sound is made three times with the lips) after admiring something, symbolically demonstrating one's possession of surplus bodily fluids to avert the drying powers of envy.

There are literally thousands of spells to turn back the evil eye in Italian folklore. Many, appropriately enough, involve water: typically, some matter (wheat seeds, salt, oil, or molten lead) is dropped into a bowl of water and the resulting shapes are interpreted to see whether an 'eye' forms. This diagnosis is often the cure as well, although some cures also involve prayers, such as this one collected by De Martino in Colobraro (Lucania):

Affascine ca vaie pe' la via
da _____ *non ci ire*
che è bona nata
battezzata, cresimata
A nome de Ddie
e della Santissima Trinitate

Fascino going along the way
don't go to _____
for she is well-born
baptized and christened
in the name of God
and the Holy Trinity [21]

Often, mothers and grandmothers knew how to resolve simple cases of the evil eye at home, since children often fell prey to this ailment. More complicated cases required the intervention of a folk healer or specialist. It was far preferable to prevent the evil eye in the first place by using amulets, and Italian folk culture, from ancient times forward, is rife with these devices.

Amulets and protective devices

Since the evil eye is fundamentally about the lack of fecundity, it should not be surprising that some of the oldest amulets against it are symbols of fertility and regeneration. The most obvious of these is the phallus. The phallus was a common motif in Roman art and sculpture, where its purpose was to bring good luck. This custom has persisted in charms and amulets found throughout Italy in the nineteenth and twentieth centuries. It is most often carved in coral, but can also be made of other materials, and is worn around the neck. Phallic symbols such as fish, roosters, daggers, snakes and keys are also commonly found on protective amulets. Many of these are also euphemisms for the penis in folk speech (e.g. *il pesce*, 'the fish'; *l'uccello*, 'the bird'; and *chiavare*, 'to 'key', to 'screw').

The horn or *corno* is a closely related symbol. It represents the sexual potency of the mature male herd animal, usually the goat or ram. Horn amulets in bronze and bone, identical in shape to contemporary ones, have been found in numerous Etruscan and Roman-era tombs, attesting to its continuous presence since very ancient times.[22] Mediterranean coral, because of its blood-red colour, has long been associated with potency and good fortune; horn-shaped amulets were often made of this material, a tradition that continues today. The cheap red plastic horns from souvenir stands that hang from the rear-view mirrors of Italian cars are the modern-day versions of the older coral horns, although they have now become general good luck charms or, in diaspora communities, symbols of ethnic pride.[23]

The *mano fica*, a fist with the thumb caught between the bent first and second fingers, is another common symbol found in amulets against the evil eye. The gesture represents the phallus inside the female genitalia (*fica*), a graphic opposition to the power of the evil eye. Like the phallus, it can be made of coral, gold, silver, tin, plastic and other materials, and is worn as a charm around the neck, on a bracelet or keychain, or, today, hung on the rear-view mirror of a car. The *mano cornuta* or horned hand – a fist with the first and little fingers extended – has long been used as a gesture to avert the evil eye, usually with the fingers pointing upwards and the hand waving side to side.[24]

The naturally branching shape of coral lent itself to the creation of multi-pronged amulets. More common in the eighteenth and nineteenth centuries, these are rarely seen today outside of museums. Since according to the logic of magic, more is always better, each branch of the small coral charms was carved with a different protective symbol. Perhaps it is from these multi-pronged coral charms, as well as from an attempt to craft a likeness of the rue flower, that the multi-branched *cimaruta* evolved. *Cimaruta* means 'top of the rue (plant)'; these amulets, usually made of silver or tin, had a different symbol on the tip of each branch. These might include phalli, horns, solar disks and crescent moons (symbols of fertility and increase), fish (a symbol of Christ, but also a euphemistic term for the phallus), a key (to protect against epilepsy, but also a phallic symbol), the Sacred Heart of Jesus, and numerous others. Such charms were generally worn under clothing, and were meant to protect from witchcraft.

Rue (*ruta graveolens*), a medicinal herb native to the Mediterranean with emmenagogue and abortifacent properties, was used by folk healers to treat colic, stomach ailments and skin eruptions.[25] It was so beneficial that it was believed to protect against witchcraft and the evil eye as well. Rue was often combined with lavender in *brevi*, small packets or bags made of fabric and worn around the neck next to the skin. Mothers often made these for their children. In addition to beneficial herbs, they might contain garlic, salt, apotropaic stones, prayers, saint's images, sacred objects, and of course amulets such as those described above.[26] A number of naturally occurring stones and found objects were thought to have apotropaic qualities, and were carried in the pocket as protection or incorporated into other amulets. For example, arrow or spear points from Paleolithic sites, known as *pietre della saetta*, were believed to be the physical manifestations of lightning, and to be both the cause of and a form of protection against strokes. In some areas of southern Italy, women would find round or kidney-shaped stones of iron-rich clay that rattled from the loose minerals trapped inside. Through sympathetic magic, these became known as *pietre della gravidanza*, or pregnancy stones, and were believed to protect pregnant women and allow them to carry to term successfully. *Pietre del sangue*, or bloodstones, were red-spotted jasper thought to stop bleeding if applied to a wound, while *pietre stregonie* (witch stones) or *pietre stellari* (star stones), polyporic pebbles whose tiny spots were popularly interpreted as 'stars,' were thought to protect against witchcraft. These stones were sometimes carved into cross-shaped amulets and combined with figures of Christian saints, the Virgin Mary or Jesus to enhance their powers.[27]

Folk healing

Generally, folk healers in Italy fell into one of two categories: ordinary people who knew one or two specific charms, and specialists who possessed a broader magical knowledge involving a variety of techniques and practices. At one time, each village had a number of folk healers who could cure a variety of illnesses. They ranged from those who cured with herbs, magic formulas and prayers to professional sorcerers who were called in serious cases of magical attack. In practice, however, these practitioners differed more in intensity than in kind: sorcerers were often individuals who had learned some cures from a family member, but who broadened their knowledge and became specialized in vernacular magic. Some, like De Martino's 'zio Giuseppe', owned books of magical formulas where, according to one of his informants, 'all knowledge was written'.[28]

The word *strega* (witch) was never used in reference to these practitioners, except to insult them. They were known as *curatori/curatrici* (curers), *guaritori/ guaritrici* (healers), or simply as *praticos* ('knowledgeable ones', akin to the English cunning-folk. Most inherited their craft from a relative, although occasionally a healer claimed to have acquired power directly from a saint. This was the case of an old woman in Castellammare di Stabia (Campania), who in the 1970s told a folklorist how she obtained her healing powers as a child by falling into a deep trance. Her parents believed her dead, but St Rita 'touched her mouth, bestowing power onto her', and she miraculously recovered.[29] Another folk healer from central Sardinia told a researcher that one could acquire magic powers by going to a sacred place (a cemetery or church) and receiving *su sinzale* (a sign), although the nature of the sign was not specified.[30]

Some of these specialized healers employed trance states in their work. Trancing healers might be consulted to discover whether an illness was caused by witchcraft, to find lost or stolen livestock, or for love magic. De Martino movingly describes how one such healer diagnosed and treated supernatural illness:

> During the course of her recitation [of the prayer], the healer immerses herself in a controlled dream-like state, and in this condition she merges with the psychic condition of her client, and suffers with him: the altered state causes the healer to yawn, and her suffering with her patient causes her to shed tears. When the healer does not yawn or weep, it means that she was

not able to discern any spell in effect, and thus her client is not bewitched, but his illness depends on other causes.[31]

In the late 1970s, folklorist Luisa Selis interviewed 'Antonia', a 75-year-old *maghiarja* (sorceress) from central highland Sardinia. Antonia reported being possessed by three spirits who helped her with her healing work: a priest, who helped her foretell the future; a physician, who helped her cure illnesses; and a bandit, who helped her recover lost livestock.[32] Trancing healers and diviners like Antonia demonstrate a link with pre-Christian practices that was often recognized by their fellow villagers. About one such healer, an informant of De Martino surmised 'these are people who were born before Jesus Christ ... [they] know ancient science, and maybe remember something that [they] tell us now'.[33]

Most healers, however, were not specialists but ordinary people who possessed some practical or magical knowledge, often in the form of single formulas and prayers, as in the case of Mario from Bessude, whose story I cited at the beginning of this chapter. Formulas are secret and proprietary; they belong to individuals in the community. In the same village, other individuals specialize in curing styes and chalazions, removing the evil eye, or keeping birds and dogs out of fields. These people belong to different families, and thus the remedies, rather than being concentrated in one individual, are diffused throughout the population. As Mario described, healing formulas are passed on from one family member to another at calendrically significant times of year such as Christmas Eve or St John's Eve (June 23). The owner of the formula passes on the power along with the knowledge; once they have been transmitted, the original owner ceases to practise. Often, it is only certain family members who can receive the knowledge, for example a descendent of the opposite sex, or the youngest daughter. It is commonly believed that healers cannot die until they have passed on their knowledge. For the most part, these kinds of healers do not require cash payments; they use their skills as part of a system of balanced reciprocity that knits the community together in an economy of mutual obligation.

The nature of folk cures is quite varied; I can include only a small sample here. Many remedies were mixtures of olive oil and various herbs. De Martino reports that in Lucania, wounds and sores were treated with a mixture of olive oil or animal fat and rue, while Antonia, the Sardinian folk healer, treated boils with an infusion of mallow leaves and olive oil.[34] For maximum efficacy, herbs were to be gathered on St John's Eve before sunrise.

In Sardinia, many *berbos* centred on the protection of the herds and crops, the principal livelihood of the community. Eagles would sometimes make off with newborn lambs during the lambing season. Selis collected from Antonia a spell to bind an eagle to a tree in order to prevent it from attacking the flock. Antonia would go to the field where the eagle had last been seen, approach the tallest tree, and recite the *presura de s'abile* (binding of the eagle):

> *Abile, abile*
> *mares fortes zires*
> *mares zires fortes*
> *pedras d'aeras bortes*
> *pedras de rivu e de mare*
> *in custa robba*
> *non torres a colare.*

> Eagle, eagle
> you circle strong seas
> you circle seas strongly
> you turn stones of air
> river and sea stones
> in this flock
> do not return to forage.[35]

To keep birds away from crops during the harvest and threshing, the following spell was used in highland Sardinia:

> *Su cane ardente*
> *non appas in mente*
> *de toccare sa robba mia*
> *in custu monte violente*
> *inie ti balles solu*
> *no appas consolu*
> *de sa robba mia.*

> The burning dog
> does not have it in mind
> to touch my crops
> in this violent mountain
> may you dance alone
> without the consolation
> of my harvest.[36]

Some folk cures took the form of narratives. Angelina, a 92-year-old native of Arsoli, a town on the border between the regions of Lazio and Abruzzo, gave folklorist Maria Rosaria Tomassi the following cure for *jermecara*, or worms. The cure would begin on Good Friday. Angelina would make the sign of the cross over the eyes, mouth and ears of her patient, reciting this narrative:

> *Ecco la settimana santa che arriva*
> *presto arriva e presto si perde*
> *Lunedì santo S. Giobbe ammazza un verme*
> *de martedì santo ne ammaza un'altro*

mercoledì santo corre S. Giobbe
e ne ammazza un'altro
Giobbe con la mano para tutto e ammazza tutto
giovedì santo ne ammazza un'altro
venerdì santo – dopo la giornata inguaribile
di Dio e di S. Giobbe benedetto –
n'ammazza un'altro e finisce tutti
Sabato santo e la resurezzione di Dio
S. Giobbe fa pulizia di tutti
Domenica è la santa Pasqua
che tutti i vermi diventino acqua.

Here comes the holy week
it quickly arrives and quickly leaves
on holy Monday, St Job kills a worm
he kills another on holy Tuesday
on holy Wednesday, St Job runs
and kills another
Job with his hand shields all and kills all
on holy Thursday he kills another
on Good Friday – that terrible day for
God and blessed St Job –
he kills another and finishes them all off
Holy Saturday is the resurrection of God
St Job cleans them all up
Sunday is holy Easter
may all the worms become water.[37]

In this story, St Job is the hero whose battle against the worms follows the story of the Holy Week, the most significant time in the Roman Catholic calendar, and therefore a most propitious time for curing illness. Some folklorists suggest that the patient's suffering is symbolically compared to Christ's passion.[38] Here we see the adaptation of Christian narrative material to a system based on sympathetic magic, illustrating the almost complete penetration of Catholic ideology in the vernacular magic of Italy.

Taking a patient's measure, a form of magical healing found throughout Western Europe, was adapted by Antonia to cure *s'istriadura* (lit. 'the stretching'; jaundice). Using string, she would measure the patient's height from head to foot, then the distance between his outstretched arms, from left middle finger to right middle finger. If the height measurement was shorter than the width of the arms, the patient was judged to be affected by *s'istriadura*. The cure involved cutting the string to pieces and burning it on a tile along with rosemary, incense, wax from a blessed candle and a white barn owl feather. The tile was passed several times over the head of the patient in the sign of the cross; then it was placed on the floor, where the patient had to jump over it three times while inhaling the fumes.[39]

Folk healer Maria Paddeu is renowned throughout Sardinia for her ability to cure neonatal hernias. Maria and her brothers are the hereditary keepers of a small shrine to St John the Baptist located just outside the town of Thiesi in north-west Sardinia. Each year on St John's Eve (23 June), women bring their babies to Maria so she can cure them. These small hernias usually resolve themselves as babies grow, but occasionally must be surgically repaired, and many mothers are reluctant to have their babies go under the knife. I was lucky enough to witness a healing during the summer of 1986. With help from her brothers, Maria makes a long vertical cut in the branch of a fig tree that grows outside the shrine. The naked baby is then passed in and out of this opening three times while Maria recites a prayer to St John.[40] Afterwards, the cleft is wrapped in burlap and sewn with twine. Maria's followers say that when the branch heals over, the child's hernia will disappear. Similar examples of this cure have been collected from several regions in Italy, suggesting that this practice is of fairly ancient derivation.[41]

Magic and counter-magic

Not all magic was healing magic. The ethnographic record is rich with instances of manipulative or aggressive magic, usually in response to claims of sorcery done against the client. *Attaccature, fascini, legature* and *fatture* are examples of this type of magical working, and share an emphasis on the domination of the victim's body through attachment, binding or fixing. The structural features of these spells were often similar, whether they were used for love or to cause illness or death. Love spells often involved the manufacture of philtres or potions using menstrual blood or semen to bind the object of affection through the principle of contagious magic.

A number of spells made use of the transformative power of the moment of the elevation of the host during Mass. A Sicilian spell to make an enemy fall ill entails taking a lemon or an orange to midnight Mass on Christmas Eve, removing a bit of peel, and piercing it with pins while reciting '*Tanti spilli infiggo in quest'arancia, tanti mali ti calino addosso*' ('As many pins as I stick in this orange, may as many ills befall you'). The fruit is then thrown into a well or cistern.[42]

Some cases of grave illness are still attributed to magic. As recently as the 1980s, folklorist Luisa Del Giudice documents that her brother-in-law's congenital blood disorder was interpreted by a folk healer in Terracina (Lazio) as the result of *sangue legato*, 'bound blood' allegedly caused by a spell put on him by a former girlfriend.[43] This diagnosis points to the fraught nature of social relations in small communities that frequently led to accusations of witchcraft and counter-witchcraft. The folk healer's diagnosis reopened an unresolved social conflict and raised suspicions about a person who in all likelihood was perfectly innocent of any wrongdoing. This case also illustrates the pervasive idea that anger and ill will alone are enough to unleash psychic and physical harm. As De Martino demonstrates, folk healers may themselves become caught in this dangerous web: 'people go to [the folk healer] to have *fatture* undone; but they also believe the old mage can weave evil spells, especially in matters of love, and occasionally he finds himself in the embarrassing situation of having to undo magic he himself made.'[44]

Tarantismo and Argismo

One of the most fascinating forms of Italian folk healing is the trance-dancing that took place in Puglie and Sardinia in response to the bite (real or imagined) of an insect or spider. These related phenomena have been studied in depth by Italian anthropologists Ernesto De Martino and Clara Gallini, and any treatment I give them here cannot do justice to their complexity.[45] Briefly put, it was believed that the bite of an insect or spider caused the victim to become possessed by the insect's spirit. In classic tarantulism, described by De Martino, the victim, usually a woman, was typically bitten by a *tarantola* (not a tarantula, but the European wolf spider, whose bite is painful but not deadly) while performing agricultural labour in the fields during the hot summer months. She might or might not be aware of the bite – in fact the bite itself could be metaphorical; but eventually she developed symptoms ranging from headache to depression and convulsions. Suspecting spider-possession, her relatives would call special musicians to the house to play a range of tunes until the woman's 'spider' recognized the particular rhythms that fit its personality. Then the afflicted woman began to dance. Dancing would continue for hours, sometimes days, until the spider's bite was temporarily exorcised. But the ritual would have to be repeated yearly at the feast of Sts Peter and Paul (29 June) in order for the woman to remain free from symptoms. The lively rhythms of the music accompanying this rite, typically played on tambourines, flute, guitar and accordion, are the origins of the tarantella folk dance. But the ritual, when it was still practised, was anything but merry. Besides the suffering that the illness and cure entailed, being *tarantata* carried a social stigma. De Martino analyses the practice as an enactment of personal and interpersonal conflicts experienced by peasant women in southern Italy in light of their situation of economic and gender oppression. Many *tarantate* in fact suffered from emotional frustration connected with love and family difficulties. Edoardo Winspeare's wonderful film 'Bitten' (1998) perfectly captures the atmosphere surrounding the affliction of a young girl when her family forbids her to marry the young man she loves.[46] In *argismo*, the Sardinian variant, the biting insect was either a spider (*Latrodectus tredecimguttatus*) or the *mutilla*, a brightly-coloured ant-like insect. Both are known in Sardo as *argia*, 'brightly-coloured', and are identified as the souls of the dead who were not received in the other-world because of their sins.[47] *Arge* retained characteristics they had while alive: they could be single, married, widowed or priestly, female or (rarely) male; they had names and towns of origin, and a story explaining their return as spider-spirits. The purpose of the ritual was twofold: to identify the possessing spirit and its story, and to placate it by acceding to its demands.[48] The ritual usually began with a musical exploration to discover, as in *tarantism*, which music pleased the spirit and would induce it to dance: lullabies for child-*argias*, love songs for single, engaged or married *argias*; funeral laments for widowed *argias*, and so on. This might be followed by a verbal interrogation of the patient by the community in order to discover the identity of the possessing spirit and the story behind its return. This often involved a tale of love, abandonment and betrayal by lovers and family members that would be partially enacted by the possessed individual and the community. In contrast to the *Puglie*, Sardinian victims were more often male than female; during the course of the ritual cure, the possessed individual might take on the characteristics of the possessing *argia*, cross-dressing and even undergoing mock childbirth in the case of pregnant *argias*. The music accompanying the ritual was performed by a specially trained flute or accordion player; the victim's family and community participated in the cure, which involved drinking, partying and dancing over a period of three days. Like her mentor De Martino, Gallini analyses the ritual in terms of its psycho-social role within the small-scale, face-to-face, tension-filled agricultural communities in which it was practised; but she cannot completely escape the survivalism of her theoretical forebears: 'We should at least ask ourselves whether the dance of the *argia* may have had as its antecedent a pre-Christian possession rite in which the summertime return of the dead was enacted.'[49]

The work of Henningsen on medieval Sicilian beliefs concerning the *donne di fuori*, as well as the research of Crapanzano on Moroccan healers (1975) and Kligman on Romanian *calus* (1981) suggest that *tarantismo* and *argismo* are variants of ecstatic dance therapies found in many parts of the circum-Mediterranean.[50] In many of these vernacular healing systems, illnesses are believed to be caused by spirits, whether embodied in insects (as in *argismo* and *tarantismo*) or in supernatural form (*iele* in Romania, *jinn* in Morocco, *exotica* in rural Greece). Certain healers specialize in communicating with these spirits in dreams and trances to discover the cause of the illness, and cures are effected through ritual enactments that may include music and ecstatic dancing.

Disappearance, survival and reclamation: vernacular magic in Italy today

Already when Gallini was conducting her research project in the 1960s and 1970s, she was dealing with a disappearing custom. By the time I arrived in Sardinia in the mid-1980s, *argism* had disappeared. 'All of the *argias* are dead,'

I was told, perhaps, informants added, because of DDT that was used extensively to kill malaria-causing mosquitoes. But DDT alone was not to blame for the general decline of the traditional folkways within which magical practice had flourished.

The unification of Italy, the establishment of an official Italian language based on the Florentine vernacular, the building of a transportation network, the development of compulsory education based on national norms, and the diffusion of mass media have all contributed to the breakdown of regional isolation and the growth of an Italian national identity. In the last twenty years, globalization and the unification of the European market have brought with them a groundswell of interest in the local, the regional and the indigenous. Yet these changes are the same ones that have led to the rupture of traditional rural folkways that were the cradle of Italian vernacular magic.

The social changes of the late twentieth century have profoundly trans-formed the peasant villages of Italy and have integrated them into a global economy. In much of Italy, post-war urbanization and immigration stripped the villages of half their population. Legal reforms abolished the old, exploi-tative landholding systems that strangled *contadini*; contemporary agriculturalists practise their trade only part-time, working in factories or in the expanding service economy as well. Women now fill positions in the labour market and in politics that the emigrating men left empty, and mass tourism, cable TV and the Internet have introduced new models of identity and consumption. The old sense of the precariousness of human life has lightened somewhat as a result of better conditions and new opportunities, bringing a decline in evil eye belief and witchcraft accusations. While some customs remain – many young mothers still put their babies' undershirts on inside-out – the explanations have changed: instead of saying this is to keep away the evil eye, my informants now tell me the purpose of this custom is to protect babies' delicate skin from the chafing of the seams. Italians who consult magical healers today are much less likely to do so because they believe themselves to be victims of the evil eye or a *fattura*; they are more likely to want information about their futures, a love affair or a job situation.[51]

But magic and occultism are not dead in Italy; they are finding new expressions in a plethora of New Age religions and practices, mostly concen-trated in urban areas that build upon Italy's magical heritage. In her 1990 survey, Cecilia Gatto Trocchi found a range of magical and occult practices in Italy, from traditional healers now located in urban areas to esoteric groups such as the Rosicrucian Brotherhood and the Theosophical Society, to New Age practices such as fire-walking and crystal healing.[52] More recently, the Puglie is seeing a renewed interest in *tarantismo*. The new *tarantati*, however, bare little resemblance to the women studied by De Martino; they are male and female, under forty, and belong mostly to the middle classes. Calling themselves '*tarantolati*', these young people gather at night to play frame

drums and dance ecstatically, striving to achieve alternate states of consciousness in a kind of rave to the rhythms of traditional folk music. Paolo Apolito
analyses their practice as a post-modern critique of rationalism, as well as an
expression of a uniquely local identity in a globalizing world.[53]

Because of its relatively late development as a modern industrial nation-
state, Italy is perhaps in a unique position in Europe, in that traditional
vernacular magic coexists with newer reclaimed forms such as those documented by Apolito.[54] In the case of folklore reclamation, it is not only the
forms of folklore previously repudiated as backwards and irrational that are
being reclaimed; it is the very interpretive structures erected by nineteenth-
and early twentieth-century folklorists and ethnologists that are being called
into question. The Sardinian folk-rock group Tazenda included in its 1992
album *Limba* ('Tongue', 'Language') a song entitled *'Preghiera Semplice'*
('Simple Prayer') that alludes, in part, to the difficulty of reclaiming alternate
spiritualities after a cultural hiatus:

> *Dansat sa majalza, sa majalza dansat*
> *archimissas in sas manos*
> *Ballu, ballu tundu*
> *abbaticamus su mundu*
> *brincamos che indianos*
> *Sa vida, sa sorte, su muscu 'e sa terra mia*
> *Sa muida 'e sa morte, sas dudas mias.*

> The sorceress dances, the sorceress dances
> Wheat sprigs in her hands
> Dance, dance the circle dance
> We tread the earth
> We jump like Indians
> Life, fate, the smell of my land
> The rattle of death, my doubts.

In this song, the sorceress dances holding wheat sprigs, symbols of the
harvest and life's potential for renewal. The circle dance, still performed at
all the summer harvest festivals in the island's small towns, is often the only
time the community gathers together, forming a chain that winds in and out,
spiralling inward, then unwinding, bringing each member of the dance face
to face with every other dancer. But in this context, the dancers trample the
earth, the source of the wheat sprigs; they jump like Indians, an allusion to
the survivalism of the early ethnologists, who compared peasant practices to
those of Third World peoples. In the end, the doubts about the very
sacredness of the dance, the power of the sorceress brought on by the
rationalist paradigm are compared to a death rattle. It is unclear whether
this is more powerful than, or equally balanced with, the life, fate and the
smell of the land – the local, the indigenous, the quick, the stuff of life itself.

Notes

1 Leonard Norman Primiano, 'Vernacular Religion and the Search for Method in Religious Folklife', *Western Folklore* 54, 1 (1995) 39, 45.
2 Primiano, 'Vernacular Religion', p. 38.
3 Primiano, 'Vernacular Religion', p. 41.
4 As Owen Davies has shown in his study of cunning-men in provincial England, many cunning-folk possessed magical texts and formularies whose material could turn up in a number of social contexts, both learned and popular: Owen Davies, *Cunning-Folk: Popular Magic in English History* (London, 2003).
5 Giuseppe Bellucci, *Il feticismo primitivo in Italia e le sue forme di adattamento* (Perugia, [1919] 1983).
6 Cecilia Gatto Trocchi, *Magia ed esoterismo in Italia* (Milan, 1990).
7 Paolo Apolito, 'Tarantismo, identità locale, postmodernità', in Apolito *et al.*, *Transe, guarigione, mito: antropologia e la storia del tarantismo* (Nardo, 2000), pp. 137–43; Luisa Del Giudice, 'Mountains of Cheese, Rivers of Wine: Paesi di Cuccagna and Other Gastronomic Utopias', in Del Giudice and Gerald Porter (eds), *Imagined States: Nationalism, Utopia and Longing in Oral Cultures* (Logan, 2001), pp. 11–63.
8 Owen Davies, *Witchcraft, Magic and Culture, 1736–1951* (Manchester, 1999); Jeanne Favret-Saada, *Deadly Words: Witchcraft in the Bocage* (Cambridge, 1980).
9 Davies, *Witchcraft, Magic and Culture*; Owen Davies, *A People Bewitched: Witchcraft and Magic in Nineteenth-Century Somerset* (Bruton, 1999).
10 See Alfredo Cattabiani, *Lunario: dodici mesi di miti, feste, leggende e tradizioni popolari d'Italia* (Milan, 1994), pp. 207–8.
11 Ernesto De Martino, *Sud e magia* (Milan, [1966] 1987), p. 71. On such nocturnal experiences see David Hufford, *The Terror that Comes in the Night: An Experience-Centered Approach to Supernatural Assault Traditions* (Philadelphia, 1982).
12 Gustav Henningsen, in his careful review of Spanish Inquisition documents from Sicily, reveals that during the sixteenth century, the term *donne di fuori* referred to both fairies and people of both genders who were believed to ride out with them at night. These individuals were usually folk healers who could cure illnesses caused by the fairies, often as a result of some unwitting offence against them. The usual cure involved a ritual supper offered to the fairies by the victim. The fairies, accompanied by the healers in spirit form, would come to the victim's home on an appointed night where they would dance, celebrate and spiritually consume the food, thus curing the afflicted person: Gustav Henningsen, '"The Ladies from Outside": An Archaic Pattern of the Witches' Sabbath', in Gustav Henningsen and Bengt Ankarloo (eds), *European Witchcraft: Centers and Peripheries* (Oxford, 1993), pp. 191–215. These medieval Sicilian beliefs have interesting parallels throughout the modern Mediterranean. In rural Greece, as recently as the 1960s, certain folk healers specialized in curing ills brought about by the fairies, known as *exotica* ('those from outside'). Anthropologist Vincent Crapanzano, working in Morocco in the 1960s, documented a belief system centred on the *jinn* (fairies) and their human followers, folk healers belonging to religious brotherhoods who could cure illness by performing a trance-dance to special music. The queen of the jinn, known as 'A'isha Qandisha, could appear either as a beautiful woman or a hideous hag, but always had a non-human feature, such as camel toes. Healers consulted 'A'isha Qandisha in their dreams, where she explained the cause of the illness and its cure: Vincent Crapanzano, 'Saints, Jnun, and Dreams: An Essay in Moroccan Ethnopsychology', *Psychiatry* 38 (1975) 145–59. In the 1970s, folklorist Gail Kligman documented Romanian brotherhoods of trance dancers who specialized in curing ailments thought to be caused by *iele* (fairies),

whose patron saint was Diana or Irodeasa: Gail Kligman, *Calus: Symbolic Transformation in Romanian Ritual* (Chicago, [1977] 1981).

13 Giuseppe Pitrè, *Usi, costumi, credenze e pregiudizi del popolo siciliano* (Palermo, 1889), pp. iv, 153.

14 Antonangelo Liori, *Demoni, miti e riti magici della Sardegna* (Rome, 1992), pp. 107–11.

15 De Martino, *Sud e magia*, p. 15.

16 Willem de Blécourt, 'The Witch, her Victim, the Unwitcher and the Researcher: The Continued Existence of Traditional Witchcraft', in Willem de Blécourt, Ronald Hutton and Jean La Fontaine, *Witchcraft and Magic in Europe: The Twentieth Century* (Philadelphia, 1999), p. 147.

17 De Martino, *Sud e magia*, p. 15.

18 See De Martino, *Sud e magia*; Alan Dundes, 'Wet and Dry, the Evil Eye', in idem (ed.), *The Evil Eye: A Casebook* (Madison, 1992), pp. 257–312.

19 George M. Foster, 'Peasant Society and the Image of Limited Good', *American Anthropologist* 67 (1965) 293–315.

20 In Roman slang, the expression *'non mi seccare [le palle]'*, literally 'don't dry up my testicles', or 'don't annoy me', is a current reflection of this underlying system of binary oppositions. Similarly, the Roman slang expression *'rimanerci secco/a'*, 'to dry up of it', is a euphemism for dying.

21 De Martino, *Sud e magia*, p. 17.

22 Bellucci, *Il feticismo primitivo*, p. 50.

23 Frances M. Malpezzi and William M. Clements, *Italian American Folklore* (Little Rock, 1992), p. 121.

24 This symbol needs to be deployed with care as it has other meanings, however. Jabbed towards another with the fingers pointing at them, this gesture is a powerful insult meaning 'cuckold.'

25 Malcolm Stuart (ed.), *The Encyclopedia of Herbs and Herbalism* (New York, 1979), pp. 256–7.

26 Alfonso Di Nola, *Lo specchio e l'olio: le superstizioni italiane* (Bari, 1993), pp. 14–15.

27 Bellucci, *Il feticismo primitivo*, pp. 80–5, 92, 87, 100.

28 De Martino, *Sud e magia*, pp. 70–2.

29 Di Nola, *Lo specchio e l'olio*, p. 40; my translation.

30 Luisa Selis, 'Prime ricerche sulla presenza delle streghe in Sardegna oggi', in Maria Bergamaschi *et al.*, *L'erba delle donne: maghe, streghe, guaritrici* (Rome, 1978), p. 139.

31 De Martino, *Sud e magia*, p. 17; my translation.

32 Selis, 'Prime ricerche sulla presenza delle streghe', p. 141.

33 De Martino, *Sud e magia*, pp. 70–1.

34 De Martino, *Sud e magia*, pp. 38–9; Selis, 'Prime ricerche sulla presenza delle streghe', p. 143.

35 Selis, 'Prime ricerche sulla presenza delle streghe', p. 141.

36 Liori, *Demoni, miti e riti magici*, p. 189.

37 Maria Rosaria Tomassi, 'La Furnicella', in Bergamaschi *et al.*, *L'erba delle donne*, p. 150.

38 Tomassi, 'La Furnicella', p. 150.

39 Selis, 'Prime ricerche sulla presenza delle streghe', p. 142.

40 I was unable to collect the words, as this is secret material that Maria can pass on only to another family member.

41 Di Nola, *Lo specchio e l'olio*, p. 116.

42 Di Nola, *Lo specchio e l'olio*, p. 49. Di Nola gives this incantation in Italian and not in Sicilian. See also the 'Conjuration of Lemons and Pins', in Charles G. Leland, *Aradia, or the Gospel of the Witches* (Custer, [1890] 1990), pp. 29–32.

43 Luisa Del Giudice, personal communication, 1999.

44 De Martino, *Sud e magia*, p. 71; my translation.
45 Ernesto De Martino, *La terra del rimorso* (Milan, 1961); Clara Gallini, *La ballerina variopinta* (Naples, 1988).
46 Recent historical research by Maria Rosaria Tamblé has revealed a possible connection between *tarantismo* and witchcraft. In the trial of Caterina Palazzo of Calabria in 1627, the folk healer is accused of having exorcised a number of clients who suffered from tarantulism. Although she denied the accusations, a story emerged during the trial linking the venomous spider with other animal familiars, such as toads and frogs, known to aid witches in their diabolical workings: Tamblé, 'Tarantismo e stregoneria: un legame possibile', in *Transe, guarigione, mito*, pp. 101–18.
47 Gallini, *La ballerina variopinta*, p. 25.
48 Gallini, *La ballerina variopinta*, p. 42.
49 Gallini, *La ballerina variopinta*, p. 96; my translation.
50 Henningsen, '"The Ladies from Outside"'; Crapanzano, 'Saints, Jnun, and Dreams'; Kligman, *Calus: Symbolic Transformation*.
51 Cecilia Gatto Trocchi, *Magia ed esoterismo in Italia* (Milan, 1990), p. 89.
52 Gatto Trocchi, *Magia ed esoterismo*.
53 Apolito, 'Tarantismo, identità locale, postmodernità', pp. 137–43.
54 For a discussion of folklore reclamation, see Sabina Magliocco, 'Coordinates of Power and Performance: Festivals as Sites of (Re)Presentation and Reclamation in Sardinia', *Ethnologies* 23,1 (2001) 167–88.

9

Curse, *maleficium*, divination: witchcraft on the borderline of religion and magic

Éva Pócs

This chapter is concerned with a special form of witchcraft that is practised, to my knowledge, only amongst Hungarians living in Transylvania. It is possible that it is common among the Romanian population of Transylvania as well, but so far I have not found any relevant information in the Romanian literature. My analysis is based on fieldwork conducted several years ago with my university students in Csíkkarcfakva and Csíkjenőfalva, two villages in the old county of Csík inhabited by Roman Catholic Hungarians.[1] The two villages are in Transylvania, in the Hungarian block of the Székely land bordering on Orthodox Romanian areas. The Hungarians here have scarce cultural contacts with Romanians; indeed, the cases described below are almost the only examples of any connection between their respective religions. The time spent in the field was unfortunately insufficient for a comprehensive survey of the system's functioning or for the elucidation of its social and mental environment. What we have managed to observe and record was in fact not so much the practice as the narratives about it, from which we can make only indirect and conditional inferences about the real situation. What follows is a preliminary overview of the findings based on around one hundred collected narratives.

Until recently, little was known about the religious variant of witchcraft described here.[2] In Csík the priest actively participates in the system of witchcraft. He not only helps remove bewitchment from the sick, but helps carry out bewitchment as well. In this form, witchcraft as a social system regulating personal conflicts, and as an ideological system, has several features that distinguish it from other forms known in Central and Western Europe including aspects of divine jurisdiction, ordeal and divination; in fact, in many respects it functions subordinated to them. The classic West European suspicion-accusation bewitchments can be found in Hungarian and Transylvanian witchcraft trials from the sixteenth to the eighteenth centuries, and some of its features are still discernible among the twentieth-century Hungarian population of both Hungary and Transylvania.[3] Witchcraft as a social system in village communities typically functions within the network of malefactor-injured-identifier-healer.[4] In most cases the role of the malefactor is fictitious. The *maleficium* (bewitchment) employed by the witch is an occult interaction between two people, and it is either accompanied by some *actual deed* or not. What this basically means is that if I have suffered some misfortune, I *attribute* the intention and performance of *maleficium* to somebody that I have good reasons to impute such plans to: I believe my misfortune to be the result of his or her *maleficium*. According to this interpretation of witchcraft, in fact, there are no actual witches: the witch is almost always the *other person*, a scapegoat selected for specific reasons. Accordingly, the bewitchment narratives, which provide the basis for the description and interpretation of Central European witchcraft, usually relate events from the perspective of the victim.

Such narratives can be found in Csík as well, and from them we can posit a minor role for 'classic' witchcraft in communities there. However, the majority of the narratives we collected through fieldwork reflect a different kind of attitude and another system of witchcraft. One of its main characteristics is the actuality of the act of bewitchment: witchcraft is not just an *accusation*.[5] People either perform it themselves or have it performed by someone else. This is what Willem de Blécourt has termed 'practised witchcraft' or 'active bewitchment', and what Per Sörlin defined as 'maleficent witchcraft'.[6] In this environment *maleficium* is a practice dispensing justice and restoring order, performed as a response to misfortunes. It fulfils the function of norm control as a 'punitive', individual kind of jurisdiction. This is particularly clear in those cases when someone is employed to perform the bewitching, which is much more frequent than its personal effectuation. Here the *maleficium*, the key factor of witchcraft, is usually not a direct (real or virtual) interaction between the two persons involved, in other words the malefactor and the victim. Instead, it is carried out through a mediator who is employed by villagers to perform the witchcraft, or to use the local term *megcsináltat* ('to have someone done in'). This mediator is in most cases a *kaluger*, a Romanian Orthodox monk or priest,[7] although sometimes a lay magician – a *guruzsló* or *gurucsáló* – from the same or a neighbouring village provides the same service. Compared to the large number of clients of the Romanian priests and monks, though, these mostly female magicians were, at least by the twentieth century, less frequently employed.

The *kaluger*'s curse, commissioned by individuals who want to harm other people, is a specifically religious method of projecting fate and divine justice, for resolving communal conflicts. Thus the usual cast in witchcraft conflicts is joined by an external mediator representing the religious sphere, thereby intertwining and integrating popular witchcraft and certain religious normative jurisdictional systems. The discrepancy between witch *beliefs* (and the related terminology) and the actual *practice* of witchcraft also implies that at least two different systems of different origins have been superimposed on each other. In spite of this discrepancy, there are several factors connecting the various coexisting systems of witchcraft as well. One such link is that the bewitchment – the 'doing in' – can be the explanation or cause of the same types of misfortune and injury. The narratives reveal the following examples: incurable and undiagnosable diseases lasting for a long time (even for decades), ataxia, paralysis, paralysed limbs, shrunken limbs, loss of eyesight and loss of speech. We also find sudden death due to accidents, estrangement of spouses or lovers, ailing animals and cows going dry. A quick succession of misfortunes can also be suspicious. As a woman put it quite expressively, 'when this devastation starts to come one after the other, somebody's hands must be in it'.

So, we can draw the conclusion that in each system – including the existing traces of the Central European type – people are 'done in' within the same social environment and due to the same witchcraft-inducing tensions and conflicts, whether the rites of *maleficium* are performed by, or attributed to priests or lay persons. In the narratives, the alleged causes of the 'doing in', the tensions and conflicts forming within a network of personal interrelations may become manifest in debates, brawls or fights. Some of the most common types of conflicts are: skirmishes about land boundaries, family conflicts, litigation, perjury in inheritance debates, the breaking-off of an engagement, jilted lovers, breach of promise, the lover's or the spouse's jealousy, bad marriages, unfaithful husbands, divorces, abortion, murder (of a family member, which has not led to criminal prosecution perhaps due to the lack of evidence); theft (of money, corn, animals, clothes, bedclothes, food, jewels); denunciations to the authorities (for example about the distillation of brandy or political denunciation), conflicts with communal leaders, hostility, hatred, brawling and fights for indefinable reasons within the family or among neighbours.

Many times the objective of the *maleficium* according to the narratives is not to cause damage but to set right the previous *maleficium* and to make up for the damage – to make the (bewitched) sick person recover, to catch the thief, to get back the stolen clothes, animals or money. In the context of 'justified revenge' the most common element is theft. In these cases the aim of the *maleficium* is basically to recover the stolen property and at the same time to punish the thief. My informants believed that this *maleficium* can be performed in several ways, and although they are essentially identical they relate to whether they perform it themselves, or they have employed someone else to do it:

(1) Manipulation with objects based on the principles of contagious magic, such as carrying out *maleficium* using the belongings of the intended victim (handkerchief and matches, for example) or other objects (such as

bone, wool, hen's heads, thread and chain), or creeping into his or her property (courtyard, house) and placing the bewitching object there so that she or he will get into contact with it unknowingly.

(2) The most characteristic personal technique is the curse. This is actually a religious form of curse, in which one does not just wish evil things to someone else but in doing it refers to a higher authority: it is the par excellence form of curse, essentially a kind of exorcism. Instead of the 'pure' form of word magic ('May you break your neck'), one must use its religious form: 'May God break your neck'. By delegating it to God, the human method of *maleficium* is elevated into the supernatural sphere, from which it strikes down upon mortal men as a divine blow even if not performed through priests: 'The scourge of God shall find him. He who deserves it shall be found.' Thus in a certain sense individual cursing can also be regarded as a characteristic element of 'religious witchcraft'. As an example, here is a curse text, which allegedly came true (the 'target person' died in a traffic accident): 'May the blessed Lord let your neck get under the wheels!' The mother of one of our informants cursed someone by kneeling down at the middle of the road, holding up her hands and asking God 'never to give her luck'. In this case we have a ritual form in which the motif of the oath's publicity itself signifies that the motives of the curse are held to be justified.[8] According to the general opinion, the curse can only fall upon the guilty. This underlines the ordeal-like character of cursing, the fatefulness of its realization instead of the interpersonal aspects of magic, and it provides, as it were, a kind exemption for the curser. Our informants talk about their wish to have their curses come true quite openly, even if it causes a serious illness or even the life of a fellow being; they do not consider it a sin or malevolence, only the just punishment of fate or God.

(3) The third important method of *maleficium* is *fasting*. Together with a curse or in itself, it can be effective to pledge a ritual fasting 'against' someone, for example, on every Tuesday, on nine Tuesdays, on three Tuesdays, etc. (on these occasions they do not eat anything during the day or until noon, they only drink water or eat everything but rich food). These may also go on as long as their objective comes true – until the target person gets sick, becomes paralysed or dies.

As for having someone done in by *another person*, our data reveal little about the techniques of magicians. Nevertheless, the beliefs related to them and their helping spirits are apparently more vivid today than their actual role in the system of witchcraft. As I have said, our data present 'doing someone in' through Romanian *priests* as the most common method of *maleficium*.

According to the common belief, people went to the *kaluger* mainly to ask for curses or to have a mass said as *maleficium*, and we have abundant data about the firm conviction in the effectiveness of the *kalugers'* rites. 'Their prayers are effective', it is said. In contrast to the Hungarian and Roman Catholic priests, the Romanian ones 'have greater power'. Thus what matters is not merely the professional skill related to the required cursing rites but often also the supernatural power of the *kalugers* as holy men, and the influence radiating from monasteries as holy places.

The people visiting the *kaluger* sometimes only want to find out the identity of the wrongdoer through the priest's divination rites. However, quite often the above-mentioned interpersonal tensions and conflicts inducing the intention to have someone done in are also revealed. In such cases they evidently know the identity of the wrongdoer, and their primary aim is personal revenge, the miscreant's just punishment through the priest's curse. As in other types of witchcraft, the purpose of the priest's *divination* may be to verify the fact of *maleficium*, to find out the identity of the malefactor, and even to discover the future fate of the bewitched person and his or her chances of recovery. When the motive of the *maleficium* is to retaliate for a theft by an unknown culprit, or to take vengeance and strike back for an earlier *maleficium*, it is the natural task of the *kaluger* to disclose the identity of the malefactor. The injured party probably has his or her own suspects, but the person to be bewitched is also selected through divination, through the 'casting of fate'. Personal interaction, one of the basic requirements of witchcraft appears to have no role in the procedure; individual responsibility is shifted over to fate. The mechanism of shifting responsibility is the same when a factual suspicion about the guilt of a given person is reinforced by the *kaluger's* divination: this way he soothes his client's conscience about the rightfulness of the *maleficium*. The most important divination rite attributed to the *kaluger* is the opening of the book, when he finds out the identity of the wrongdoer from the Bible – i.e. *sortes biblicae*. Other methods include *katoptromantia*, *hydromantia* as well as pouring hot lead into water or burning candles.

The *kaluger's* most important activity is holding masses, saying prayers and casting curses according to the wishes of his clients who pay the money for the mass in advance and tell him what they want with it. According to the narratives, *maleficium* is an act consciously carried out by the priest.[9] The narratives mention instances of *maleficium* that came true: the target person became paralysed, lame, blind, mute, divorced his/her spouse, became a beggar, the marriage was never celebrated, and the family came to decline. The most severe 'objective' is total destruction: the person 'done in' pines away, becomes weak and dies. Family members may also be mentioned in connection with sickness and death; it was especially against sons-in-law and daughters-in-law that such steps were taken within the family.

Those who go to the *kaluger* must tell him what the prayer, curse or mass should be *for*; and they have to define the exact degree of misfortune – 'she gave the money so that he should become lame'; or somebody gives money for a mass to have his wife die. According to my informants the *kalugers'* curse was a prayer in which they asked for 'the punishment of the guilty'. The ritualistic forms of the priest's curse legitimize individual cursing and the whole system built upon it. By delegating it to God, the human method of *maleficium* is elevated into the supernatural sphere, from which it strikes down upon mortal men as a divine blow even if not performed through priests: 'The scourge of God shall find him. He who deserves it shall be found.' According to the general opinion, the curse can only fall upon the guilty. This underlines the ordeal-like character of cursing, the fatefulness of its realization instead of the interpersonal aspects of magic, and it provides, as it were, a kind exemption for the curser. My informants talk about their wish to have their curses come true quite openly, even if it causes a serious illness or even the life of a fellow being. They do not consider it a sin or malevolence, only the just punishment of fate or God. An important aspect of this ritualistic curse is that it can only affect the wrongdoer and never the innocent.

As a technique of harmful magic, the *priest's curse* can function by itself or with other methods of magic. The people ordering the *maleficium* quite often bring some object of the future victim to the *kaluger*: a piece of clothing, a kerchief or some earth from his/her garden, and the *kaluger* 'says a mass', 'recites', 'sheds a curse' on it. The *kaluger* curses this object, and it then has to be placed in the garden or around the threshold of the future victim, from where it can exert its evil effect. In a quite serious and mortal version of this, the curse is pronounced upon some earth taken from the graves of nine dead people. The devices of black magic, also used in individual *maleficium*, thus become a kind of negative version of the church sacraments: 'religious' objects, parts of a 'sacred', more effective system. The mass has, according to the narratives, a distinctly black mass-like variant, which is held at night and considered particularly evil in its effect – it causes death.

Besides the curse-rite performed by himself, the priest may prescribe for his clients various individual methods of black magic such as a fasting vow mentioned above, while at the same time he undertakes and performs the mass or the curse. The fast may include the burning of candles or lamps in a prescribed way: with this, through analogy, the victim's life is, as it were, burnt out. This has the same 'negative sacrament' function as the objects mentioned earlier. The ordeal-like quality of having someone done in is quite evident in the case of the fast prescribed by a priest as well. The fast 'vowed for evil' functions the same way as cursing. It can only make someone sick if he or she 'deserved it', if he or she had 'done something bad earlier'. If it is directed towards an innocent person, it will eventually harm the fasting person's family instead.

The priest's curse does not exclude the alternative of a 'good' solution. According to one informant, a *kaluger*, who had recited a mass against a thief, told his client that if his geese did not turn up within thirty days, he was to go back to the *kaluger* to have the wrongdoer 'done in' again. However, this had the desired influence on the thief, as the geese arrived home just in time. Ordering a curse-mass could be motivated only by the wish to alarm the wrongdoers. In fact, they could be scared with mere threats of such masses. According to the narratives, during a quarrel the malefactor may utter threats and thus proclaim his or her resolution to have her opponent done in. This threat is again something of a 'call of fate'; it is the first step towards elevating the everyday act of *maleficium* into the sphere of divine jurisdiction. During a quarrel about the boundaries of a hayfield one of the parties uttered the following threat: 'Don't you say so, for I will see justice done, for I will go to the *kaluger*!' According to the logic of the narratives, this kind of threat allows for certain alternative solutions such as the wrongdoer 'undoing' the damage that has aroused the conflict. This textual motif again highlights the ordeal-like character of the whole process of 'having someone done in'. In a narrative about the theft of dress-materials, the curser knew the identity of the thief and threatened her with the following words: 'hear me, good woman, if you took it ... tell me ... because I will put a black mass on you'. In a story about a stolen lamb, the old woman from the injured family deliberately put it around the village that they would have the thief done in so that he should hear about it. He returned the stolen lamb the next night. These narratives concerning theft make it particularly clear that the mere threat of having someone done in can fulfil the priestly curse's function of restoring order and dispensing justice in itself.

Some of our stories, mostly about having thieves 'done in', also feature the motif, perhaps a legendary one, of withdrawing the *maleficium*; an act towards restoring the equilibrium, this serves to reinforce the fiction of '*maleficium* as just punishment', which is deeply embedded in the villagers' consciousness. If the wrongdoers make amends for their transgressions, the punishment will be stopped. In such cases the person ordering the *maleficium* may go to the *kaluger* to take it back. Thus as a result of the mass ordered against the thief of three lambs, one bewitched wrongdoer went to the gate of the curser: 'Oh, Vilma! Oh, oh, Vilma, don't you say masses any more, don't you order masses any more ... for it was I who stole the three lambs.' It is clear from such data that in the world-view of Csík the rite of 'doing in' also constitutes a system of ethical norms and of sanctions against those who transgress against them.

The divination-like quality of having someone done in is strengthened by the prediction of the patient's fate, which, according to the narratives, takes place simultaneously with the process of divination. Based on whether they have been done in 'with good intentions' or 'with evil ones', the priest announces whether the sick persons will recover or die, when they will recover (after forty days for example), when the damage will be compensated, or predicts a speedy degradation of the victim's health. In the case of the latter, a frequent motif of narratives is that the *kaluger* hurries his clients so that they should not find the target person already dead, lame or mute upon arriving home. He urges, for example, that the client drive fast, 'because the old woman will be dead by the time you get home'.

Unfortunately, we cannot as yet see clearly the degree to which the everyday life and world-views of the given society are affected by the belief system and ritual of having someone 'done in'. The greatest problem is that we can only see the co-operation of the 'holy persons' from 'below', from the point of view of the malefactors employing these services and their victims. We cannot make any final statement on this topic until we conduct a detailed research at the site of the priests' *maleficium*, among priests and monks, in Romanian monasteries, to find out how they see this system and what exactly they consider it to be; how they take part in it according to their reality, in their interpretation. For the time being, there are still many vague areas about the actual role of the Orthodox priests and monks in taking upon themselves the performance of curses and masses 'with evil purposes' – in essence, the active participation in witchcraft.

At present the real points of connection between the ideas and practice of the villagers related to *maleficium* and the system of priestly rituals are unclear; but my data imply a closely interwoven system and shared principles between the participants of the ritual's sacred and profane spheres. This phenomenon cannot be studied in itself. We must also consider the other services of the priests performing these rites, and, more generally, the broader context of the religious systems into which, as I believe, the system of popular witchcraft became integrated.

The benediction and healing activities of the priests and *kalugers* are not limited to the mental sphere and system of connections here referred to as witchcraft. It is in fact more general in its scope. Our narratives show that as a person who divines and heals, the Orthodox priest (and in this respect the Hungarian Catholic priest as well) exercises his influence over a wide range of everyday life experiences. It is not only to order black masses that the Hungarians in Csík went to the Romanian *kalugers*. They also had other positive objectives: to achieve the recovery of a person 'done in', to ask for blessing upon the restoration of family peace and, in general, the maintenance of peace and prosperity – though they could also receive these services from the Hungarian and Roman Catholic priests, and at the nearby shrine of Csíkszentdomokos. From the marriage of a daughter to the successful future of the family, from a peaceful and easy death to the recovery of stolen objects, 'masses for good purposes' were held for a wide variety of purposes. Priestly healing also had its place in the Csík system of religious witchcraft; as we have seen, the mediator-priest could also act as healer in a given case of *maleficium*. Clients quite often requested two services from the *kaluger* simultaneously: to heal someone who has been 'done in', for example, and also to recite a curse in revenge upon the person they suspected. According to our data, for instance, the *kaluger* recites seven 'benevolent' masses on the sick person whose clothes or photos are taken to the church by his or her family members. The *kaluger* blesses these objects, recites a mass upon them and thus brings recovery and blessing to the sick person. In another type, oil or sugar is taken to the priest, who confers a blessing upon it. By this means it becomes a kind of sacrament, which helps when the family uses it to cook food for the sick person. The opening of the Bible 'for luck or for health' and the priest's prescription of magical fasting 'for good purposes' also appear in this context.

All this is the positive equivalent of the bewitching activities the *kaluger* is commissioned to conduct, and in many instances their actual alternative. This is evident in several bewitchment-narratives in which *maleficium* and healing, curse and benediction appear as solutions that alternate and merge into one another. In a narrative from Karcfalva, for example, somebody's animals died one after the other until he went to the *kaluger* who 'opened the book' and told him who the malefactor was. Then his client had to pay for masses for nine days to repair the damage and to bring some earth and salt from his home to have them blessed. After this, he buried the earth and the salt, now conferred with a healing power, into the foundation of his house – and the problem was indeed solved and the animals stopped dying.

The most characteristic feature of religious witchcraft in Csík is the integration into the system of the holy person's ordeal and rites conferring blessing and curse. The good and evil alternatives of the same system are in the hands of the priest acting as the instrument of fate. An archaic ambivalence is manifested in his person; he is simultaneously a *blessing* and *cursing* priest, who balances the personal inner relations of witchcraft from outside and from above. With his practice of ordeal, he is one of the pillars of the villagers' world order especially with regard to ethical norms. The Western examples of church rites make it all the more clear that here the system of popular witchcraft has been integrated into an actual religious system run by priests. We have two systems, sanctioning grievances by different ways and punishing with different methods those who upset the moral equilibrium of the community.

The system of priestly curses functioning in Csík has some parallels in both Eastern and Western Christianity. These shed more light on the religious systems into which popular witchcraft was, in our presumption, integrated in some of the realms of Orthodoxy in south-east Europe. We have parallels from present-day south-east Europe about the intertwining systems of popular and church divination, but such parallels are even more frequent in the medieval and early modern period of Western Catholicism. Todorova-Pirgova has writen about 'religious magicians' in Bulgaria, who conduct their divining activities with the priests' moral support. Similarly, the explicit role of priestly divination in the identification of *maleficium* is not without parallels – even from modern Western Europe.[10] Although scattered, our contemporary European parallels seem to imply that the coexistence of populations with differing nationalities and religions must have played a major role in the survival of such sacred services. In the century of the Reformation German Protestant peasants secretly visited Catholic holy places to seek cures or participated in processions aimed at averting hail. It is all the more remarkable that in the twentieth-century Netherlands in Utrecht and Gelderland with a mixed Catholic and Protestant population the Protestants were especially inclined to employ the services of Catholic witch doctors.[11] Todorova-Pirgova describes similar interconnections between Bulgarian Muslims and Orthodox Bulgarians.[12]

With his practising of magic, healing and divination, the figure of the Romanian priest resembles the 'Christian magicians' of the Western Middle Ages, as Valerie Flint termed those figures working on the borderline of magic and religion. Flint describes magician-priests from the fourth to the fifth centuries, who conducted 'sanctified magical activities', prophesied from the Bible and identified thieves by divination.[13] Some of the methods of priestly magic and divination found in Csík have direct parallels with the realms of Western Catholicism. The type of Bible divination known as 'the opening of the book' has a long medieval tradition. Schreiner's research on the subject suggests it is rooted in ancient traditions from the sixth century.[14] Prohibitions of divining from the Bible as well as data on the use of the Bible and the Psalms for divination and magic, such as finding the identity of a thief with the help of a suspended Bible or psalm, reoccur throughout the medieval and early modern periods.[15] According to Richard Kieckhefer, methods for spotting a thief or finding stolen goods were in common use during the medieval period, though they were often considered a subtype of demonic magic.[16] It is telling that from the Council of Laodicea to the sixteenth century it was not only the Western churches that felt obliged to denounce repeatedly priestly magic and divination.[17] Ryan's research on early modern data on Russian priests accused of *maleficium* and magic, as well as the large number of prohibitions of priestly magic and divination from the same period, attest to a very lively priestly practice in Russia.[18]

Another important area where witchcraft and priestly practice interconnected concerns the clerical activity of healing and conferring benediction, which has survived to this day in Orthodox Eastern Europe. Indeed, in this region it seems to exist with almost the same intensity in the twentieth century as we know it did in medieval Western Christianity. The medieval church could satisfy the various everyday magical needs of the laity by healing and averting natural catastrophes.[19] The sacred place provided a kind of social shield for the community surrounding it. For the medieval person it was a basic need to be in a constant state of baptism, as it were, through repeated benediction as a protection against the demonic outside world. As Gur'evich observes, blessing was essentially a form of protective magic, an amulet against curses.[20] In Western Europe priestly healing through church benediction was quite common until at least the seventeenth century, after which the memory of healing priests and monks were still kept alive in Protestant areas by popular incantations that had originally been benediction texts said over various diseases. In Orthodox Eastern Europe, along with village healers, priests and monks continued to have a much stronger role in healing, blessing, some types of cursing, as well as exorcism, which was practised by Western priests as well.[21]

By providing a sacred protection benedictions are, as we saw in the system of Csík, the alternative of curses. The two can easily change places in a system of divine ordeal where the priest conferring the blessing or curse is only an instrument of higher powers, and where curse formulae related to exorcism are originally parts of a legitimate rite.[22] Furthermore the priest legitimizes the idea that the cursing of humans is directed against the work of Satan, against the sins imparted to man by Satan, and is a just punishment meted out in the name of God. There are several medieval forms of ritual cursing in the realms of Western Christianity that are almost exact equivalents of the Csík system of 'having someone done in' through priests. The most important of these is the *clamor*, the ritual curse upon those who committed an offence against the religious community or church property. Its formulae were recorded from the ninth century, and are known to have been in use in Frankish territory (present-day Western France) from the eighth century to the twelfth century.[23] The malefactor was publicly denounced and his punishment requested in prayer, which, at least in the final section of the *clamor*, took the shape of a curse. The *clamor* ritual could be complemented with fasting,[24] just as magical fasting is found in Csík.

Even before the standardization of the *clamor* ritual we have data on cursing as a liturgical threat from the sixth and seventh centuries. Lester Little quotes a number of stories, most of them about punishing thieves of the church property, from this period.[25] From the eighth to the thirteenth centuries there are a strikingly large number of stories about the sanctioning or threatening of thieves with curses. Keith Thomas even describes cases from late medieval England in which thieves of church and monastery property, or people who failed to pay back loans, were punished by curses or threatened in a public cursing rite.[26] The public threats served partly to appease the injured party's thirst for revenge: the wrongdoer got sick, perished, his animals died – justice was done. In other cases the *clamor* was a warning shot. The harmful act could be reversed, stolen goods returned without the realization of the curse; the equilibrium was restored between the injurer and the injured, whether a private person or the community of a monastery.[27] Thus the *clamor* was in essence a divine ordeal just like the priest's curse in the system of Csík witchcraft. Both served as a form of compensation as well as a means of maintaining or restoring social stability. As Little writes, 'the *clamor* was a ceremony in which social disorder and concomitant suffering were acted out and accepted hierarchies were inverted'.[28]

The data from Csík also reveals a form of priestly magic that is less legitimate than the *clamor* rite, in other words the celebration of a black mass to cause disease and death. According to Klaus Schreiner's research, the saying of requiems for the living, as well as the practice of *Totbeten* or *Mordbeten*, in other words the recital of mortal curses within prayers, was a recurring phenomena in medieval Western Europe.[29] The requiem celebrated for the living is pure black magic. It could be accompanied by such similarly 'common' magical acts as fasting to provoke misfortune. According to thirteenth-century data, mendicant friars were specialists in this field.

Advocating the avoidance of untimely death and the preparation for death, the more spiritual Christianity of the late Middle Ages conflicted with the magical service of the requiem for the living.[30] It nevertheless survived for a long time. This must have been due to the strong popular traditions of cursing and black magic with the same kind of duality of church and secular traditions that we find in twentieth-century Csík. This question of a duality of popular and church rites has been raised by those who have researched curse-rites in the medieval Church.[31] We may agree with Little's opinion that the various European popular curse traditions cover a widespread, perhaps universal phenomenon, which provided a mental framework for the more formal, studied religious cursing.[32] The role of cursing is quite important in medieval and early modern village societies, both in a religious context and more generally as a means of verbal conflict regulation, to use Eva Labouvie's phrase.[33] As we have seen, in Eastern Europe the duality of secular and church usage of ritual curses has survived until the modern age. In the light of this duality, it appears quite natural that, just as cursing has a priestly religious variant, the popular system of witchcraft, which is to a large extent based on communal forms of cursing, should also have a parallel 'priestly' layer. Furthermore, the two layers are not unrelated: as we have seen in Csík there are ritual, public forms which appear in witchcraft as well.

We can find, then, several close similarities between religious-magical practices in the contemporary Orthodox sphere of influence and the medieval rituals of the Western church. These correspondences are probably due to the fact that Orthodox Christianity has preserved until the modern period – legitimately or illegitimately – ritual forms that have already become extinct in the West. Although it is the Orthodox priestly practice, among others, that has preserved them, we still cannot consider them specifically Eastern

European or Orthodox (let alone Hungarian) features, although we can evidently account for local characteristics and differences that have developed through temporal deferments and cross-cultural encounters. The Western examples of church rites make it all the more clear that here the system of popular witchcraft has been integrated into an actual religious system run by priests. We have two systems, sanctioning grievances in different ways and punishing with different methods those who upset the moral equilibrium of the community. The reason why they could merge so easily is that a common element in both is the damage caused by a person within the community: this is the common factor that could connect the category of individual *maleficium* or revenge and that of the 'just' punishment restoring order in the community. In medieval Europe, and apparently in Eastern Europe in the modern period, the priests' role in satisfying everyday 'magical needs' involved the act of *maleficium* causing death and sickness, but only in an ambivalent system subordinated to divine ordeal.

In the light of our medieval Western examples, the curse ritual performed by priests in Csík could and can exist *without* witchcraft, just as popular systems of cursing could exist without it. No witchcraft ideology was needed to proceed, for instance, against offenders of property, which was the most frequent motive in Western *clamor* cases. The important role of having thieves 'done in' in Csík is defined here as witchcraft only for the reason that the explanation of individual problems in terms of *maleficium* involves the presumption of a person with bewitching powers 'entering' the system. We may suppose that this rural system of witchcraft, cursing, and black magic as a form sanction is the result of the merging of two factors with differing origins: Hungarian popular witchcraft and a Romanian curse-ritual similar to the Western *clamor*. What we do not know is whether a similar Romanian-Romanian fusion has ever taken place; in other words, whether Romanian popular witchcraft has had a system like the Hungarian one or whether a *clamor*-like institution was sufficient there to satisfy all the relevant needs.

These rites of curse-blessing within ordeal systems have an important ideological basis in the archaic, one could say Old Testament-like concepts of sin, punishment and justice, which disappeared from Western Christianity earlier than from its Orthodox form. That these systems survived longer in the Orthodox east was most likely due to several factors. I can mention two of these in connection with the material under scrutiny here. One of them is the greater importance accorded to the role of the Devil in Eastern liturgy. In relation to this, in Orthodox Eastern Europe the peasants' world-views and the popular beliefs of witchcraft are closely related to the church demonology's concept of the Devil. In Western and Central Europe the heyday of the demonological concept of witchcraft, and the identification of *maleficium* with possession by the Devil, was in the sixteenth and seventeenth centuries. In the east these beliefs – perhaps due to the proximity of Orthodox

Christianity – survived or revived. Possession by the Devil is still a cause and explanation for diseases among the villagers of Csík, and they go to Romanian monks and priests to have the Devil exorcised in the same way as in the requests discussed above.[34] The priest is in a constant struggle with Satan, who tries to gain ascendancy over men. It is a part of his everyday practice to purify people and their environment with benedictions, sacraments and exorcisms, and thereby limit the Devil and the Devil's sphere. The other factor is the clearly more populist attitude of Orthodox priests: their greater readiness to cater to the concrete, daily magical needs of the people, to employ magical methods based on face-to-face relationships. It seems that Roman Catholic Hungarians have a need for these services which Hungarian priests may not provide but Orthodox priests are ready to perform.

As for the Romanians, our discussion so far may also suggest one more interesting connection related to Orthodoxy. One theory developing from the research on European witch persecution was that the discontinuation of the 'magical' services of the medieval Church may have provided an impetus to the blooming of witchcraft and witch persecution in the West. In Orthodox Eastern Europe, or at least in the Orthodox areas of Romania, these services have continued, and there was no official witch persecution. In the light of our analysis, it is understandable that by taking an active role in the popular system of witchcraft, the Orthodox Church never persecuted witches. The priests rather than the laity would be the most prone to accusations if a witch-persecution was set in motion.

Notes

1 As well as the data collected by myself, I have used some of my students' data, for which I would like to express my gratitude here.
2 In recent years a few studies have been published from various parts of Transylvania. In each case they focus on Hungarians living close to Romanians, who have integrated, like the people from Csík, the activities of Romanian priests/monks into their system of punishment and divination. See Vilmos Keszeg, 'A román pap és hiedelemköre a mezőségi folklórban [The Romanian Priest and His Belief Circle in the Folklore of the Mezőség.]', *Ethnographia* 107 (1996) 335–69; Tünde Komáromi, 'Rontásformák Aranyosszéken. A gyógyító román pap [Forms of Maleficium in Aranyosszék. The Romanian Priest as Healer]', *Néprajzi Látóhatár* 5 (1996) 87–98; Dóra Czégényi, 'Magyar–román interetnikus kapcsolatok vallási vetülete. A román pap alakja egy erdélyi közösség hiedelemrendszerében [Religious Aspects of Hungarian–Romanian Inter-Ethnic Contacts. The Figure of the Romanian Priest in the Belief System of a Transylvanian Community]', in Éva Borbély, and Dóra Czégényi *et al.*, *Változó társadalom* (Kolozsvár, 1999), pp. 29–43; Gyula Tankó, *Életvitel a Gyimesekben* [Way of Life in the Gyimes Region] (Székelyudvarhely, 2001).
3 For a general survey of Hungarian witch persecution and early modern witchcraft see Gábor Klaniczay, 'Hungary: The Accusations and the Universe of Popular Magic', in Bengt Ankarloo and Gustav Henningsen (eds), *Early Modern European Witchcraft, Centres and Peripheries* (Oxford, 1990), pp. 219–55; Klaniczay, 'La chasse aux sorcières

en Europe Centrale et Orientale', in Robert Muchembled (ed.), *Magie et sorcellerie en Europe du Moyen Age à nos jours* (Paris, 1994), pp. 275–91.

4 One of the first European descriptions of the system is Alan Macfarlane, *Witchcraft in Tudor and Stuart England* (London, 1970), but see also Keith Thomas, *Religion and the Decline of Magic* (London, 1971); Christine Larner, *Enemies of God: The Witchhunt in Scotland* (Baltimore, 1981); Robin Briggs, *Communities of Belief: Cultural and Social Tensions in Early Modern France* (Oxford, 1989). On the characteristics of Hungarian witchcraft see, Éva Pócs, 'Maleficium-narratívok, konfliktusok, boszorkánytípusok (Sopron vármegye 1529–1768)' ['Maleficium Narratives – Conflicts – Witch Types, Sopron County, 1529–1768'], *Népi Kultúra – népi társadalom* 18 (1994) 9–66; idem, *Between the Living and the Dead: A Perspective on Witches and Seers in the Early Modern Age* (Budapest, 1999); Ildikó Kristóf, *'Ördögi mesterséget nem cselekedtem'. A boszorkányüldözés társadalmi és kulturális háttere a kora újkori Debrecenben és Bihar vármegyében* ['I Did No Devilish Deed'. The Social and Cultural Background of Witch Persecution in Early Modern Debrecen and Bihar County] (Debrecen, 1998).

5 Evidently, we do not know as yet the proportion between effectuated *maleficium* cases and those that were only narrated, or the real dimensions of the actual cases of black magic.

6 Willem de Blécourt, 'The Witch, her Victim, the Unwitcher and the Researcher: The Continued Existence of Traditional Witchcraft', in Willem de Blécourt, Ronald Hutton and Jean La Fontaine, *Witchcraft and Magic in Europe: The Twentieth Century* (London, 1999) pp. 188–91; Per Sörlin, *'Wicked Arts'. Witchcraft and Magic Trials in Southern Sweden, 1635–1754* (Leiden, Boston and Cologne, 1999), pp. 128–77.

7 From the Romanian word *călugăr* (monk).

8 The literature of witchcraft persecution features the role of cursing as *maleficium* causing physical problems, views on the rightfulness and justification of cursing and more generally the importance of cursing in medieval Europe as well. Thomas describes the significance of ritual cursing in early modern England, which can be traced back to the Middle Ages. He also mentions views on 'relapsing' curses similar to those from Csík: Thomas, *Religion and the Decline of Magic*, pp. 598–611. In certain situations these were permitted or tolerated by the Church as well.

9 According to the description in Tankó, *Életvitel a Gyimesekben*, p. 155, the monks of Romanian monasteries in Moldva and Gyimes or the wandering *kalugers* appearing in the fairs to collect the orders are usually entrusted by Hungarians in Gyimes with the practice of black magic and with holding curse-masses – as a form of dispensing justice or as a solution of family and social conflicts in a way very similar to Csík.

10 For twentieth-century data of priests and monks fulfilling the role of witch doctors, see Jeanne Favret-Saada, *Deadly Words: Witchcraft in the Bocage* (Cambridge, 1980), pp. 141–5; de Blécourt, 'The Witch, her Victim, the Unwitcher and the Researcher', p. 185; Inge Schöck, *Hexenglaube in der Gegenwart. Empirische Untersuchungen in Südwestdeutschland* (Tübingen, 1978), pp. 99, 143; 187–200; Ton Dekker, 'Witches and Sorcerers in Twentieth Century Legends', in Marijke Gijswijt-Hofstra and Willem Frijhoff (eds), *Witchcraft in the Netherlands from the Fourteenth to the Twentieth Century* (Rotterdam, 1991, pp. 183–201.

11 Dekker, 'Witches and Sorcerers in Twentieth Century Legends', pp. 187–200. See also the contribution of de Blécourt in this volume.

12 Iveta Todorova-Pirgova, 'Witches and Priests in the Bulgarian Village: Past and Present', in Gábor Klaniczay and Éva Pócs (eds), *Demons, Spirits, Witches: Church Demonology and Popular Mythology* (Budapest, forthcoming). This principle is more widespread in Hungarian–Romanian (and Catholic/Protestant–Orthodox) relations than the discussion above indicates. Vajkai mentions other parts of Transylvania

where Orthodox Romanian shrines are visited by Hungarian Protestants: Aurél Vajkai, *Népi orvoslás a Borsavölgyében [Popular Healing in the Borsa Valley]* (Kolozsvár, 1944), p. 45.

13 Valerie Flint, *The Rise of Magic in Early Medieval Europe* (Princeton, 1991), pp. 247–73, 375–80.

14 Klaus Schreiner, 'Volkstümliche Bibelmagie und volkssprachliche Bibellektüre. The-ologische und soziale Probleme mittelalterlicher Laienfrömmigkeit', in Peter Dinzel-bacher and Dieter Bauer (eds), *Volksreligion im hohen und späten Mittelalter* (Paderborn, Munich, Vienna and Zurich, 1990), pp. 337–8.

15 Schreiner, 'Volkstümliche Bibelmagie', pp. 335–72.

16 Richard Kieckhefer, *Magic in the Middle Ages* (Cambridge, 1989), p. 84.

17 Klaus Schreiner, 'Tot- und Mordbeten, Totenmessen für Lebende. Todeswünsche im Gewand mittelterlicher Frömmigkeit', in Martin Kintzinger, Wolfgang Stürner and Johannes Zahlten (eds), *Das andere Wahrnehmen. Beiträge zur europäischen Geschichte* (Cologne, Weimar and Vienna, 1991), pp. 341–5. For Eastern Europe see W. F. Ryan, *The Bathhouse at Midnight: An Historical Survey of Magic and Divination in Russia* (Stroud, 1999), pp. 408–17.

18 Ryan, *Bathhouse,* pp. 408–17.

19 Adolph Franz, *Die kirchlichen Benedictionen im Mittelalter I-II* (Breisgau, 1909).

20 Aron Gur'evich, *Problemy srednevekovoi narodnoi kul'tury* (Moscow, 1981), p. 84.

21 See on the practice of incantation in monasteries, Fritz Pradel, *Griechische und südi-talienische Gebete, Beschwörungen und Rezepte des Mittelalters* (Giessen, 1907); V. J. Man-sikka, *Über russische Zauberformeln mit Berücksichtigung der Blut- und Verrenkungssegen* (Helsinki, 1909).

22 Richard Kieckhefer mentions several medieval Western European examples of the alternative usage of blessing and curse, priestly benediction and exorcism 'on the same level of consciousness': Kieckhefer, *Magic in the Middle Ages,* pp. 69–84.

23 Lester K. Little, *Benedictine Maledictions. Liturgical Cursing in Romanesque France* (Ithaca and London, 1993). Thanks to Gábor Klaniczay for calling my attention to this book.

24 Little, *Benedictine Maledictions,* pp. 20–5.

25 Little, *Benedictine Maledictions,* p. 84.

26 Thomas, *Religion and the Decline of Magic,* pp. 599–600.

27 See also Gur'evich, *Problemy srednevekovoi narodnoi kul'tury,* pp. 88–92.

28 Little, *Benedictine Maledictions,* p. 142.

29 Schreiner, 'Volkstümliche Bibelmagie'; Schreiner, 'Tot- und Mordbeten'. For a sum-mary of the sources see Dieter Harmening, *Superstitio. Überlieferungs- und theoriege-schichtliche Untersuchungen zur kirchlich-theologischen Aberglaubensliteratur des Mittelalters* (Berlin, 1979), pp. 222–5. For relevant data from Ireland see Little, *Benedictine Mal-edictions,* pp. 168–70.

30 Schreiner, 'Tot- und Mordbeten', pp. 340–3.

31 Gur'evich, *Problemy srednevekovoi narodnoi kul'tury,* p. 66; Little, *Benedictine Maledic-tions,* pp. 154–85. Little mentions Greek, German, Scandinavian, and especially Irish pagan popular prototypes.

32 Little, *Benedictine Maledictions,* p. 154.

33 Eva Labouvie, 'Verwünschen und Verfluchen: Formen der verbalen Konfliktregelung in der ländlichen Gesellschaft der frühen Neuzeit', in Peter Blickle (ed.), *Der Fluch und der Eid. Die metaphysische Begründung gesellschaftlichen Zusammenlebens und politi-scher Ordnung in der ständischen Gesellschaft* (Berlin, 1993), p. 122. See also Thomas on the role of cursing in early modern village societies and in this context in witchcraft, *Religion and the Decline of Magic,* pp. 599–611.

34 For witches possessed by the Devil and for the most important related works, see
   Éva Pócs, 'The Popular Foundations of the Witches' Sabbath and the Devil's Pact
   in Central and Southeastern Europe', *Acta Ethnographica* 37 (1991–92) 343–6; Pócs,
   'Patterns of Possession in Central-East Europe', in Klaniczay and Pócs (eds), *Demons,
   Spirits, Witches*. It is especially the Serbian and Romanian witches that are believed
   to be people possessed by devils or evil spirits, who obtain their power of *maleficium*
   through the possessing Devil.

10

Spooks and spooks: black magic and bogeymen in Northern Ireland, 1973–74[1]

Richard Jenkins

On 5 August 1973, the *Sunday News*, published in Belfast, printed an article about the Copeland Islands, a popular spot for day trips and picnics just off the North Down coast. Adorned with drawings of a Baphomet-like goat's head, the headline screamed 'Black Magic Ritual Killings on Copeland Island Beach'. Quoting an anonymous expert on the occult and the local Ulster Society for the Prevention of Cruelty to Animals Inspector, the story described the purported ritual sacrifice of sheep and the discovery of a symbol-decorated site where a ceremony of some sort had apparently taken place.

On 8 September events took a more sinister turn. The burned and badly mutilated body of ten-year-old Brian McDermott, who had been missing from his home for nearly a week, was retrieved from the River Lagan in Belfast. Within days of his body being found, there were suggestions in the press, referring back to the Copeland Islands incident, that witchcraft might have been involved in the murder.[2]

Between then and the end of 1973, an unprecedented rash of articles referring to local witchcraft, black magic and satanism appeared in the press, north and south of the Irish border. I have located over seventy, unfolding in a spatial and chronological pattern. During the second half of October the stories were concentrated in the south-east of the area: south Down, north Armagh and north Louth. During the first fortnight of November they shifted north and west, to Armagh, south-east Tyrone, Fermanagh, and south and mid-Antrim. During the rest of November and early December they concentrated in mid-Ulster, particularly Tyrone. From an examination of the television news archive index at Broadcasting House, Belfast, there does not seem to have been any noteworthy TV coverage of these matters, at least on the BBC.

A few further stories appeared during early 1974. The most spectacular appeared in March: 'Witchcraft brew found in gruesome ritual cave', relating to a find in Island Magee, Co. Antrim.[3] There were also stories about the film *The Exorcist* – culminating in autumn 1974 when it opened in Belfast – and evangelistic campaigns confronting teenage 'dabbling' in the occult.[4] By then the episode was over: after that there was only occasional press coverage, such as could be matched anywhere.[5]

Different kinds of press coverage can be identified: reports of apparent specific instances of black magic rituals or whatever,[6] reports of the circulation of local rumours about black magic,[7] articles focusing on the denial of rumours by the police, churchmen or the newspaper itself (which, of course, provided another opportunity to repeat the rumours),[8] editorial comment of various kinds,[9] reports of sermons dealing with the matter,[10] religious advertisements and church notices mentioning these subjects,[11] and readers' letters.[12] Worth mentioning in their own right, as quite distinct from the 'over ground' press, are the, typically Loyalist, paramilitary news-sheets and publications.[13] Finally, there are consistent motifs and themes in the press coverage: the Brian McDermott murder,[14] animal sacrifice, typically involving cats, dogs, sheep and goats,[15] the threat of child abduction (particularly of a blonde, blue-eyed girl),[16] the problem of young people and others experimenting with the occult,[17] and the spoiling, particularly for children, of traditional Hallowe'en celebrations.[18] In one sense, this sequence of, often closely-connected, newspaper stories was the main thing that happened. If that had been *all* that happened, however, this would only be a minor story of troubled times. As I will show, however, there was more to it than that – certainly more than met the eye at the time.

How can we understand what happened?

Social science offers several closely related interpretive frameworks. For example, these events seem to fit the classic pattern of a 'moral panic': a period of sustained public discourse, created and dominated by politicians, the media or other moral entrepreneurs, which creates or dramatizes a particular public issue or problem.[19] Bringing the issue to prominence may resolve, redefine, or consolidate it. A consistent feature of moral panics as they are described in the literature is the illumination or redrawing, through the stigmatization or stereotyping of marginal groups and categories, of collective boundaries of inclusion and exclusion. A sense of 'us' is strengthened by the imagining of 'them' during the collective conjuring of 'folk devils'.

These satanism stories can also be analysed as rumour[20] or 'improvised news':[21] an informal or popular attempt to clarify 'what's going on' in times of ambiguity or uncertainty. When significant matters are not clear, rumour at least is definite enough to fill the vacuum. It is only a short step from rumour to contemporary or urban legends, in which motifs and themes of contemporary concern are articulated and elaborated in oral narratives, which may be worked and reworked versions of long-standing tales.[22] Here, too, imagination colonizes the spaces of uncertainty in everyday life. In this context, there is evidence of later contemporary legends, particularly in North America, addressing the themes – adolescents and the occult, satanism and child abduction – which the northern Irish rumours of 1973–74 made their own.[23]

Finally, the social anthropological literature on witchcraft and sorcery is also relevant. One influential strand in this analytical tradition argues that accusations, and the symbolism, of supernatural aggression follow and reveal contours of collective and individual tension within groups. They are believed to give voice to, and provide an acceptable vocabulary of blame for, conflicts that cannot easily be expressed, let alone acted on or resolved, in face-to-face communities.[24] In this framework, witchcraft beliefs have been described as a 'social-strain gauge'.[25]

It is easy to criticize these approaches for their explicit or implicit functionalism, in that moral panics, rumours and contemporary legends are believed to express the underlying problems of society, and perhaps to contribute to their solution. It is not, however, productive,[26] and overlooks what these approaches share with some resolutely anti-functionalist approaches to similar topics.[27] In particular, there is a widespread recognition that conflict and violence, ambiguity and uncertainty, are collectively expressed and worked through in narrative and symbolism. Some kind of interpretation along these lines is almost irresistible. Before exploring this further, however, other interpretations of what happened are present in the material itself and are a necessary part of any account of these events.

Was black magic going on?

A rumour with a foundation is quite different from one with none. There are at least three places to look for that foundation. First, Northern Ireland, like many other places, had long played host to muttered intimations of black magic and satanism, supposedly often practised – in best Dennis Wheatley style – by people in high places. There may be more to this than rumour. The peninsula of Islandmagee, in Co. Antrim – source of the last of Ireland's few witchcraft trials, in 1711 – enjoyed a sinister reputation during my childhood in nearby Larne. In October 1961, a collection of occult paraphernalia, apparently disused for some time but seemingly authentic, was discovered in a cave there.[28] In March 1974, a similar find in the same area may, as we shall see below, require a different interpretation. Nevertheless, it is possible that there were practising occultists, if not actual satanists.

There was also the tragic reality of Brian McDermott's murder. This was a killing for which, in the tender innocence of its victim and its savagery, it was difficult to find a place in the local classificatory scheme of violence: 'Even among the black crimes that have been committed in this area in these last indelible years, the murder of the Belfast child, Brian McDermott, is surely the blackest of them all'.[29] An account that refers to this as a black magic killing was collected by Feldman in the 1980s and the story persists today.[30] However, another, no less persistent, account of Brian McDermott's murder makes a different set of connections: with paramilitary violence and the sexual abuse of children. This was clear at the time, when RUC Assistant Chief Constable William Meharg speculated about a 'sex fiend'[31] or 'juvenile terrorists'.[32] Although no one was arrested for the murder, that the security forces knew the killer but could not prove it has long been believed locally: the individual concerned, now dead, has even been named in print.[33] All of the evidence that I have collected, whether documentary or in interviews, points away from satanism. Even so, it is easy to understand how the murder contributed to the subsequent rumours.

Finally, a persistent theme in the rumours was that teenagers and others were 'dabbling' in the occult, using ouija boards and the like to contact spirits. Putting to one side the specifically local aspects of these stories – particularly attempts to contact the spirits of local people, sometimes paramilitary heroes, who had met violent deaths[34] – there is no reason to doubt that some of this was happening. It went on in my youth, it has been documented elsewhere, and teenagers are still doing it.[35] That pranks and experiments of this kind are common suggests that, in themselves, they do not explain much. Even so, there was at least a small amount of grit around which the imaginings of rumour could accrete. The narrative pearls which subsequently emerged, however, were out of all proportion to any observable reality, and had taken on many different hues. To understand those stories we will have to look elsewhere.

Was something else going on?

Another secret reality may have contributed to the creation and spread of the rumours. On 28 October, the front page of Dublin's *Sunday World* was dominated by a banner headline: 'Black Magic Fear in Two Border Towns'. The story concerned rumours in Dundalk, in the Republic, and Newry, in Northern Ireland, and the supposed ritual sacrifice of a goat in the latter. Some local opinion was reported as suggesting that the Army was spreading these rumours, pointing out that a similar tactic had been used in the campaign against the Mau-Mau in Kenya. Versions of this interpretation of the situation emerged in a couple of other places during the following week.[36]

This theory was elaborated in greater detail in *Republican News* on 24 November. The centre piece of their evidence was the British Army's Brigadier Frank Kitson, a counter-insurgency expert who had recently served in Belfast and written a 'little book' detailing his part in the Mau-Mau campaign, revealing how accusations against the insurgents of ritual brutality and 'barbaric magic' had been fostered as black propaganda:

> It is not surprising that the same trick should be played on Irish people during their struggle. The British counter-insurgency team has been working very hard on the black magic theme for some time now ... their purpose is clear. It is first to suggest that diabolical influences are at work in the freedom struggle ... Secondly, it is an attempt to impose a voluntary curfew on the anti-imperialist population and make them live in fear.[37]

Conspiracy theories were two a penny in the North, and at the time this story didn't stand out as more plausible than the rest. However, in 1990 Paul Foot published *Who Framed Colin Wallace?*, about a British Army intelligence officer – a local man – who claimed to have been persecuted following his refusal to spread black propaganda against Labour politicians. Foot described Wallace's 'Information Policy' section, based at Army headquarters, Lisburn, as 'instrumental in setting off the witchcraft hysteria'.[38] This involved the fabrication of supposed black magic ritual sites, complete with black candles and pentacles. According to Wallace in this book, the objectives were to tar paramilitary organizations with the brush of Satan, and to keep young people in at night, particularly in the vicinity of Army observation posts.

I interviewed Colin Wallace in 1993. He described the black magic activities as one aspect, and not the most important, of a wider black propaganda strategy aimed at smearing paramilitary organizations in the eyes of their own supporters as communist, embezzling money, engaged in drug dealing, and linked to satanism. With respect to black magic, the principal tactic was the mock ritual site. He mentioned locations in the Ardoyne in north Belfast, Newry (the episode described in the *Sunday World*), Islandmagee, and another in County Antrim. This activity may have started as early as late 1972, and it continued into early 1974. They did not do many:

> the idea was to create, manufacture a number of situations that then would be reported in the press. But more important, we weren't aiming at briefing the press on this, but the idea was to try to get local people to talk about it in the hope that the fact that sites had been found would generate rumour and give the impression it was much more widespread than it was ... one of the things we were trying to do was to blur the edges ... In case we came across somebody that was an expert on witchcraft and satanic rites, that any differences in ritual in what we were doing, people would say, oh that's a fake. So we never did anything that was particularly detailed, just left clues that would get people guessing.

Other tactics included briefing enquiring journalists – the anonymous expert on the occult in the Copelands Island report in August 1973 was probably an intelligence officer – and placing fake religious advertisements[39] and readers' letters in the press.[40] Wallace could not remember the Copeland

Island incident, although there is evidence to suggest that it was a deliberate hoax.[41] He was also definite that there was no direct connection between the black propaganda and the Brian McDermott murder. Stories about sacrificed dogs and cats may have had a different Army source: local knowledge insists that some units killed dogs and cats, to make their patrols quieter and terrorize the neighbourhood.

Wallace wanted to create something that would develop and spread on its own. To this end, he drew on his knowledge of his own background. So, although the campaign was aimed at both communities, it was perhaps aimed more at Protestants than Catholics. He mentioned several sources for the basic idea and the detail: his grandmother's supernatural tales during his childhood in Randalstown, Co. Antrim, newspaper coverage of a case in Britain at this time, and a few books, such as Montague Summers's *The History of Witchcraft and Demonology*. Although he knew Kitson's books, he did not remember them, or Kitson himself, influencing this project. Looking at the two relevant books (Kitson 1960, 1971), and a later Kitson text on counter-insurgency (1977), this is not surprising.[42] Although Kitson discusses the role of 'pseudo Mau-Mau' under Army control, and says that they had to administer the occasional 'Mau-Mau oath' in order to maintain their cover, he nowhere says that his 'counter-gangs' carried out atrocities or rituals to blacken the name of the Mau-Mau. Kitson writes about those things only as authentic Mau-Mau behaviour. While the *Republican News* and the *Sunday World* got the basic story right, the reference to Kitson is wrong (and we are entitled to ask where the information came from).

Can Wallace's account be trusted? He is an ex-member of an occupational community of professional liars, so we should entertain doubt. However, I am inclined to believe him, if not on the fine detail – he insisted that the passage of time had rendered his memory unreliable – then with respect to the larger picture. I have several reason for my confidence. First, I revealed nothing of what I had already discovered until we had exhausted what he knew. Only then did I produce various press cuttings as prompts to further discussion. Second, his tale didn't appear slick or rehearsed. His testimony was full of the inconsistencies and contradictions that might be expected from someone remembering events which occurred amid the hurley-burley of many other things, twenty years earlier. Finally, a number of points of detail, which he got more or less right, suggested that he knew what he was talking about. There were also enough things of which he denied knowledge to reinforce that judgement.

On balance, therefore, it is plausible that the Army played a part in starting and encouraging the rumours. This is a useful reminder that conspiracy theories should not always be dismissed: in this case, it seems that there was a conspiracy. But we still need to ask why this particular disinformation 'took off' to the extent that it did. To answer that question we must explore a range of other issues.

The role of the newspapers

Local newspapers fed the flames in several respects. First, some journalists seem to have been very reliant on official sources for information: the 'anonymous expert' in the Copeland Islands story is but one example. It is, of course, true that in many cases those official sources, in the shape of the police in particular, were denying the witchcraft stories. In other cases, however, they were not. While it is possible to sympathize with the difficulties faced by journalists in Northern Ireland during the 1970s, some seem to have been too close to their official sources for comfort. Disinformation readily found its way into print. Wallace and his colleagues also planted bogus readers' letters and other decoys in the press. In December 1973, for example, an advertisement appeared in the *Belfast Telegraph*, the *News Letter*, and local papers elsewhere in the Province:

PROTESTANTS AWAKE!!

Politicians and others have lied and deceived. (And lies permit entrance to evil spirits, Eph. 4: 25, 27. Is this why there is a fearful increase of witchcraft in Ireland, North and South?).
WE HAVE BEEN BETRAYED INDEED.[43]

Unusual in that it was published on a weekday, and does not identify its source or sponsor, this 'advertisement' is black propaganda in action.

Over-reliance on official sources is but one symptom of shoddy journalism. Particularly, although not exclusively, in the very local, small-town papers, there sometimes also seems to have been a credulity – or at least a preparedness to print anything for a 'good story' – that is remarkable. A significant part of this problem were those local papers which were owned by the same Province-wide group, and appear to have been poorly resourced in terms of news journalism. In these papers, the same story could appear in a number of towns over a period of weeks. One such story appeared in the *Ballymena Chronicle and Antrim Observer*, 8 November 1973:

WITCHCRAFT RUMOURS DISTRESS PARENTS

Rumours about witchcraft now rife in Mid-Ulster, are terrifying children and causing grave concern to parents.
 Stories circulating all over the country claim that witchcraft is being practised in some areas and that a blonde, blue-eyed girl, aged from between three and eleven, is to be abducted this weekend for use in a black magic ritual.
 Frightened parents are now keeping their children indoors after school

because of the fear that those engaged in the witchcraft practice might lure youngsters away. In some instances parents are accompanying their children to and from school.

Teachers in some schools have warned children to be careful about accepting lifts or talking to strangers in the streets. They have also advised their pupils to stay in their homes after darkness falls.

Meanwhile the rumours continue abated and gain greater significance as each new detail is added.

This is identical in every respect to items which had appeared in the *Dungannon Observer*, the *Mid-Ulster Observer* and the *Fermanagh News* the previous Saturday, 3 November. If nothing else in the story, one should be sceptical of the precision of 'this weekend'. All of these titles were owned by Observer Newspapers (NI), Dungannon. Given journalism of this calibre, it is little wonder that rumour spread (or at least appeared to).

Other examples of the 'wandering story' phenomenon could be cited – and not all from the Observer group – but this example is interesting because in Ballymena at that time three papers were battling to survive. The witchcraft rumours became part of this struggle; in the process they were dramatized and consolidated. The following Thursday, 15 November, the *Ballymena Guardian and Antrim Standard*, the closest competition to the *Chronicle*, went on to the offensive on its front page. The article begins with an introduction which sets the national scene and denies the truth of such rumours:

TOWNS IN GRIP OF BLACK MAGIC FEAR

Many people are alarmed at what is supposed to be going on and some are indeed frightened almost to the stage of panic.

Indeed one such couple called at our Ballymena office last Friday afternoon. They had read a report in a weekly newspaper about Black Magic and arrived at the conclusion that since a story had got into print there was perhaps truth behind the other tales they had heard.

The young parents – they had a charming little blond [*sic*] girl with them in a pram – came to us to ask if we had any definite proof that such wicked things as they had been told of were in fact happening in the area.

DEEPLY AFFECTED

Obviously deeply affected by what she had heard, the young mother volunteered the information that only that day a pupil at a local school had been kidnapped and the police were searching for her.

A quick telephone to the local police while the mother was still in the office confirmed that such was not in fact the case.

Pity others would not try to kill such stories at source.

The article concludes by emphasizing the absence of evidence for rumours in Antrim and Ballymena, and encouraging readers to question strange tales before repeating them: 'No doubt it is comfort of some sort to be able to say one is not the lie-maker, but even to be the lie-teller in the light of current feeling should be a heavy burden on each man's conscience.' The target – the *Chronicle* – could not be clearer. The same day, the town's long-established *Ballymena Observer*, without alluding to the *Chronicle*'s original story of the week before, also printed a story that detailed local rumours and denied their basis in fact.

Thus newspapers contributed to the situation as conduits for disinformation, in the low standard of evidence which sometimes seems to have been required to make a story, in the recycling of stories around the province, and in the familiar journalistic imperative, to print something – anything almost – when everyone else was on to the story.[44] The press coverage, rather than reflecting or documenting what happened in some straightforward sense, is thus, at least in part, actually 'what happened'. It was certainly influential in creating anxieties and rumours which, at the time, were real for some people.

External influences?

Local interest in the occult, the scattered activities of the Army, and amplification by the local press do not explain everything. For example, where did the story about the sacrifice of blonde, blue-eyed children come from? Were there external sources for these stories and images?

Returning to Colin Wallace, his remark during the interview about a case in Britain suggests a number of possibilities. The 'Highgate Vampire' case, which came to trial in June 1974, had been in and out of the newspapers for years.[45] Wallace may have had in mind other newspaper reports.[46] Black magic and the desecration of churchyards were matters of public discussion. A more general set of influences, mentioned in the Northern Irish press coverage of *The Exorcist*,[47] is the ready local availability of literature on the occult. Less esoteric popular authors such as Dennis Wheatley – *The Satanist*, *To the Devil – A Daughter*, *The Devil Rides Out*, and so on – and horror films were also obvious inspirations for the imagery of the Black Mass, the sacrificial virgin, demonic goats, and the like.

The United States might also have been a source. *Rosemary's Baby* was a cinema hit in 1968, and *The Exorcist* was contemporary with the end of the period under discussion here. In 1973 the evangelist Maurice Cerullo published *The Back Side of Satan*, an early text for the growing new-right, Christian anti-satanism campaign that contributed during the 1980s to the creation of a moral panic about satanic abuse.[48] There were rumours the same year about cattle mutilation, often attributed to satanists, in the American mid-west.[49] A satanism rumour in Idaho in November 1973 was followed in 1974 by similar rumours in Montana, both featuring the abduction and murder of a virgin girl child.[50] These could have provided grist for the northern Irish rumour mill, but I have seen no evidence to suggest this. If anything, the northern Irish rumours are evidence in support of Ellis's argument that current American anti-satanist mythologies derive originally from Britain. While it is true that 'satanic abuse' is an American invention, subsequently imported to Britain, the local roots of the northern Irish rumours require emphasis, as does their early appearance.[51]

Ritual murder

One of those roots directs our attention back to the press. Black magic sacrifice was not the only kind of 'ritual killing' which was in the news in Northern Ireland at this time. Between 1972 and 1974, Belfast, in particular, was the arena for a campaign of random assassination, mainly by members of Protestant paramilitary organizations, which at its height saw bodies being discovered almost daily. In 1972 alone, 121 murders were classified as assassinations, two-thirds of the victims being Catholic.[52] That is an imprecise statistic, but it makes the point.

Whether this was a co-ordinated, deliberate strategy or not, it was effective in terrorizing large areas of Belfast, especially at night.[53] Most victims were shot, but a small number were tortured, mutilated or disfigured – signs of the cross being cut on their body, for example – and/or stabbed to death, often with notable savagery. These murders were the work of Protestants. In response, two local journalists on *The Belfast Telegraph*, Martin Dillon and Denis Lehane, began to write about 'ritual killings', culminating in the publication on 25 October 1973 of their book, *Political Murder in Northern Ireland*. Although Dillon later identified some of these 'ritual' murders as the early handiwork of Lenny Murphy, leader of the 'Shankill Butchers',[54] the earlier book focused on a juvenile gang based in East Belfast, led by the man whose name has been persistently linked to the Brian McDermott murder.[55]

According to Dillon and Lehane the 'ritual killings' began as early as May 1972, with a murder which was significant for 'the use of the knife and the fact that the killing involved a ritual in which more than one person used the knife on the victim'.[56] Just before the witchcraft rumours began to circulate, on 26 June 1973, the double murder of Catholic politician Paddy Wilson and Irene Andrews was widely reported as involving horrific multiple knife wounds. In a newspaper interview that July, this killing was described as a 'ritual killing' by a man claiming to represent the Ulster Freedom Fighters, the group claiming responsibility.[57]

Whether Dillon and Lehane were correct in their characterization either of particular murders, or of the relentless toll of assassination victims, is not the point. What matters is that in their journalism, and the book, they tapped into or established a public discourse about 'ritual killings': killings which were actually happening, with the corpses to prove it. Furthermore, the assassinations themselves, combined with press comment of this kind, created a powerfully sinister local atmosphere of uncertainty, menace and mystery. Combined with the Brian McDermott murder, it is not surprising that fears of another kind of ritual killing were credible to at least some people. The possibility was not wholly outlandish.

An enchanted world: 'traditional' belief

Colin Wallace also mentioned the supernatural stories that his grandmother had told him as a child. With respect to 'traditional' folk belief, one of the most striking things about this pattern of rumours and newspaper stories is their timing. They cluster around Hallowe'en, the 31 October: thirty-three of the relevant newspaper items fall into the four-week period, 18 October to 14 November.

Some of these mention Hallowe'en, particularly with respect to the witchcraft rumours spoiling the 'traditional fun' of the festival. What was that traditional fun? One of the best-documented northern Irish calendar festivals, Hallowe'en was and is celebrated by Catholics and Protestants.[58] During my childhood in Co. Antrim in the 1960s it involved bonfires, fireworks, dressing up in 'false faces' (grotesque masks), playing 'Hallowe'en knock' – a distant relative of 'trick or treat' – around the doors, games such as bobbing for apples, fortune-telling, and food. And we knew that it was about witches and ghosts, even though it may be more closely identified with the fairies in tradition.[59] It was a supernatural moment, a moment not just for fun, but also of other-worldly power and a frisson of fear, even if we didn't *completely* believe in it. This is no doubt why it has long featured in American satanism rumours and legends.[60]

Satanic rumours notwithstanding, local newspapers at this time were also full of lighthearted features about the 'traditional' trappings of Halloween: festive recipes, communal parties and bonfires, ghost stories, and so on.[61] Not all of the trappings, perhaps – fireworks had been banned three years earlier, not wholly successfully, by the Explosions (Control of Fireworks) Order – but the festival was still very much in evidence. Nowhere in this kind of coverage were black magic rumours mentioned. Kids, too, were still up to their usual tricks, despite the rumours. In Portadown, for example, at the heart of the 'rumour area' at this time, two teenagers were caught by the police, dressed in a sheet, 'spooking' motorists on the Tandragee Road.[62] Similarly, the field archives of the Ulster Folk and Transport Museum contain a delightful 1976 account of a Hallowe'en play, complete with witches, devised by a twelve-year-old girl from Newtownards, Co. Down and her friends.[63] This material warns us against presuming that people were 'in the grip' of either a pervasive fear about witches and black magic, or unofficial beliefs – 'superstition' – more generally. They clearly were not. *At most* this was a partial and uneven phenomenon.

However, this is not the whole picture either. There are other indications that in Northern Ireland at the time many people actively believed – or at least *half*-believed – in the presence or proximity of another world, enchanted in one way or another. There were, for example, newspaper articles and advertisements devoted to 'healers', whether they were explicitly Christian[64] or something else, 'traditional' or otherwise.[65] This too is well documented.[66] During the early 1970s Danny Gallagher, a 'seventh son of a seventh son', in competition with another of that ilk, Finbarr Nolan, was attracting significant crowds to healing sessions all round the North. In an advertisement that appeared in various versions in local papers during 1973 and 1974, Gallagher, describing himself as a 'faith healer', reminded readers that 'Persons requiring treatment are requested to bring earth from the grave of a relative or clergyman'.[67] It is denying the testimony of the evidence *not* to see this as magical (although nor should we necessarily presume the faith of those who turned up to be healed).

An enchanted world: symbolizing 'the trouble'

Ghosts and fairies also make their appearance in the newspapers at this time. The *Strabane Chronicle* and the *Ulster Herald*, for example, both carried, on 6 October 1973, the same article about a man whose house in Corbally, Co. Tyrone, was apparently plagued by the fairies. While the fairies may be a belief whose time had passed – and this story thus exceptional – ghosts were, and are, a different matter.

The 'Troubles' in the North since 1969 have produced ghost legends which dramatize and memorialize the death and violence of the times. On All Soul's Day 1973, the day after Hallowe'en, there was, for example, an enigmatic story about the suppression of a ghost story by 'Dublin security chiefs' who were worried that 'IRA terrorists' would exploit it.[68] Other stories are more clearly based in events. One of the better known examples of this genre concerns the eighteen soldiers who were blown up at Warrenpoint in 1979: newspaper reports began to emerge the following year about 'the ghostly patrol which appears from nowhere, stops cars, vanishes into the night without trace'.[69] The field recording archives of the Ulster Folk and Transport Museum contain a number of 'troubles'-related ghost and banshee stories and others have been published.[70] Burton's ethnography of the Ardoyne, north Belfast, during 1972–73, mentions local ghost stories, suggesting that 'the troubles increase the probability of such tales becoming conversational currency'.[71] Feldman, too, documents ghost stories as the 'genealogies of the dead': 'In the community where these stories were collected, the intensified presence of ghosts since the advent of the Troubles is attributed to the sheer frequency and randomness of violent death within a limited space and time'.[72]

The message is clear: the violence and emotion of the Troubles find expression in narrative and the symbolic domain. Another striking example of this is 'The Black Man', who, to my knowledge, first appears in print in Morris Fraser's *Children in Conflict* (1974). Fraser, a child psychiatrist, presents the case of 'Anne', an eleven-year old from the Lower Falls area of Belfast, who began to experience hallucinations in late 1969. When he saw her in 1971: 'She said that the figure she saw was a tall man in a big hat, brightly coloured coat and frightening eyes. He varied in size from being only a couple of inches high to being "ten times as big as a house". He was, she said, a Protestant, because he was evil and trying to kill her ... Sometimes he whispered to her and told her to do "bad things".' [73] For Fraser this was a matter of dealing with trauma through projection and displacement, drawing on the historical imagery of the Devil.[74]

Be that as it may, it was not to be an isolated phenomenon. In October 1972, a year before the rumours which we have so far been discussing, the youngsters of the Catholic area of the Ardoyne were full of stories about a 'Black Man' who stalked the streets after dark. Pictures drawn by local informants of his close relative, 'the Big Man of Arden Street', complete with banshees and witches,[75] show a clear relationship to Anne's hallucinations (not to mention anticipating Freddy Kruger by more than a decade). For a fortnight before Hallowe'en, the area was full of stories about black magic and the Black Man. Drawing in the Catholic Church, Protestants and the British Army, these talked of butchered dogs, black candles, upside-down crosses and victims of violence coming back to life.[76] Largely a discourse of young people, some scoffed openly at the rumours, others went to the priest for holy water. The rumours died away soon after Hallowe'en, and Burton interprets them as youthful pranks, an excuse for boys to leave girls at home.

In the context of Fraser's account of 'Anne', and Colin Wallace's identification of the Ardoyne as one of the Army's phony satanist sites, Burton's is not a sufficient explanation (although there is doubtless something in it). This view is reinforced by Feldman's evidence that 'Black Man' stories – once again drawing upon motifs of butchered pets, the Army, and satanic ritual – were still current in the mid-1980s.[77] Feldman's explanation of these stories is that they both reflect the actual counter-insurgency tactics of the British Army's Parachute Regiment and are a 'cultural elaboration of terror', a symbolic reworking of violence and its practitioners.

The 'Black Man' genre means two things in the context of this chapter. First, stories about black magic and sacrificed pets were current as a collective discourse in the Ardoyne a good year before they begin to show up in the newspapers. This adds credence to Colin Wallace's testimony, and suggests the possibility that such tales may have been a source on which the Army black propagandists drew. Second, with ghost stories and the like, they are further evidence of an enchanted universe within which the Troubles were experienced and interpreted, and within which the black magic rumours circulated and found a degree of credence.

An enchanted world: religion

Northern Ireland in 1973–74 was far removed from the disenchantment that Max Weber predicted as the miserable fate of scientific, rationalized modernity. Nowhere is this more apparent than in organized religion, the most important symbolic and moral framework within which political violence was and is interpreted: Northern Ireland is by any yardstick – observance, belief, or attitudes – a very religious place.[78]

The general point about religiosity applies to both Protestants and Catholics. However, with a few exceptions – an editorial in *The Derry Journal* inspired by the Brian McDermott murder and dramatizing the 'flood gates of evil' which the Troubles had opened,[79] and some anti-rumour preaching and comment by Catholic clergy[80] – the religious discourse about satanism is largely Protestant. Colin Wallace thought that, on balance, Protestants were the primary target. On balance, he may have been right. Protestant worries about these matters surface in the early 1970s, with the publication of *The Dark Arts in Bible Light* by W. J. McK. McCormick.[81] While this also lambasted idolatry, 'spiritism', Freemasonry and hypnotism, a good part of the book is devoted to a scriptural attack on occultism and magic. The real target, however, is probably Roman Catholicism more than satanism.[82] In response to the Brian McDermott murder, we find a distinctly liberal Protestant discourse about moral decline, evil and the 'Troubles', linked also to the possibility of collective social and political redemption; Ian Paisley's fundamentalist *Protestant Telegraph*, however, made sectarian political capital out of the tragedy.[83]

Probably more to the point is the concentration of the rumours in south Down, Armagh, and mid-Ulster. These are marginal farming areas, socially conservative and economically disadvantaged, with long histories of inter-ethnic conflict, where fundamentalist Protestantism and loyalism bump right up against Catholicism and militant republicanism. This is Northern Ireland's 'Bible belt'. Banbridge is at this area's heart, so it is interesting to read contemporary accounts of the Rev. Samuel Workman's 'Special Evangelical Mission' to Scarva Street Presbyterian Church, Banbridge. Beginning on 21 October 1973, this was extended due to popular demand to 16 November, when extra seating had to be installed to accommodate the throng.[84]

The Outlook, published in nearby Rathfriland, carried an account on 2 November 1973 of 'Belfast preacher on Black Magic and Armageddon':[85] the Rev. Workman had preached a 'challenging and startling sermon on "the last days"'. After discussing the Middle East and the Common Market, he posed the question – drawing on 1 Tim. 4: 1, on the 'the latter days' – 'what makes anybody think that satanic activity can be safely dismissed as nothing more than human addiction to rumour-mongering and proneness to credulity?' The theme of black magic was elaborated further in a long piece entitled 'The Black Art', which may have been the text of a sermon, contributed the same day to the *Banbridge Chronicle* by the Rev. J. T. Hagen, the minister of Scarva Street Presbyterian Church:

> there is in our day a real revival of the black art and other associated evils. Much of the difficulty, trouble and evil in the world today is caused by the devil … The devil is real and devil worship is real. There are those who are selling their very souls to satan. There are those who are being robbed of their peace and very sanity because of this evil. Two forces are at work in our world, the forces of Christ and the forces of the devil. The forces of the devil are out to destroy and bring misery and unhappiness, the forces of the Lord Jesus Christ are out to bring peace.[86]

This brief extract lets us taste something of the atmosphere of a packed soul-saving mission meeting, and the preaching about black magic that went on there. Some people, fundamentalist Protestants, were taking the matter very seriously.

The Outlook's report suggests that more than black magic was being taken seriously. For some this was a time of heightened religious fervour and foreboding. This is also clear from the, solely Protestant, church notices and announcements in the Saturday edition of the *Belfast Telegraph*. Sampling the months of September, October and November, in 1971 there were on average 8.57 broadsheet columns of Church notices every week; in 1972 this was 8.32, rising to 10.21 in 1973, 10.25 in 1974, and falling back to 8.96 in 1975. Nor is it simply a matter of level of enthusiasm. The themes dramatized in these advertisements for special meetings and crusades are also significant. For some Northern Irish Protestants, millenarianism was in the air in the autumn of 1973, and Armageddon was on the horizon if not actually being played out then and there. The 'end times' and the 'last days' are consistent themes, their signs and portents, drawing on interpretations of the Book of Revelations and other Biblical sources, being the entry of the UK into the European Common Market in 1972, the Arab-Israeli War of 1973, and the Northern Ireland conflict itself.[87]

It is not original to observe that uncertainty, masked by an apparently rock-solid, inflexible confidence in their own righteousness, characterizes Ulster Protestants.[88] This view resonates here because, in part, the black magic rumours can be interpreted as a Protestant discourse about moral uncertainty, about the overturning of an established and axiomatic moral order that had been manifest in the Northern Irish state and the Protestant way of life. This is particularly so with respect to the murder of Brian McDermott, almost certainly committed by Protestants but impossible to 'own up to' within local canons of acceptable violence. It is also so with respect to the assassinations, particularly the 'ritual murders': guns are one thing, knives are another. The killings may have been done in the name of Protestantism, but not all Protestants could accept or acknowledge them.

This uncertainty should also be understood in the context of the prorogation of the local parliament, Stormont, by the British government in December 1972. The Protestants' bulwark, and the source of the legitimacy of their local sovereignty, had been removed at a stroke. Further themes, which emerged in the black magic rumours and the church material, and which there is no space to discuss here, mingle in drugs and sex. These dramatize the equally abrupt modernization of Protestant Ulster, and the corruptions of permissiveness – tame though they appear in retrospect – which were enthusiastically embraced by a younger generation who saw the outside world on television and wanted a life different from that of their parents. The Protestants of the 'Bible belt' weren't just threatened by Popery and Republicanism, they were also threatened by the God-less English, who would happily sell them down the river, and, from within, by their own children. It is perhaps little wonder that a dominant motif in the rumours was the threatened child.

Why did the rumours stop?

Although there is no defining moment, by the early months of 1974 the episode was effectively over. There were a few articles on witchcraft and black magic in the Northern Ireland press during this period, but nothing more. They were either probable Army disinformation [89] or reports of evangelistic attempts to capitalize on the issue.[90] After March 1974 no more rumours of the type discussed in this chapter appeared in the press: the issue was dead. Why?

The most obvious answer is that rumour needs something on which to feed and nothing actually 'happened'. Fears about the abduction of a child for sacrifice, for example, can only remain current so long in the absence of at least an attempt to snatch someone's son or daughter. Facts are not everything in these matters, but they do matter. Furthermore, such 'evidence' as there was evaporated when it was examined. The Copelands Island episode, for example, had been publicly disproved, and in detail, by the end of September 1973.[91] Similarly, 'the sudden appearance' in Banbridge at the end of October 'of a black circle which was found burned on land near a spot named Solitude', apparently turned out to have been caused by horses, exercised on a lunging rein.[92] Millenarian prophecy and portent also needed something concrete to feed them: the end of the 1973 Arab-Israeli war in

Israeli victory – not to mention the more general reluctance of Armageddon to materialize – took some of the wind out of those who saw themselves as living in the 'last days' (for the moment anyway).

The final answer is that during the spring of May 1974, both the press and Army intelligence had other, if not better, things on which to concentrate. Loyalist resistance to the cross-community, power-sharing Executive – the British attempt to fill the local political vacuum created by the demise of Stormont and provide a basis for non-sectarian politics – was gathering and organizing. William Craig was reviewing fascist-style parades and adopting apocalyptic rhetoric, Ian Paisley was marching and fulminating, and there was conflict and discord within the Unionist Party. Alliances and marriages of convenience were forged between Protestant trade unionists, paramilitary organizations and politicians. Plans were laid against a backdrop of continuing violence.

In two weeks during May 1974 those plans came to fruition in the Ulster Workers Council strike. The immediate upshot of the strike was the collapse of the Executive, and, in the face of Harold Wilson's misjudged televised accusation of 'spongeing', the opening up of a consensual ground upon which a wide range of Protestant opinion could meet to assert itself and oppose the present state of affairs. In the medium term, Protestants reasserted their local power and forged a new relationship with Britain. They were back inside the gates again, which suggests a final answer to my question. If the witchcraft rumours were nurtured by a crisis of confidence within the Northern Irish Protestant community, the easing of that crisis will have made a difference.

Understanding what happened

The black magic rumours were not a moral panic in the classic sense, if only because there were few if any clear-cut moral entrepreneurs. Colin Wallace clearly doesn't count, and the newspapers followed rather than led the way in this matter. Other than in the limited operations of the Army, there doesn't seem to have been an organized or co-ordinated plan of campaign on the part of anyone. The word 'panic' is, anyway, an over-statement: many people disregarded the rumours or simply laughed at them. Many more probably only believed in them occasionally, in the dark. While the evidence from Banbridge leaves no doubt that many others *did* believe in the possibility of satanists and devil worship, and the reality of Satan, ordinary life went on all around them.

To understand what happened we must appreciate the coming together of a number of factors: the reality of occultism, however trivial or rare; the Brian McDermott murder; the Army's disinformation tactics; local journalism and newspaper practices; external influences; public discourse about 'ritual' assassinations; the everyday reality of an enchanted world which combined 'traditional folk belief', the symbolized expression and working-through of terror and violence, and fundamentalist, millenarian Protestantism; and a crisis of morale and moral confidence within the Protestant community. Thus the black magic rumours open a privileged window on to a revealing and unique moment in the north of Ireland's recent history. If we are to understand the view through that window, light must be brought to bear on the matter from a range of different directions.[93] In return, the story casts its own light into other dark corners.

Notes

1 This research was supported financially by the University of Wales Swansea, for which I am grateful. The following were enormously helpful: BBC Northern Ireland; Belfast Central Library; the British Library Newspaper Library, Colingdale; Derry Central Library; the Linenhall Library, Belfast; Magee College Library; and the Ulster Folk and Transport Museum. The Royal Ulster Constabulary and the Ulster Society for the Prevention of Cruelty to Animals answered my questions as best they could. The following are also owed thanks: Linda May Ballard, Robert Bell, Pia Christensen, Kate Ingram, May McCann, Noel McGuigan, David McKittrick, Richard Norton-Taylor, Geraldine and Liam O'Dowd, Ciarán O Maoláin, and Colin Wallace. Versions of this paper have been aired in front of helpful and critical audiences at Aarhus University, University of Aberdeen, Queen's University of Belfast, University of Bristol, Copenhagen University, University College Cork, University of Manchester, University of Plymouth, University of Sheffield, University of Southampton, and the University of Wales Swansea.
2 BNL and IN, 11 Sep. 1973. The following abbreviations will be used: BNL, *Belfast News Letter*; BT, *Belfast Telegraph*; IN, *Irish News*; IT, *Irish Times*; SN, *Sunday News*; SW, *Sunday World* (Dublin).
3 *East Antrim Times*, 8 March 1974.
4 See, BT 4 March 1974; SN 31 March 1974; SN 24 Apr. 1974; BNL 22 Oct. 1974; BT 22 Oct. 1974; BT 23 Oct. 1974; BT 24 Oct. 1974; BT 25 Oct. 1974; BNL 29 Oct. 1974; BT 29 Oct. 1974; BT 2 Nov. 1974.
5 There are occasional press stories, not all of which are reporting local stories, covering such matters. For example, BT 16 July 1975; BNL 23 March 1977; BNL 19 Sep. 1987; BNL 25 Jan. 1988; IT 12 March 1988; IT 14 March 1988; BNL 19 Sep. 1988; BNL 25 Sep. 1988; IN 1 Nov. 1989; BNL 3 May 1990; BT 19 Sep. 1991; SW 25 July 1993; BT 2 Oct. 1993; *Sunday Life* 17 Oct. 1993.
6 For example, *Evening Press* (Dublin) 1 Oct. 1973; BNL 2 Oct. 1973; *Sunday Press* (Dublin) 14 Oct. 1973; SN 28 Oct. 1973; SW 28 Oct. 1973; *Lurgan Mail* 1 Nov. 1973; IN 24 Nov. 1973; *Dungannon News and Tyrone Courier* 28 Nov. 1973; *Mid-Ulster Observer* 29 Nov. 1973; *Mid-Ulster Mail* 1 Dec. 1973; *WDA News* vol. 1 no. 42 (mid Dec.); *East Antrim Times* 8 March 1974.
7 See, for example, BT 22 Sep. 1973; *WDA News* vol. 1 no. 32 (Sep. 1973); *Irish Independent* (Dublin) 16 Oct. 1973; *WDA News* vol. 1 no. 35 (mid Oct. 1973); BNL 23 Oct. 1973; *Lurgan Mail* 25 Oct. 1973; *Banbridge Chronicle* 26 Oct. 1973; SN 28 Oct. 1973; *Down Recorder* 2 Nov. 1973; *Northern Standard* (Monaghan) 2 Nov. 1973; *Dungannon Observer* 3 Nov. 1973; *Fermanagh News* 3 Nov. 1973; *Mid-Ulster Observer* 3 Nov. 1973; *Sunday Citizen* 4 Nov. 1973; *Carrickfergus Advertiser* 8 Nov. 1973;

Ballymena Chronicle and Antrim Observer 8 Nov. 1973; *The Outlook* (Rathfriland) 9 Nov. 1973; BT 23 Nov. 1973; *Gown* 12 Dec. 1973; BNL 19 Nov. 1974.

8 For example, BT 24 Sep. 1973; *County Down Spectator* 28 Sep. 1973; BNL 16 Oct. 1973; SN 21 Oct. 1973; *Down Recorder* 26 Oct. 1973; *Mourne Observer* 26 Oct. 1973; *Portadown Times* 31 Oct. 1973; *Armagh Guardian* 1 Nov. 1973; *Ulster Gazette and Armagh Standard* 1 Nov. 1973; BNL 2 Nov. 1973; *Ulster Star* (Lisburn) 2 Nov. 1973; *The Argus* (Drogheda and Dunkalk) 2 Nov. 1973; *Dundalk Democrat and People's Journal* 3 Nov. 1973; *Dungannon Observer* 10 Nov. 1973; *Fermanagh News* 10 Nov. 1973; *Ballymena Guardian* 15 Nov. 1973; *Ballymena Observer* 15 Nov. 1973; *East Antrim Times* 16 Nov. 1973; *Impartial Reporter* (Fermanagh) 22 Nov. 1973; *Fermanagh Herald* 24 Nov. 1973; *Republican News* 24 Nov. 1973; BNL 30 Nov. 1973; *Fermanagh News* 1 Dec. 1973; *Strabane Weekly News* 1 Dec. 1973; *Impartial Reporter* (Fermanagh) 6 Dec. 1973; *Ballymena Guardian* 6 Dec. 1973.

9 See, *Derry Journal* 14 Sep. 1973; *Protestant Telegraph* 15 Sep. 1973.

10 See, *Banbridge Chronicle* 2 Nov. 1973; *The Outlook* (Rathfriland) 2 Nov. 1973; *The Argus* (Drogheda and Dunkalk) 2 Nov. 1973.

11 See, BT 12 Dec. 1973; BT 13 Dec. 1973; BT 14 Dec. 1973; BT 15 Dec. 1973.

12 See *Lurgan and Portadown Examiner* 8 Nov. 1973; *Armagh Observer* 10 Nov. 1973; *Fermanagh News* 10 Nov. 1973; *WDA News* vol. 1 no. 38 (mid Nov.).

13 See *WDA News* vol. 1 no. 32 (Sep. 1973); *WDA News* vol. 1 no. 35 (mid Oct. 1973); *Ulster Loyalist* 15 Nov. 1973; *WDA News* vol. 1 no. 38 (mid Nov.); *Republican News* 24 Nov. 1973; *WDA News* vol. 1 no. 42 (mid Dec.).

14 See *Derry Journal* 14 Sep. 1973; *Protestant Telegraph* 15 Sep. 1973; BT 22 Sep. 1973; *WDA News* vol. 1 no. 32 (Sep. 1973); *Evening Press* (Dublin) 1 Oct. 1973; *Sunday Press* (Dublin) 14 Oct. 1973; *WDA News* vol. 1 no. 35 (mid Oct. 1973); SN 28 Oct. 1973; *Dungannon News and Tyrone Courier* 31 Oct. 1973; *Ulster Star* (Lisburn) 2 Nov. 1973; *Sunday Citizen* 4 Nov. 1973; *Ballymena Guardian* 15 Nov. 1973; *East Antrim Times* 16 Nov. 1973.

15 For example, *Evening Press* (Dublin) 1 Oct. 1973; BNL 2 Oct. 1973; *Sunday Press* (Dublin) 14 Oct. 1973; BNL 16 Oct. 1973; *Irish Independent* (Dublin) 16 Oct. 1973; *WDA News* vol. 1 no. 35 (mid Oct. 1973); *Lurgan Mail* 25 Oct. 1973; *Banbridge Chronicle* 26 Oct. 1973; *Mourne Observer* 26 Oct. 1973; SN 28 Oct. 1973; SW 28 Oct. 1973; *Portadown Times* 31 Oct. 1973; *Lurgan Mail* 1 Nov. 1973; *Armagh Guardian* 1 Nov. 1973; *Ulster Gazette and Armagh Standard* 1 Nov. 1973; BNL 2 Nov. 1973; *Ulster Star* (Lisburn) 2 Nov. 1973; *Northern Standard* (Monaghan) 2 Nov. 1973; *Dundalk Democrat and People's Journal* 3 Nov. 1973; *Sunday Citizen* 4 Nov. 1973; *Carrickfergus Advertiser* 8 Nov. 1973; *Dungannon Observer* 10 Nov. 1973; *Fermanagh News* 10 Nov. 1973; *Ulster Loyalist* 15 Nov. 1973; *Ballymena Guardian* 15 Nov. 1973; *Ballymena Observer* 15 Nov. 1973; *Impartial Reporter* (Fermanagh) 22 Nov. 1973; *Fermanagh Herald* 24 Nov. 1973; *Republican News* 24 Nov. 1973; BNL 7 Feb. 1974; *Sunday Press* (Dublin) 24 Nov. 1974.

16 For example, *Irish Independent* (Dublin) 16 Oct. 1973; BNL 23 Oct. 1973; *Lurgan Mail* 25 Oct. 1973; *Mourne Observer* 26 Oct. 1973; SW 28 Oct. 1973; *Dungannon News and Tyrone Courier* 31 Oct. 1973; *Northern Standard* (Monaghan) 2 Nov. 1973; *Dungannon Observer* 3 Nov. 1973; *Fermanagh News* 3 Nov. 1973; *Mid-Ulster Observer* 3 Nov. 1973; *Ballymena Chronicle and Antrim Observer* 8 Nov. 1973; *Ballymena Guardian* 15 Nov. 1973; *Ballymena Observer* 15 Nov. 1973; *East Antrim Times* 16 Nov. 1973; BT 23 Nov. 1973.

17 For example, BT 22 Sep. 1973; *WDA News* vol. 1 no. 32 (Sep. 1973); *Evening Press* (Dublin) 1 Oct. 1973; BNL 2 Oct. 1973; *Sunday Press* (Dublin) 14 Oct. 1973; *Banbridge Chronicle* 26 Oct. 1973; SN 28 Oct. 1973; *Sunday Citizen* 4 Nov. 1973; IN 24 Nov. 1973; *Dungannon News and Tyrone Courier* 28 Nov. 1973; *Mid-Ulster Observer* 29 Nov. 1973;

Mid-Ulster Mail 1 Dec. 1973; *WDA News* vol. 1 no. 42 (mid Dec.); BNL 6 March 1974; SN 31 March 1974; BNL 7 Nov. 1974; BT 13 Nov. 1974; BNL 19 Nov. 1974; *Sunday Press* (Dublin) 24 Nov. 1974.

18 For example, SN 28 Oct. 1973; *Dungannon News and Tyrone Courier* 31 Oct. 1973; *Northern Standard* (Monaghan) 2 Nov. 1973; *Ulster Loyalist* 15 Nov. 1973.

19 S. Cohen, *Folk Devils and Moral Panics: The Creation of the Mods and Rockers* (London, 1972); E. Goode and N. Ben-Yahuda, *Moral Panics: The Social Construction of Deviance* (Cambridge, Mass., 1994); S. Hall, C. Critcher, T. Jefferson, J. Clarke and B. Roberts, *Policing the Crisis: Mugging, the State and Law and Order* (London, 1978); K. Thompson, *Moral Panics* (London, 1998).

20 A. Corbin, *The Village of Cannibals: Rage and Murder in France, 1870* (Cambridge, Mass., 1992); A. Farge and J. Revel, *The Rules of Rebellion: Child Abductions in Paris in 1750* (Cambridge, 1991); J.-N. Kapferer, *Rumour: Uses, Interpretations and Images* (New Brunswick, 1990); E. Morin, *Rumour in Orléans. Jews Accused of White Slaving: A Modern Myth Examined* (London, 1971); P. A. Turner, *I Heard it Through the Grapevine: Rumor in African-American Culture* (Berkeley, 1993).

21 T. Shibutani, *Improvised News: A Sociological Study of Rumour* (Indianapolis, 1966).

22 G. Bennett and P. Smith (eds), *Contemporary Legend: The First Five Years* (Sheffield, 1990); J. H. Brunvand, *The Vanishing Hitchhiker: American Urban Legends and Their Meanings* (New York, 1981); idem, *The Choking Doberman and Other 'New' Urban Legends* (New York, 1984); idem, *The Mexican Pet: More 'New' Urban Legends and Some Old Favourites* (New York, 1986).

23 J. Best, 'Endangered Children and Antisatanist Rhetoric', in J. T. Richardson, J. Best and D. G. Bromley (eds), *The Satanism Scare* (New York, 1991); B. Ellis, 'Legend-Trips and Satanism: Adolescents' Ostensive Traditions as "Cult" Activity', in Richardson *et al.*, *The Satanism Scare*; J. S. Victor, *Satanic Panic: The Creation of a Contemporary Legend* (Chicago, 1993).

24 A. Sanders, *A Deed Without a Name: The Witch in Society and History* (Oxford, 1995), pp. 73–129.

25 M. Marwick, 'Witchcraft as a Social-Strain Gauge', in M. Marwick (ed.), *Witchcraft and Sorcery* (2nd edn, London, 1982).

26 J. S. Victor, 'The Sociology of Contemporary Legends: A Review of the Use of the Concept by Sociologists', *Contemporary Legend* 3 (1993) 75–8.

27 A. Feldman, *Formations of Violence: The Narrative of the Body and Political Terror in Northern Ireland* (Chicago, 1991); M. T. Taussig, *The Devil and Commodity Fetishism in South America* (Chapel Hill, 1980).

28 BT 3 Oct. 1961; see also P. F. Byrne, *Witchcraft in Ireland* (Cork, 1967), p. 75.

29 *Derry Journal* 14 Nov. 1973, editorial: 'The Flood-Gate of Evil'.

30 Feldman, *Formations of Violence*, p. 82.

31 BNL 11 Sep. 1973.

32 IN 11 Sep. 1973.

33 BNL 1 March 1982; M. Dillon, *The Shankill Butchers: A Case Study in Mass Murder* (London, 1990), p. 23.

34 See, BT 22 Sep. 1973; *WDA News* vol. 1 no. 32 (Sep. 1973).

35 Ellis, 'Legend-Trips and Satanism'.

36 *The Argus* (Drogheda and Dundalk) 2 Nov. 1973; *Sunday Citizen* 4 Nov. 1973.

37 *Republican News* 24 Nov. 1973.

38 P. Foot, *Who Framed Colin Wallace?* (London, 1990), p. 145.

39 See, BT 12 Dec. 1973; BT 13 Dec. 1973; BT 14 Dec. 1973; BT 15 Dec. 1973.

40 See, *Lurgan and Portadown Examiner* 8 Nov. 1973; *Armagh Observer* 10 Nov. 1973; *Fermanagh News* 10 Nov. 1973; *WDA News*, vol. 1 no. 38 (mid Nov.).

41 *County Down Spectator* 10 Aug. 1973 and 24 Aug. 1973; BT 24 Sep. 1973; *County Down Spectator* 28 Sep. 1973; BT 12 Oct. 1973.

42 F. Kitson, *Gangs and Counter-Gangs* (London, 1960); idem, *Low Intensity Operations: Subversion, Insurgency, Peace-keeping* (London, 1971); idem, *Bunch of Five* (London, 1977).

43 See, BT 12 Dec. 1973, 13 Dec. 1973, 14 Dec. 1973, and 15 Dec. 1973.

44 For another good example of this see, *East Antrim Times*, 16 Nov. 1973.

45 B. Ellis, 'The Highgate Cemetery Vampire Hunt: The Anglo-American Connection in Satanic Cult Lore', *Folklore* 104 (1993) 13–39.

46 For the *News of the World* during 1973, see P. Jenkins, *Intimate Enemies: Moral Panics in Contemporary Great Britain* (New York, 1992), p. 156.

47 See, BNL 19 Nov. 1974.

48 M. Cerullo, *The Back Side of Satan* (Carol Stream, 1973).

49 B. Ellis, 'Cattle Mutilation: Contemporary Legends and Contemporary Mythologies', *Contemporary Legend* 1 (1991) 39–80.

50 R. W. Balch and M. Gilliam, 'Devil Worship in Western Montana: A Case Study in Rumor Construction', in Richardson *et al.*, *The Satanism Scare*.

51 Ellis, 'The Highgate Cemetery Vampire'; J. La Fontaine, 'Satanism and Satanic Mythology', in W. de Blécourt, R. Hutton and J. La Fontaine, *Witchcraft and Magic in Europe: The Twentieth Century* (London, 1999), p. 124.

52 R. Deutsch and V. Magowan, *Northern Ireland 1968–73, A Chronology of Events*, vol. 2 *1972–73* (Belfast, 1974), p. 255.

53 S. Bruce, The *Red Hand: Protestant Paramilitaries in Northern Ireland* (Oxford, 1992), pp. 54–6.

54 Dillon, *The Shankill Butchers*, pp. 16–30.

55 M. Dillon and D. Lehane, *Political Murder in Northern Ireland* (London, 1973), pp. 192–3.

56 Dillon and Lehane, *Political Murder*, p. 67.

57 Dillon and Lehane, *Political Murder*, p. 285.

58 P. Robinson, 'Harvest, Halloween, and Hogmanay: Acculturation in Some Calendar Customs of the Ulster Scots', in J. Santino (ed.), *Halloween and Other Festivals of Life and Death* (Knoxville, 1994); J. Santino, *The Hallowed Eve: Dimensions of Culture in a Calendar Festival in Northern Ireland* (Lexington, 1998).

59 See, R. P. Jenkins, 'Witches and Fairies: Supernatural Aggression and Deviance among the Irish Peasantry', *Ulster Folklife* 23 (1977) 45.

60 B. Ellis, '"Safe" Spooks: New Halloween Traditions in Response to Sadism Legends', in Santino, *Halloween and Other Festivals*.

61 See, *East Antrim Times* 12 Oct. 1973; BNL 26 Oct. 1973; *East Antrim Times* 26 Oct. 1973; *Irish Weekly* (Belfast) 27 Oct. 1973; BNL 29 Oct. 1973; IN 30 Oct. 1973; BT 30 Oct. 1973; *Derry Journal* 30 Oct. 1973.

62 Portadown Times 31 Oct. 1973.

63 Ulster Folk and Transport Museum, field transcripts archive: M3/2.

64 See, *County Down Spectator* 10 Aug. 1973; BT 19 Sep. 1973; *Londonderry Sentinel* 19 Sep. 1993; *Londonderry Sentinel* 17 Oct. 1973; *The Outlook* (Rathfriland) 19 Oct. 1973; *East Antrim Times* 19 Oct. 1973; BT 27 Oct. 1973; *Londonderry Sentinel* 31 Oct. 1973; BT 10 Nov. 1973.

65 See, *Newtownards Chronicle* 16 Aug. 1973; *Mid-Ulster Mail* 8 Sep. 1973; *Strabane News* 8 Sep. 1973; *The Outlook* (Rathfriland) 5 Oct. 1973; *Newry Reporter* 25 Oct. 1973; *Mid-Ulster Observer* 25 Oct. 1973; *Newry Reporter* 25 Oct. 1973; *Mid-Ulster Mail* 27 Oct. 1973.

66 A. D. Buckley, 'Unofficial Healing in Ulster', *Ulster Folklife* 26 (1980) 15–34; P. W. Nolan, 'Folk Medicine in Rural Ireland', *Folk Life* 27 (1988–89) 44–56.

67 East Antrim Times 15 Nov. 1974.

68 BNL 1 Nov. 1973.

69 SN 30 March 1980. See also S. St Clair, *The Step on the Stair: Paranormal Happenings in Ireland* (Sandycove, 1989), pp. 98–100.

70 Ulster Folk and Transport Museum, field transcripts archive: M3.8(10), M3.8(22); L. M. Ballard, 'Tales of the Troubles', in P. Smith (ed.), *Perspectives on Contemporary Legend: Proceedings of the Conference on Contemporary Legend, Sheffield, July 1982* (Sheffield, 1984).

71 F. Burton, *The Politics of Legitimacy: Struggles in a Belfast Community* (London, 1978), p. 26.

72 Feldman, *Formations*, p. 67.

73 M. Fraser, *Children in Conflict* (London, [1973] 1974), p. 91.

74 Fraser, *Children in Conflict*, p. 92.

75 Burton, *Politics of Legitimacy*, pp. 180–1.

76 Burton, *Politics of Legitimacy*, pp. 26–8.

77 Feldman, *Formations*, pp. 81–4.

78 S. Bruce and F. Alderdice, 'Religious Belief and Behaviour', in P. Stringer and G. Robinson (eds), *Social Attitudes in Northern Ireland: The Third Report* (Belfast, 1993).

79 *Derry Journal* 14 Sep. 1973.

80 e.g. *The Argus* (Dundalk and Drogheda) 2 Nov. 1973.

81 W. J. McK. McCormick, *The Dark Arts in Bible Light* (Belfast, n.d.). Although this book is not dated, the photocopy of it in my possession bears a price sticker for 25 pence (metric money was introduced in 1971), and there was an advertisement for it in vol. 1 of the *Ulster Bulwark* dated June 1971.

82 In this vein see also: *Ulster Bulwark* vol. 2. no. 9, 2/73 and vol. 3 no. 5 (Oct. 1973); *Protestant Telegraph* 1 Sep. 1973.

83 BT 10 Sep. 1973, 13 Sep. 1973; *Protestant Telegraph* 15 Sep. 1973.

84 *The Outlook* (Rathfriland) 19 Oct. 1973; *Banbridge Chronicle* 9 Nov. 1973, 16 Nov. 1973, 7 Dec. 1973.

85 *The Outlook* (Rathfriland) 2 Nov. 1973.

86 *Banbridge Chronicle* 2 Nov. 1973.

87 For example, *Ulster Star* (Lisburn) 19 Oct. 1973; BT 27 Oct. 1973, 3 Nov. 1973.

88 S. McKay, *Northern Protestants: An Unsettled People* (Belfast, 2000); S. Nelson, *Ulster's Uncertain Defenders* (Belfast, 1984).

89 BNL 7 Feb. 1974; *East Antrim Times* 8 March 1974.

90 BNL 6 March 1974; SN 31 March 1974.

91 BT 24 Sep. 1973; *County Down Spectator* 28 Sep. 1973.

92 SN 28 Oct. 1973; BNL 19 Nov. 1974.

93 For examples of similarly multi-factorial interpretations of early modern witchcraft episodes, see J. Demos, *Entertaining Satan: Witchcraft and the Culture of Early New England* (New York, 1982) and A. Macfarlane, *Witchcraft in Tudor and Stuart England: A Regional and Comparative Study* (London, 1970).

INDEX